New Ways of Classroom Assessment, revised

James Dean Brown, Editor

New Ways in TESOL Series

Innovative Classroom Techniques
Jack C. Richards, Series Editor
TESOL International Association

Typeset in Bitstream Aldine 401 and Humanist 777

by BrightKey

and printed by Gasch Printing

TESOL International Association

1925 Ballenger Avenue

Alexandria, Virginia 22314 USA

Tel 703-836-0774 • Fax 703-836-7864

Publishing Manager: Carol Edwards

Design: BrightKey

ISBN: 9781931185981

Library of Congress Control Number: 2012953102

Contents

Part I: Alternative Methods of Assessment 1 – 50

Portfolios

Journals, Logs, and Conferences

Online Assessments

Dynamic and Continuous Assessments

Individual Differences

Part II: Alternative Feedback Perspectives 5|–126

Self-Assessment

Peer Assessment

Self-Assessment Combined With Peer Assessment

Part III: Alternative Ways of Doing Work-Based Assessment

121-194

Group Work

Pair Work

Group and Pair Work

Part IV: Alternative Ways of Accomplishing Classroom Chores 95-250

Preparing Students for Tests

Creating Assessment Procedures

197-222
IV- Creating

Making Grading Easier

Evaluating Curricula

Part V: Alternative Ways of Assessing Written Skills 251-310

Reading

Reading and Vocabulary

Vocabulary

Writing and Grammar

Part VI: Alternative Ways of Assessing Oral Skills

Listening and Note-Taking

Speaking

Pronunciation and Connected Speech

INTRODUCTION TO THE REVISED EDITION

In my years as an ESL/EFL teacher within and outside the United States, my colleagues and I often discussed and complained about the quality of various standardized tests and the effects of those tests on our teaching. Indeed, teachers often feel helpless when confronted with large-scale standardized testing practices. In this revised edition, teachers have once again been given an opportunity to answer back and show how they do assessment in their classrooms on an everyday basis.

My goal was to step out of the way and let teachers tell their stories about how they do assessment in their classrooms. I have a fairly strong psychometric and statistical background, which serves me well in developing norm-referenced tests for proficiency and placement purposes. But my training and work in the area of criterion-referenced tests has taught me to listen carefully to what teachers are saying about their teaching and the testing they want to do in their classrooms. As a result, my mind is not closed to new types of tests just because they do not fit well in my psychometric/statistical world. What I am saying is that this book offers a collection of classroom testing ideas created by teachers with as little interference as possible from a so-called testing expert.

At the same time, the fact that I include a particular assessment technique in this book does not constitute an endorsement of that technique on my part from a psychometric perspective. Instead, each contribution is included here because (a) a teacher found it useful, (b) I thought it made sense from a classroom perspective, and (c) the description clearly and adequately explained the technique.

I learned in doing this project (and the previous edition) that, almost universally, the teachers who contributed to this book expressed the aims of their contributions in terms related directly to helping students learn. Indeed, the contributors themselves appear to have had difficulty separating the teaching from the measurement, and the lesson from the assessment. I say this because I find that most of the assessment ideas described in this book also describe the lessons that go with them. In some cases, the assessment is indistinguishable from a regular classroom activity until the teacher, or the students themselves, do some form of scoring or other feedback.

Consequently, this book is a series of teachers' contributions that looks more like assessment activities than like tests, and I will consistently refer to all of these contributions as assessment activities. To me, assessment *activities* are different from tests in that they are not easily distinguishable from other classroom activities, largely because they are thoroughly integrated into the language teaching and learning processes. In other words, assessment activities do not stand out as different, formal, threatening, or interruptive. At the same time, *assessment* activities are different from ordinary classroom activities in that they provide a way of observing or scoring the students' performances and giving feedback in the form of a score or other information (e.g., notes in the margin, written prose reactions, oral critiques, teacher conferences) that can enlighten the students and teachers about the effectiveness of the language learning and teaching involved.

In each of the assessment activities, a great deal is said about feedback. But why is feedback important in the classroom? My guess is that feedback derives its importance from the fact that it is one of the teacher's most powerful tools for shaping how students approach the learning process and for finding out what is going on in the students' minds.

Traditionally, the feedback in classroom assessment settings has come from the teacher's perspective, and you will indeed find that the teachers give feedback in many of these contributions. Additionally, many other contributions utilize other feedback perspectives including self-assessment, peer assessment, and outsider assessment strategies. Most often, these alternative scoring perspectives are used in conjunction with the teacher's feedback or in pairs, perhaps because the contributors knew intuitively that combining two or more feedback perspectives would increase the reliability (and credibility from the students' perspectives) of the resulting information.

The activities in this book are organized according to the primary or predominant emphasis of the activity. Part I focuses on alternative methods of assessment; Part II, on alternative feedback perspectives; Part III, on alternative ways of doing task-based assessment; Part IV, on alternative ways of doing classroom chores; Part V, on alternative ways of assessing written skills; and Part VI, on alternative ways of assessing oral skills.

Certain conventions have been followed in order to make the assessment activity descriptions as compact as possible. For instance, based on experience, I am assuming that most classrooms have blackboards or whiteboards and chalk or markers, and that the students have paper, pencils, and pens available. As a result, such items are not mentioned in the lists of resources needed for each assessment activity.

In browsing through this collection of assessment activities, you may notice that the contributions come from a wide variety of geographic locations. Indeed, contributions come not only from teachers in the United States but also from Japan, Jordan, Venezuela, Zimbabwe, and elsewhere. You may also notice that there are fairly heavy clusters of contributions from Hawai'i in the United States, and from Venezuela and Japan internationally. This seemingly strange pattern results from the fact that my home base is the University of Hawai'i at Mānoa, that I taught regularly for over 20 years at Temple University in Japan, and that I had the good fortune to teach in the TESOL Summer Institute at the University of Carabobo in Valencia, Venezuela. Naturally, wherever I went, I tried to generate interest in contributing to this volume. Equally fortunate, however, was the fact that many contributions also arrived by mail, fax, and e-mail from many other locations.

I would like to thank all of the contributors to this book. They were universally cooperative and understanding. More importantly, they created the content of this book, and quite obviously, the book would not exist without them.

Part I

Alternative Methods of Assessment

- **Portfolios**

- **Journals, Logs, and Conferences**

- **Online Assessments**

- **Dynamic and Continuous Assessments**

- **Individual Differences**

Part I: Alternative Methods of Assessment

EDITOR'S NOTE

The contributions here in Part I provide good examples of alternative methods of assessment. In this case, *methods* means ways of gathering assessment information, which here include portfolios; journals, logs, and conferences; online methods; dynamic and continuous methods; and methods that account for individual differences.

Portfolios are collections of students' work selected by students (with the teacher's guidance) to represent their learning experiences. Portfolios usually involve students gathering samples of their L2 use (such as compositions or video clips) into a folder, box, website, and so forth, to show to peers, parents, outsiders, and others, much in the way a photographer gathers exemplary photographs in a portfolio to show to prospective clients. Portfolios provide a type of personal assessment that is directly related to the activities in the classroom, and they are particularly appropriate for assessing language learning processes. Portfolios may also enhance students' learning, improve their view of the teacher's role in the classroom, and involve everyone in the assessment processes.

The first three contributions provide generally useful information about portfolios: a guide to planning portfolios ("Planning Portfolios"), a general introduction to the ideas behind using portfolios ("ESL Language Portfolios: How Do They Work?"), and a concrete method for assessing portfolios ("Self-Assessment: Preparing an *English* Portfolio"). The other two portfolio contributions provide examples of how to apply the portfolio method for different purposes: listening to newscasts ("Portfolio Assessment of Newscast Listening"), and selecting reading texts ("Using Portfolios in the EFL Reading Class").

Journal assessments typically require students to make regular entries in a diary or journal at home or in class. Journal writing can be used to encourage students to practice writing, or to assess their writing ability and its growth over time, or to collect information on students' views, beliefs, attitudes, and motivations. Two contributions explain how to use journals as assessment activities: one for self-evaluation at the midterm ("Using Journals for Self-Evaluation at Midterm") and the other to help students think and write about their reading processes ("Don't Talk About It, Write It Down").

Logs are somewhat different from portfolios and journals in that they afford students a chance to record experiences with English use outside the classroom. Many details may be logged, including when and where the language was used, what was involved linguistically, and why certain experiences occurred the way they did. Two contributions show how to use logs to encourage students to figure out which learning strategies, materials, and contexts work best for them ("Self-Assessment: Keeping a Language Learning Log") and to perform a variety of different communicative activities and keep track of what they've done ("Passport: A Log").

Conferences usually involve students visiting the teacher's office alone or in groups for brief meetings to get personalized assessment directly related to the classroom learning, to learn about their own learning processes, to develop a better self-image, or to afford teachers an opportunity to inform, shape, observe, and gather information about students. Although a number of contributions in this book mention conferences, only one focuses solely on using conferences to assess students' conversational abilities in a nonthreatening environment ("Eat, Drink, and Be Merry: Lunchtime Student Assessment").

Online assessments are distinguished by the fact that they take advantage of computer technology, particularly online resources. Much has been written about the role of technology in language assessment, including elaborate discussions of new computer delivery systems, ways to use computers to test different language skills, new software and hardware tools/resources, or examples of computer-based assessments being used in practice (for an overview of this literature, see Brown, 2013). Two of the contributions in this section focus on using online resources for developing activities that assess listening comprehension ("Exploiting Online Recordings to Test Academic Listening Ability") and writing ("Using Glogs and Comic Strips to Assess Academic Content"), while the third involves downloading, installing, and using free software to help in assessing the students' speed in processing words ("Speed in Processing Words: Antonyms or Synonyms").

Dynamic assessments come in two forms in this volume. *Interventionist dynamic assessment* seeks to predict the problems that learners are likely to come across in learning or using the language and then create prearranged mediation possibilities. These options include implicit to explicit strategies and, only if necessary, overt explanations ("Interventionist Dynamic Assessment: Feedback on a Timed Reading"). In contrast, *interactionist dynamic assessment* is integrated into the learning process with the goal of understanding students' abilities and supporting their development, including unrestricted use of all available forms of mediation ("Interactionist Dynamic Assessment: Feedback on Essay Writing").

Continuous assessment thoroughly integrates assessment into the curriculum, assessing and giving feedback to the students in constant, cyclical, and cumulative ways (including daily classwork, ongoing project work, portfolios, etc.), all of which is taken into consideration in grading or otherwise evaluating the students. This form of assessment is often contrasted with final examination systems. In this section, one activity involves continuous reflection by the students on their strengths and weaknesses in performing business English communicative tasks or simulations ("Continuous Reflection on Business Simulations"). Another focuses on helping students continuously use recorded audio journals to develop their abilities to judge their own discourse accuracy ("Audio Journaling for Self-Assessment").

Individual differences assessment typically involves assessing differences among students in terms of motivation, anxiety, personality, multiple intelligences, willingness to communicate, learning preferences, learning strategies, literacy, and more. Knowing the students' strengths and weaknesses in terms of any of these factors allows teachers to then tailor their assessments to individual abilities and preferences. In this section, five approaches to individual differences are offered. One activity appeals to strengths of kinaesthetic (as opposed to visual, or auditory-dominant) learners, who are often disadvantaged by tests that are largely visual (or sometimes auditory) in nature ("An A-maze-ing Assessment"). The second activity will appeal to the often neglected sense of smell ("Matching Scents"), whereas the third allows students to choose the form of assessment that most appeals to them from among a variety of assessment options ("'Choose One' Activity Menus Using Multiple Intelligences"). The fourth activity can be used to diagnose the level of literacy in preliterate ESL learners by easing them from recognizing small picture shapes to letter shapes, then to word recognition, and word-to-picture matching ("Assessing and Placing the Preliterate ESL Learner"). The final activity appeals to students' visual and aesthetic sensibilities in assessing their speaking abilities ("Do You See What I See? Using Works of Art in Oral Assessment").

In short, teachers can benefit in a number of ways from using portfolio, journal, log, conference, online, dynamic, continuous, and individual differences assessments. My inner psychometrician, however, compels me to warn that all of these advantages come at a price. These forms of assessment generally require more effort from teachers and are more time-consuming than more conventional assessment activities. For teachers who care about their students' learning, however, the advantages of using these alternative methods of assessment should more than compensate for the amount of time and effort teachers will need to invest. It's well worth the effort to make it possible to assess communicative speaking and writing (or the interactions of reading, writing, speaking, and listening), to individualize the assessment for specific students, and to integrate assessment and classroom learning.

REFERENCES AND FURTHER READING

Brown, J. D. (2013). Computer-assisted language testing. In M. Thomas, H. Reinders, & M. Warschauer (Eds.), *Contemporary computer-assisted language learning*. London, England: Bloomsbury.

Burke, K. B. (2009). *How to assess authentic learning*. Thousand Oaks, CA: Corwin.

Cambridge, D. (2010). *E-portfolios for lifelong learning and assessment*. San Francisco, CA: Jossey-Bass.

Chapelle, C. A., & Douglas, D. (2006). *Assessing language through computer technology*. Cambridge, England: Cambridge University Press.

Poehner, M. E. (2008). *Dynamic assessment: A Vygotskian approach to understanding and promoting second language development*. Berlin, Germany: Springer.

Stefanakis, E. H., & Meier, D. (2010). *Differentiated assessment: How to assess the learning potential of every student (Grades 6–12)*. San Francisco, CA: Jossey-Bass.

Planning Portfolios

Lorraine Valdez Pierce

Levels	*High beginning +*
Aims	*Assess own progress*
Class Time	*3–6 hours*
Preparation Time	*Variable*
Resources	*Nothing additional*

This activity helps teachers plan assessment portfolios that can encourage students to monitor their own progress while providing teachers with feedback on instruction. This planning process helps relate assessment activities directly to instructional activities, thereby reducing the amount of time necessary for student portfolios. When portfolios are planned with assessment purposes in mind, the information is much more manageable and useful to both the teacher and the student. This planning activity and worksheet (see the Appendix) guide teachers step by step through the portfolio planning process, and teachers can use the completed worksheet to get started using assessment portfolios.

PROCEDURE

1. Specify your purpose in using portfolios. Is the portfolio for assessment of oral language? Reading? Reading and writing? A content area, such as social studies? Choose a purpose that reflects your students' greatest learning needs. Starting with a clear purpose can ensure success.

2. Decide how you will use the information in the portfolio. Do you need the information to monitor students' progress? To show you where the students' greatest needs are so that you can plan activities to meet those needs? For program placement? Being clear about how you plan to use the information generated by portfolios can help you see the big picture for their use.

3. Identify the portfolio type:

   • Collection portfolios consist of all of the students' writing or other work, reflection on that work, and your observations of the students' work.

- Showcase portfolios contain only the students' best work.

- Assessment portfolios are selective, systematic collections of the students' work, reflection on that work, and your observations of the students' work.

The type of portfolio you choose will help determine the entries and criteria for assessment. If you have been using collection or showcase portfolios, you may now be ready to move on to assessment portfolios, although they are not prerequisites.

4. Match the portfolio entries to your purpose. Keeping in mind your assessment purpose, think of routine classroom activities in which your students engage. Then think of how you can use these same activities for assessment. You can do this in several ways:

    - Record students' performance on a checklist, scoring rubric, or rating scale.

    - Keep anecdotal records.

    - Administer surveys and questionnaires on students' attitudes.

    - Teach the students how to engage in peer assessment and self-assessment.

5. Plan on requiring the students to collect several entries for their portfolios every quarter or semester. For yearlong portfolios, either you or the students, or both, can maintain portfolios by keeping selected entries from the beginning and the end of the year to pass along to the next teacher. You can also suggest optional entries that complement and broaden the scope of the required entries rather than repeat them.

6. Plan how you will record students' progress and provide feedback for each entry in the portfolio. A single letter grade is not as useful as clearly specified criteria in the form of a scoring rubric, rating scale, checklist, or anecdotal record. Surveys of the students' attitudes as well as peer assessment and self-assessment forms also document the students' progress. The students, their parents, and other teachers will all benefit from records that interpret and evaluate the students' performance in terms of specific criteria.

7. Involve the students in the design of their own portfolios in one or more ways:

    - Ask for their input into the criteria and standards for assessment.

    - Teach them to engage in peer assessment and self-assessment.

    - Guide them in selecting entries for their portfolios.

    - Invite them to participate in portfolio conferences.

8. Plan creative ways to make time for assessment portfolios. Options include

- using learning centers, including a portfolio center

- teaching the students how to work responsibly in cooperative learning groups

- assessing a select number of students each day or week through staggered cycles

- giving the students time for peer assessment and self-assessment activities.

FEEDBACK AND SCORING

Communicate the results to the students, parents, and other teachers.

- Design a cover sheet with spaces for the nature of each entry, the date it was created, and comments on the portfolio as a whole.

- Write a narrative summary indicating what the portfolio reveals about the student's strengths and weaknesses.

- Write a letter to parents describing the portfolio process in general or providing individualized feedback on each student.

- Hold parent–teacher conferences.

CAVEATS AND OPTIONS

1. Beginning-level or low-level students need time to acquire enough language to work with self-assessment and portfolio assessment. Give them and yourself time before involving them in these processes. Teachers of beginning-level ESL students have indicated that waiting one–two quarters (9-week grading periods) is sometimes necessary before involving them in portfolio assessment.

2. Use portfolios to gather information on how your class is progressing and to develop mini-lessons aimed at helping the students turn weaknesses into strengths.

3. Give yourself time to implement assessment portfolios. Initially, the process will probably take more time than it will once you have experience in managing your time, resources, and students.

REFERENCES AND FURTHER READING

Clemmons, J., Laase, L., Cooper, D., Areglado, N., & Dill, M. (1993). *Portfolios in the classroom: Grades 1–6.* New York, NY: Scholastic Professional Books.

O'Malley, J. M., & Valdez Pierce, L. (1996). *Authentic assessment for English language learners: Practical approaches for teachers.* Reading, MA: Addison-Wesley.

APPENDIX: *Portfolio Planning Outline*

STEP 1: Specify purpose of portfolio (Check one.)

❏ Assess oral language

❏ Assess reading/writing

❏ Assess content area

❏ Other

STEP 2: Specify use for assessment information (Check one or more.)

❏ Place students

❏ Monitor student growth

❏ Diagnose strengths and weaknesses

❏ Direct instruction

STEP 3: Identify portfolio type (Check one.)

❏ Showcase

❏ Collection

❏ Assessment

STEP 4: Match entries to purpose (Propose types of entries to match your instructional goals and objectives.)

Required entries

1. _____

2. _____

3. _____

4. _____

5. _____

Optional entries

1. _____
2. _____
3. _____
4. _____

STEP 5: Record students' progress (Specify the type of record for each portfolio entry.)

1. Scoring rubric
2. Rating scale
3. Checklist
4. Anecdotal record
5. Survey
6. Peer- and self-assessment form

STEP 6: Get the students involved (Check one or more.)

❏ Selection of entries
❏ Input into criteria or standards
❏ Peer assessment
❏ Self-assessment
❏ Portfolio conferences

STEP 7: Manage time (Check one or more.)

❏ Learning centers
❏ Cooperative learning activities
❏ Staggered cycles
❏ Peer assessment or self-assessment, or both

STEP 8: Communicate results (Check one or more.)

❏ Narrative summary
❏ Cover sheet or student profile
❏ Letter to parents
❏ Parent-teacher conference

ESL Language Portfolios: How Do They Work?

Kate Wolfe-Quintero

Levels	*Any*
Aims	*Assess own language use*
Class Time	*Variable*
Preparation Time	*Minimal*
Resources	*Folders or containers*

Language portfolios, a variation of the writing portfolios developed within both L1 and L2 teaching, are collections of selected pieces of students' work that show how they have developed in language use and understanding, during a single course or for the duration of their stay in a language program. Language portfolios are much more than a folder containing students' work; the students carefully select, revise, and reflect on the pieces (e.g., compositions, homework exercises) and increase their understanding of their own language development in the process. Language portfolios can be shared with peers and can include peers' reflections as well. The primary benefit of using language portfolios is that they allow students a chance to assess their language use, which leads to greater awareness of and growth in language. The portfolios can also be used for classroom assessment or subsequent program placement.

PROCEDURE

1. Tell the students about the language portfolios at the beginning of the course. As they do their course work, tell them to think about whether a particular assignment is one they would like to include in their portfolio or not, and whether or not they would like to revise it.

2. Make the guidelines for the portfolio clear. Decide if it will include different representative examples (e.g., a listening log entry, a dialog journal entry, a grammar assignment, a revised essay, the preparation materials for an oral report, a video recording) or if the students have complete freedom in the choice of representative work. Either negotiate the requirements for

the portfolio during the course, or determine them beforehand based on the program and its assessment needs.

3. After the students have completed a number of assignments, give them each a folder or container. Tell them to choose some examples of their work that they would like to (or need to) include in the language portfolio.

4. Have the students consult you and their peers and then revise the pieces, if desired.

5. Make sure the students justify their choices and explain any revisions, usually by writing a letter to any readers of the portfolio about what a particular piece shows about their language development, or by answering self-assessment questions (see the Appendix).

FEEDBACK AND SCORING

1. At some point, particularly if the portfolio is going to be used for more than self-assessment, give the students feedback on the developing portfolio, either from you and the students' peers, or from a group of teachers within the program.

2. If either you or a group of teachers will make a final assessment (for subsequent program placement), then indicate fairly early in the course how the portfolio measures up to any established standards and what the student can do to improve it.

CAVEATS AND OPTIONS

1. Language portfolios are not content portfolios or writing portfolios. In content-area classes (like math or social science), the students may collect examples and analyze work related to their understanding of the concepts of these fields and in the process develop a content portfolio. Similarly, writing portfolios demonstrate knowledge of writing as a discipline. In contrast, a language portfolio focuses on the language used in the students' work, that is, where the strengths and weaknesses of language use are, what the students think the pieces show about their language knowledge in various situations, and how the teacher evaluates the language use. A portfolio that relates to content or writing knowledge could also include an analysis of language use.

2. If portfolios are used for self-assessment and credit is given for having completed the portfolio, the students have more freedom in the way that they pursue it. If portfolios are used for course grading, then more time will be required for evaluation, but other forms of grading can be eliminated altogether. If portfolios are used for program assessment, then the students

must meet the standards set by the program or the teacher and will have far fewer choices about what they do.

3. In some programs, placement into the next level depends partially on an exit examination and partially on the language portfolio developed in the course. In other programs, it may depend solely on the teacher's judgment, in which case the language portfolio would be a major factor, or it may depend solely on an exit examination, in which case the language portfolio would have little to do with the placement decision.

4. Language portfolios are developed throughout a course both in and outside class. Allow class time regularly for assembling and discussing the portfolios. In this way, the students can come to appreciate what they are doing by getting clear answers to their questions about the portfolios. Looking at each other's portfolios helps the students understand what makes a good language portfolio. How much time portfolios require in class will vary with the aims of each course and with how much the portfolio affects the final grade or subsequent placement in the program.

5. Language portfolios can be used in any course designed for language teaching—speaking, reading, or writing courses; grammar, pronunciation, or vocabulary courses; and content-based or EAP courses—and can benefit all L2 learners, regardless of level or age.

6. Although language portfolios require little special preparation time, they do require you to think through how to integrate portfolios into the class process, the students' work, and the students' assessment. You must guide the process of self-assessment for it to be maximally beneficial. Initially, you will struggle with the students to define what will happen with the portfolios. Once their use has been established, ask permission to copy sample portfolios for subsequent students to examine, which will require some photocopying time at the end of the course. Evaluating the portfolios at the midpoint and end of the course will require a large amount time if the course grade depends upon this evaluation. And if teachers share evaluation duties, they will need extra time to read additional portfolios and work out shared standards of evaluation.

7. If you want to use language portfolios but have little extra time available, use them primarily for student self-assessment. Make the students largely responsible for the evaluation, which can begin in class with the students working together to provide modeling and feedback for each other. There is no set format for self-assessment, but try to develop thoughtful questions that lead the students to reflect on what they have done (see the Appendix).

REFERENCES AND FURTHER READING

Black, L., Daiker, D., Sommers, J., & Stygall, G. (Eds.). (1994). *New directions in portfolio assessment*. Portsmouth, NH: Boynton/Cook.

Fradd, S., & Hudelson, S. (Eds.). (1995). Alterative Assessment [Special Issue]. *TESOL Journal, 5*(1).

Hewitt, G. (1995). *A portfolio primer: Teaching, collecting, and assessing student writing*. Portsmouth, NH: Heinemann.

APPENDIX: *Sample Self-Assessment Questions*

1. How would you compare your [area of language use] now with the way it was at the beginning of this course? Has your thinking about [area of language use] changed in any way? What pieces of work in your language portfolio show your development in this area? How did any revisions of these pieces contribute to your growth? In what specific ways has your language changed?

2. Everyone has a personal learning style. What kinds of activities in this course did you find useful for improving your [area of language use]? Which did you not find very useful? What pieces of work in your language portfolio show this?

Self-Assessment: Preparing an English Portfolio

Martha J. McNamara and Debra Deane

Levels	*High intermediate +*
Aims	*Reflect on progress made in an English course*
	Assess strengths and weaknesses in learning English
	Establish goals and plans for future independent learning
Class Time	*5 hours*
Preparation Time	*60 minutes*
Resources	*Folders or binders*

Many teachers have used writing portfolios to promote self-assessment among students and to focus students on progress they have made over time. Our assignment is somewhat different: it is an *English* portfolio. Done as the culminating activity for an integrated skills course, the English portfolio gives students a chance to look back over the work they have done during the course and reflect on what they have learned.

PROCEDURE

1. Explain the concept of a portfolio to the students. If possible, bring in examples: an artist's portfolio, your own if you have one, or previous students' portfolios.

2. Describe what the students should include in their portfolio. Ask the students to go back over all the work they did during the course and decide which activities (either course work or experiences outside class) were the most meaningful for them and taught them the most.

3. Ask the students to choose one or two representative samples of their work during the term that show their ability to use English in each of the four skill areas: listening, reading, writing, and speaking. These samples should show their progress in English as well as their range of English usage in the four skills.

4. For each piece of evidence that the students include, have them prepare a brief written explanation of what the sample shows about their progress and development as a user of English—in other words, how the sample is significant to their development in English. This written explanation is the cover sheet that introduces the evidence that they are presenting in their portfolio.

5. As part of the portfolio, have the students write a letter to the teacher, describing

   • the area in which they made the most progress this semester and the reason they improved so much

   • their strongest area in English and the reason they feel it is a strength

   • their weakest area in English and the reason they feel it is a weakness

   • their plan for improving their weakest area

   • an assessment of their effort in the class this term

   • the grade they would give themselves for the course

6. As a final organizing step, have the students prepare a table of contents for the portfolio and present the portfolio materials in a folder or binder.

FEEDBACK AND SCORING

Although you can assign a grade to the finished portfolio (see the Appendix), the true value of the activity for the students is the process of doing it. The value of the portfolio for you is the insight gained into your students' learning processes.

CAVEATS AND OPTIONS

1. The materials in the portfolio can be direct or indirect evidence of the students' use of English. Examples of direct evidence are a list of books they read, a paper they wrote, and a video recording of an oral presentation they made. An example of indirect evidence is a short written description of a time they used English (e.g., a telephone call, a conversation with an American friend).

2. If you wish, have the students compile the materials for their portfolio outside class. Usually students complete their portfolio in class during the last week of the term.

REFERENCES AND FURTHER READING

Graves, D. H., & Sunstein, B. S. (Eds.). (1992). *Portfolio portraits.* Portsmouth, NH: Heinemann.

O'Malley, J. M., & Chamot, A. U. (1990). *Learning strategies in second language acquisition.* Cambridge, England: Cambridge University Press.

APPENDIX: *Assessment Criteria for English Portfolios*

The portfolios are read holistically with the three criteria below in mind, and a grade (such as A, B, C, D, or F) is assigned. Typically, the portfolio is equivalent to two major assignments.

1. Does the student include all the required material in the portfolio?

    •   Are there representative samples of the student's work during the semester in listening, reading, writing, and speaking?

    •   Is there a written explanation for each sample describing its significance to the student's progress?

    •   Is there a letter to the teacher describing the student's progress during the semester, including strong and weak areas, the student's plan for improving weak areas, and a self-assessment of work during the semester?

2. Do the representative samples and the written explanations demonstrate the student's progress during the semester?

3. Does the portfolio show evidence of the student's thoughtful reflection on the material and activities of the course and careful assessment of progress and learning in the course?

Portfolio Assessment of Newscast Listening

Brian Asbjornson

Levels	*Intermediate +*
Aims	*Demonstrate ability to understand content and organization of TV news reports*
Class Time	*20 minutes*
Preparation Time	*Variable*
Resources	*Video recordings of news broadcasts*

Portfolios used to measure students' progress over time are well-suited to assessing their ability to understand newscasts—programs that are readily available in most countries, are of high interest, and follow fairly clear organizational patterns. Over time, students can learn to recognize these patterns and develop a core of vocabulary common to newscasts. The television news-viewing portfolio was designed to measure students' progress in understanding and learning language, with repeated exposure to a set of activities.

PROCEDURE

1. Build a library of video recorded local, national, or international news broadcasts. This step will take some time, but the advantages of selecting content and having one set of materials from which the students can choose reports will be worth the time.

2. Define the criteria you will use to allot points in the Portfolio Record (see the Appendix). For example, how many points will you assign for something that is factually correct but grammatically incorrect? What criteria will you set for partial credit on summaries and reactions?

3. Set the criteria for the end-of-term evaluation by determining how many total points will earn a grade of A, B, or C, if you are using a letter-grade system. Give each student a copy of the Appendix or a similar Portfolio Record, and discuss each of the items and your criteria for evaluation.

4. Tell the students to watch a newscast from the video library outside class.

5. Have the students complete the Portfolio Record for a report as best they can during class time. Go over any difficulties the students have in understanding the activities.

6. Tell the students to continue watching newscast videos and filling out Portfolio Records. Explain that they will be assessed over time on both volume (how much they watch) and accuracy (how well they understand newscasts). Stress that the more they watch and try, the better they will become.

FEEDBACK AND SCORING

1. Throughout the course, review the students' portfolios, providing feedback on specific problems. You may need to spend classroom time on summarizing and other skills the students need to work on.

2. Base the final assessment on cumulative points as described above and in the Appendix.

CAVEATS AND OPTIONS

1. Be sure the students have access to a video recording device or media center. If all the students have such access, consider allowing the students to record their own material for their portfolio. This reduces teacher control over content and makes assessment more difficult, but it might set the students on the road to more extensive listening.

2. At the end of the term, use the "Understanding the Report" section of the Portfolio Record as an achievement test of the students' abilities to get the main idea, recognize tone and organization, and summarize. Be careful, however, to avoid giving students that have special content knowledge an advantage. To help overcome this problem, have the students view at least three reports with different content.

APPENDIX: *Portfolio Record*

DIRECTIONS: Complete these activities for reports from television newscasts. Write your answers on a separate sheet of paper. You do not have to do all of the activities! (NOTE: Do not forget to write the name of the news program on your answer sheet, as well as the date and time you saw the report.)

Points received	Points possible		Activity
		UNDERSTANDING THE REPORT	
	15	1. Main idea	Write one sentence describing the main idea of the report.
	5	2. Tone	What is the tone of the report? • serious • entertaining • informative • dramatic • other_____
	10	3. Organization	How is the report organized? • presents two or more sides of a controversy or issue • presents one side of a controversy or issue • presents no controversy • describes or talks about something
	35	4. Summary	Summarize the report in one paragraph.
	35	5. Reaction	Write one paragraph describing your reaction to the report.
		LANGUAGE BUILDERS	
	15	1. Listening vocabulary	Write down five words or phrases that you heard in the report. Provide a definition, a synonym or antonym, and a sentence demonstrating the meaning of each of the words or phrases.
	15	2. Visible vocabulary	Write down in your native language the names of five things you saw in the report but do not know how to say in English. Use a dictionary to find the English word, and provide a definition or drawing. Then use the word in a sentence that demonstrates its meaning.
	20	3. Dictation	Write out 10 sentences from the report.

Using Portfolios in the EFL Reading Class

Javier García

Levels	Any
Aims	*Select reading texts for the EFL class*
	Monitor reading process and progress
Class Time	*20–30 minutes*
Preparation Time	*None*
Resources	*Folders, one per student*

One of the problems many EFL reading teachers face is that their students are bored or uncomfortable with the texts they have to read in class. Portfolios can be used to tailor reading texts to students' needs and preferences, and to make students aware of their reading process and progress. Such portfolios can also serve as a text bank to help teachers write reading materials and tests.

PROCEDURE

1. Give each student a folder. Ask the students to put in their folders copies of texts they would like to read. The texts can be selected from newspapers, magazines, textbooks, or other sources.

2. Once a week, have the students sit in groups of three, open their folders, and talk for 20–30 minutes about the texts they have collected. Make sure the students say where they found the texts and why they were selected. In addition, encourage the students to write comments to accompany the texts.

3. Ask the students to hand in their portfolios once a week. Take the portfolios home, look at the texts the students have selected, select one text from each folder, and write five content questions for each text. Put the questions in the folders.

4. Return the portfolios to the students, and give them 30 minutes to answer the questions in each of their folders.

FEEDBACK AND SCORING

1. Collect the portfolios as soon as the students finish answering the questions, and grade the reading exercises. Give 4 points for each correct and complete answer, and partial credit (2 points) for each correct but ungrammatical answer. Write comments about each student's performance on a separate sheet of paper, and put it in the folder.

2. Return the portfolios to the students. Let them look at the exercise and read the comments.

3. Set up individual biweekly interviews with the students to talk about their reading progress and performance.

CAVEATS AND OPTIONS

1. Use some of the texts in the students' portfolios to write additional reading exercises for class, as homework, or to test students in other courses. Use different texts to write their reading tests.

    *   Use the reading exercises to test vocabulary, cohesion, and other objectives. Be sure to select the right text for the purpose of the test. Adjust the grading system according to the number and complexity of the items.

    *   Include the name of the student that contributed the text on all class reading exercises and tests. This will not only motivate the students to collect more reading material but also show them that their ideas are taken into account.

2. Some of the texts may not fit the students' proficiency level. Adapt the texts, or use them in higher-level courses.

3. Ask higher proficiency students to design reading exercises for the texts they have chosen (allow 30–40 additional minutes). Ask the other students to put the exercises in their folders, take the folders home, and write comments about the advanced-level students' exercises.

Using Journals for Self-Evaluation at Midterm

Joan Blankmann

Levels	*High beginning +; university*
Aims	*Reflect on progress in the course before formal evaluation*
Class Time	*30–50 minutes*
Preparation Time	*None*
Resources	*Class syllabus*

Students are often unprepared for midterm evaluations and conferences. This activity gives students the opportunity to review course goals and requirements, and assess their standing in the class using the same criteria that the teacher will use.

PROCEDURE

1. Ask the students to discuss the following questions in small groups: What is the purpose of midterm evaluations? Why are evaluations necessary? What do you like and dislike about evaluations?

2. Ask the students to review the class syllabus and discuss it in their groups.

3. Answer any questions the students have regarding the grading system. Make sure the students clearly understand the items that are considered for grading and the way the grades are computed.

4. Present the journal topic *Self-Evaluation of My Progress in This Course.* Tell the students first to identify and write about their areas of strength (what they are doing well) in the course, using the syllabus to guide their writing, and, second, to identify and write about their areas of weakness (what they need to improve).

5. Allow the students to write for 20–30 minutes.

FEEDBACK AND SCORING

1. Respond to the journals either in writing or orally at the conference. Note any major discrepancies between your own evaluation and the student's self-evaluation. Discussing these differences in perception can provide the student with very valuable information.

2. After the students have received their midterm evaluations, ask the students to write in their journals on this topic: *My Plan for Improvement in This Course.*

CAVEATS AND OPTIONS

1. To help this activity proceed smoothly, ask the students to locate their syllabi in advance. Have extras on hand for students who have misplaced theirs.

2. If journal writing is not part of the class, present this activity as a writing assignment in the form of a worksheet.

3. A good follow-up is an informal course evaluation. Ask the students to write about what has been most helpful and least helpful in the course and to suggest ways the second half of the course might be improved.

4. Consider using journal writing for a self-evaluation at the end of the course.

Don't Talk About It, Write It Down

Javier García

Levels	*Any*
Aims	*Think and write about the reading process and attitudes toward reading in English*
	Improve writing skills
Class Time	*15–30 minutes*
Preparation Time	*None*
Resources	*Notebooks, one per student*

Having students keep journals is no longer just a way to evaluate writing skills. Journal writing is also a powerful tool with which teachers can collect information on students' reading processes and strategies, assess those processes and strategies, and learn about students' attitudes toward and motivations for learning English.

PROCEDURE

1. Distribute notebooks to the students, or ask each of them to buy one.

2. Once a week, ask the students to write in their notebooks comments, feelings, ideas, and likes and dislikes related to texts or topics in their reading class. Encourage the students to write specifically about the difficulties they encounter while reading texts written in English, the ways in which they think they can improve their reading strategies, and their attitudes toward learning English.

3. Ask the students to hand in the notebooks once a week. Read the students' comments, and write responses in the notebooks. Advise the students about their reading strategies, make comments on their reading process and progress, and add any other information, as desired.

FEEDBACK AND SCORING

1. Grade the students' journal writing.

2. Return the notebooks to the students so that they can read all teacher responses, revise their written comments, and continue recording their ideas.

3. Allow the students to hand in revised versions of their English writing. Regrade them if desired, and return the journals to the students.

4. Keep a record of the students' comments. As the students become more used to writing their journals, bring up their ideas and comments as discussion points in class. Encourage other students to voice their opinions and ideas.

5. Take advantage of the students' comments to revise the objectives and materials used in the reading class to better suit the students' reading needs.

CAVEATS AND OPTIONS

1. At first the students will probably need to be encouraged and guided in writing in their journals. Be patient; they will eventually mention the topics you want to know about.

2. Have the students write in their journals at home.

3. Be sure to read and comment on the journals regularly.

4. Be careful when talking about the students' ideas and comments in class. Preferably do not mention the students' names but rather talk about the ideas and comments in general.

5. Combine the activity with the idea of a portfolio in which the students include not only written comments but also favorite texts, as well as others they have read or plan to read.

6. Set up biweekly interviews with individual students to talk about their English reading process and progress, English writing skills, as well as any other topic desired by teacher or student.

Self-Assessment: Keeping a Language Learning Log

Martha J. McNamara and Debra Deane

Levels	*High beginning +*
Aims	*Learn to self-assess*
	Identify strengths and weaknesses in English
	Determine which language learning strategies, materials, and contexts work best
	Document progress
	Establish goals for future independent learning
Class Time	*60 minutes*
Preparation Time	*60 minutes*
Resources	*Spiral notebooks, one per student*

This version of the language learning log is a regular, ongoing assignment. Students keep a record of situations in which they have used English (e.g., in class work, homework, or outside-of-class activities), describe those situations, and analyze their success or problems in comprehension and communication. Both the teacher and classmates can give feedback. Keeping a language learning log provides students with a concrete record of their activities and progress during the course.

PROCEDURE

1. Ask the students what they think *self-assessment* means. Discuss with the students the rationale for having learners examine their own learning processes and evaluate their own abilities.

2. Explain what a learning log is and why it is helpful for the students to keep one.

3. Give the students each a notebook. Ask them to write three entries each day in their notebook about situations in which they use English in class activities, on homework assignments, or during out-of-class activities. Give

examples of possible experiences that the students might describe, including watching TV programs; listening to an audio recording in class; reading newspapers and magazines; writing letters, notes, or a journal in English; doing grammar homework exercises; and talking with friends or transacting business in a bank or post office. For each entry, tell the students to record the date, the activity, the amount of time they used English, the location, and a description and an analysis of their use of English. Tell the students to focus the analysis on the ease or difficulty of the activity and the reasons for that ease or difficulty.

4. Give the students about 30 minutes in class to start the first entry. To create a climate for extended, thoughtful writing, write in a notebook along with the students. In the last 10 minutes, circulate to spot-check entries and answer individual questions.

5. At the end of each week, have the students evaluate their progress and make plans for future practice. To do this, they should reread their entries for that week, note where they succeeded and where they still have difficulties, determine their weak areas, and plan how to improve them during the following week.

6. Collect the logs and provide feedback.

FEEDBACK AND SCORING

1. Give three types of written feedback:

   - *Cheerleading* feedback which celebrates successes with the students or encourages them to persevere through difficulties.

   - *Instructional* feedback suggests strategies or materials to try, recommends ways to fine-tune strategy use, or instructs students on their writing (e.g., helps with word choice or selectively corrects grammar if the student requests help; however, grammar is not usually corrected in the entries).

   - *Reality-check* feedback helps the students set more realistic expectations for their language abilities if they are being too hard (or not hard enough) on themselves.

2. Assess the quantity and quality of log entries:

   - For a quantity score, record the percentage of entries completed.

   - For a quality score, determine whether or not the students have adequately described the situations in which they used English and thoughtfully analyzed their success or difficulty in comprehending or communicating in English. We give letter grades (e.g., A, B, C) for the quality score.

CAVEATS AND OPTIONS

1. Decide whether the students will log their experiences with English in their class work, on homework assignments, or in their extracurricular uses of English. This will depend on the environment in which the students are learning English and their access to native English speakers and authentic materials outside class.

2. Determine which language skills or strategies your students will assess:

   - one language skill (e.g., reading, writing, listening, or speaking)

   - the use of a particular language learning strategy (e.g., guessing the meaning of vocabulary from context while reading or listening)

   - their success or failure with a specific teaching/learning point. For example, after writing an essay, the students could examine the way they used verb tenses in the essay and analyze the success or failure of their editing process.

3. Decide how often the students will write in their logs. Writing daily entries is a good way to begin the log assignment. Once self-assessment becomes routine for the students, they may write entries on a less frequent basis.

4. Consider how often you want to collect the logs and who will be reading the entries:

   - Collect them all once a week or every other week, or collect a few each day.

   - Develop log buddies or log study groups, and have the students read and respond to each other's log entries. These options enable the students to get peer feedback, and they lessen your paper load.

REFERENCES AND FURTHER READING

Bromley, K. (1995). Buddy journals for ESL and native-English-speaking students. *TESOL Journal, 4*(3), 7–11.

Carroll, M. (1994). Journal writing as a learning and research tool in the adult classroom. *TESOL Journal, 4*(1), 19–22.

Oxford, R. L. (1990). *Language learning strategies: What every teacher should know.* New York, NY: Newbury House.

Passport: A Log

Jonice Tovar

Levels	*Intermediate +*
Aims	*Assess writing skills through experiential comments*
	Build confidence in thinking processes
	Express ideas freely
	Identify learning strategies and weaknesses in written communication
	Lower affective filter
	Receive positive reinforcement
Class Time	*20 minutes*
Preparation Time	*60 minutes*
Resources	*Nothing additional*

I n this assessment activity, the students improve their English writing skills and their grades by completing a series of student-centered, communicative activities every day (or after each class). This activity is called *Passport* (after Hart, 1994) because the students bring the passports to class (or better yet, store them at school) and do something different with them in each activity.

PROCEDURE

1. Tell the students they will each receive a passport with a list of activities. Give each of the students a passport (see Appendix A), and have them fill in their names in the place provided.

2. Read all the instructions in the passport to the students, and clarify any questions they have.

3. Pass out the Passport Activities handout (see Appendix B), and read all the activities aloud.

4. Tell the students they can begin working on any activity they want. Give them a specific deadline by which they must hand in all the passport activities,

and tell them they will each receive a reinforcement award (e.g., stamps for activities done correctly and stickers for those done incorrectly) and that each activity is worth a different number of stamps or stickers depending on how well it is done.

FEEDBACK AND SCORING

1. Record the score for each task in the passport as shown in Appendix B.

2. Alternatively, score each writing assignment 1–5 on the following basis:

   - 1 point: The writing has a personal style; spelling and punctuation are not graded.

   - 2 points: The writing has a personal style; the words chosen are clear; spelling and mechanics are correct.

   - 3 points: The writing is coherent; all necessary information is included; words and phrases are combined effectively; spelling and mechanics are correct.

   - 4 points: Use of supporting information is clear and convincing; the structure is clearly developed; the words chosen are clear, accurate, and precise; there are no errors in spelling or mechanics.

   - 5 points: The writing shows very a complete and detailed structure; there is good use of words and expressions; words and phrases exhibit good patterns of language; there are no errors in spelling or mechanics.

CAVEATS AND OPTIONS

1. Adjust the time limit for the activities depending on their difficulty.

2. If desired, at the end of each week have the students write their own opinions of each week's class on a form (see Appendix C).

3. Write a response to each student's feedback form.

REFERENCES AND FURTHER READING

Hart, K. (1994). Passports give students responsibilities for their own learning. *TESOL Journal, 3*(4), 26–27.

Sharkey, J. (1994/1995). Helping students become better learners. *TESOL Journal, 4*(2), 18–22.

APPENDIX A: *Sample Passport*

Name: Grade: PASSPORT PASSPORT PASSPORT Total grade: _____	**Improve your English and your grade using the passport activity** This is how to use it: 1. Read all the activity choices. 2. Select the ones you prefer to do. The total number of points is 40, but you only have to complete 20. 3. Each activity is worth 1–5 stamps. 4. Each stamp = 1 point. 5. Your passport grade will be averaged with your classroom participation. 6. Need help? Talk to the teacher. ☺

APPENDIX B: *Passport Activities*

TASK 1: Talk to your teacher for 1 minute (free topic), and write a 25-word paragraph on what you two talked about (*1 stamp*)

TASK 2: Talk to any other English teacher. Write whether or not you understood him and how different it was from the conversation with your teacher. (*2 stamps for free topic, 3 stamps for current events*)

TASK 3: Read something in the newspaper and talk about it for a minute in class. Then list those things you easily talked about, as well as those that were a bit complicated for you (*4 stamps*)

TASK 4: Go to the library.

- Read an article and summarize it. (*4 stamps*)

- Read an article and write two questions that are answered in it. (*2 stamps*)

- Read an article and write the main idea. (*3 stamps*)

TASK 5: Go to an English language library and look for an article in a magazine.

- Find 20 verbs in past tense. (*1 stamp*)

- Find 10 sentences in a specific verb tense. (*2 stamps*)

- Write three questions that are answered in the article. (*2 stamps*)

TASK 6: Use an encyclopedia as a reference.

- Write a 10-line comment about a famous personality. (*4 stamps*)
- Write 10 lines about a concept. (*2 stamps*)

TASK 7: Bring the lyrics of a song to class.

- Write a description of the characters. (*2 stamps*)
- Write a description of the plot, setting, and message. (*2 stamps*)
- Write your personal opinion. (*5 stamps*)

APPENDIX C: *Weekly Feedback Form*

Adapted from Sharkey (1994/1995)

Name _____ Week_____

1. How was class this week? Why? (Write complete sentences using the simple past tense and other tenses that you know.) _____

   _____

2. What was one activity (including one from the passport) that you liked? Why did you like it?_____

   _____

3. What was one activity (including one from the passport) that you did not like? Why didn't you like it? _____

   _____

4. How was the homework this week? Was there too much? too little? _____

   _____

5. Which activities (including those from the passport) would you like to do more of? Why? _____

6. Can you think of other activities to include in the passport? _____

   _____

Eat, Drink, and Be Merry: Lunchtime Student Assessment

David R. Neill

Levels	*Any*
Aims	*Demonstrate conversational ability in a nonthreatening environment*
Class Time	*30 minutes (lunchtime)*
Preparation Time	*15 minutes*
Resources	*Nothing additional*

This activity is an evaluative or diagnostic tool that the teacher can use to gain a better picture of the students' abilities and progress. In a large conversation class, it is often difficult for the teacher to assess how the students are doing. The same few students usually volunteer to answer questions while everyone else sits quietly. By having lunch with the teacher in a relaxed atmosphere, students tend to open up more, providing a better opportunity to evaluate their progress in the class. The natural flow of the conversation allows the students to ask questions that they may have been afraid to ask in class. Students who are quiet and shy in the class tend to become less afraid of making mistakes during this time. After having lunch together, the students seem to open up more in class as well.

PROCEDURE

Before the Class Begins

1. Prepare a sign-up sheet for students to schedule a lunch with you.

    *   Start the lunch schedule after the first month of class to allow for a better assessment of the students.

    *   Have at least two—but no more than four—students sign up for each lunch hour. (The number of students in the class will determine how many lunch hours to allot.)

First Day of Class

1. Tell students—after you have explained the overall class requirements—that they will be required to bring a lunch and eat it with you at least once during the term (or semester, or year).

2. Reassure the students by explaining that they will eat lunch in your office or in another location where they will not attract attention to themselves. Give directions to the location.

3. Show the students the sign-up sheet, and tell the students they can schedule their lunches with you on a first-come, first-served basis. If your class is divided into groups, have all the members of the group come on the same day.

4. Stress that the lunch is a class requirement and that you want to have lunch to get to know the students better.

Lunch

1. Before the students arrive, make a mental list of their possible language weaknesses to help you guide the flow of the conversation and decide on areas to focus on during lunch.

2. When the students arrive, greet them and have everybody start eating. Start the conversation.

3. During lunch:

   - Ask each student questions if necessary to get the conversation going.

   - Gear the discussion to the level of the students. Control the flow and content of the conversation.

   - Keep in mind certain points you have covered or will cover in class, and help steer the conversation in order to include those points.

   - Bring subject matter covered in class into the conversation so that the students have the chance to practice using it. For example, have the students ask for and give information on such topics as their future plans, hopes, and dreams

FEEDBACK AND SCORING

1. If you wish, use this session as the basis for part of each student's grade. The grading will probably be more subjective than it is for a paper test. Because the students speak in a small group, you can more reliably evaluate their productive skills. Students whom you regard as average in class may turn out to have much higher productive skills at lunchtime because you have more time to interact and because the student–teacher ratio is much better than in class.

2. Evaluate the students' listening skills by judging the quality of the responses the students give to your questions and comments and to those of the other students.

CAVEATS AND OPTIONS

This activity works best with at least four students to a group. The more students there are eating lunch with the teacher, the livelier the conversation tends to be. The activity does not work well with too few students.

Exploiting Online Recordings to Test Academic Listening Ability

Jeff Popko

Levels	*Intermediate to advanced*
Aims	*Ability to catch key words and concepts in context using authentic materials found online.*
Class Time	*8–10 minutes*
Preparation Time	*60 minutes*
Resources	*Listening passages (from online authentic recordings at the target level)*
	Projector with sound system and speakers
	Computer with Internet connection
	Photocopies of the adapted transcript

PROCEDURE

At the beginning of the course, demonstrate the idea of reading while listening (Popko, 2011) by playing a recording while projecting the transcript (e.g., a laptop connected to a ceiling projector, or any projection system). Online sources such as Voice of America or iTunesU work well, and many news organizations now have videos with transcripts available online. Also, many textbooks now come with transcribed recordings or recordings of their reading texts.

1. Choose a listening passage of the appropriate level, with a corresponding transcript, that takes 2–3 minutes to play. Create a response sheet by removing key terms and phrases in each segment of the transcript. This should create 10–15 items for the students to fill in.

2. Play the listening passage once, instructing students to listen for the main points. Distribute the adapted transcripts face down. When all of the students are ready to listen, instruct them to turn their papers over and read along with the recording, filling in the blanks, as needed. Play the recording a second time so students can check their work.

FEEDBACK AND SCORING

Score the assessment like a cloze test or dictation, using either the exact-word (i.e., only the word that was originally deleted) or the acceptable-answer (i.e., the exact word or a synonym) methods, but use the same method consistently.

CAVEATS AND OPTIONS

1. Most students are familiar with and have access to YouTube and online news sources. Students may need to be introduced to iTunesU or other sources for academic listening, however.

2. Students should practice reading while listening prior to the assessment.

3. One extension activity is to have students choose a listening passage (alone or in groups) and create their own assessments to share with their peers online (i.e., via a class shell). Longer recordings can be used as sources of listening (e.g., PBS and NPR have many 45–50 minute recordings available free online). However, 5 minutes is the longest passage suggested for assessment purposes. The longer recordings could be divided into smaller pieces for a series of, say, 10–12 weekly assessments using one recording, for the sake of continuity during an ongoing assessment process.

4. In theory, a similar effect could be achieved by the teacher reading a transcript as a type of dictation fill-in. The added value of using Internet sources is that they provide authentic texts from a wide variety of sources, on a wide range of topics, allowing students access to individualized practice activities.

REFERENCES AND FURTHER READING

Popko, J. (2011). Reading while listening to build receptive fluency. In N. Ashcroft & A. Tran (Eds.), *Teaching listening: Voices from the field*. Alexandria, VA: TESOL.

Using Glogs and Comic Strips to Assess Academic Content

Susan L. Schwartz

Levels	*Intermediate +*
Aims	*Demonstrate knowledge of academic concepts and vocabulary taught in mainstream classes*
	Use correct mechanics, spelling, and grammar in writing
Class Time	*Two class periods of 45–60 minutes each*
Preparation Time	*Variable*
Resources	*Internet access to: Glogster, MakeBeliefsComix, ComicLife2*

PROCEDURE

1. Tell students that they will use a computer application to create a poster or comic strip about the topic they have been studying. Give the students a handout (see Appendix A) that describes the project and go over it with them. Tell students they will

    *   demonstrate their knowledge by writing text and inserting images (and perhaps also inserting audio or video if creating a Glog) that describes a minimum of four important ideas or concepts about the content

    *   include a certain number of vocabulary words from the unit they have been studying

    *   include designated features of the application they are using, such as Glog decorations or speech bubbles

2. Distribute another handout (if not included with the project description); see Appendix C that explains how the project will be evaluated and go over it with the students. Tell them they will be assessed on

    *   whether the required number of facts or concepts is included and the accuracy of the information

    *   whether the required number of vocabulary words is included and used correctly

- how well the graphics and text support each other (i.e., how appealing the final product looks)

- the accuracy of the language used—the fewer the errors, the higher the score

3. Have computers booted up and the target application open before the start of the class if possible. Otherwise, instruct the students to access the Internet and then go to the application.

4. Depending on how many class periods you have allocated, give students a suggested timeline for completing their projects; for example, if two periods have been designated, let students know that by the end of the first period, they should be about halfway done.

5. Tell students to start creating their project.

6. Monitor students' progress.

7. Periodically remind students to save their work and to refer to the handout to ensure that all required elements are included.

8. At the end of each class period, tell students to save their work.

9. Evaluate the students' projects using a rubric or checklist designed specifically for the application being used (see Appendices B, C, and D).

CAVEATS AND OPTIONS

1. This assessment activity assumes that the students already know how to use these applications and can immediately begin working on their projects after receiving the directions.

2. Teachers can use these websites with students at lower language proficiency levels or who are younger than middle school age, as long as they modify the requirements and assessment criteria.

3. Students may work in groups of 2–3 if 1:1 computer availability is not possible.

4. If time allows, students may peer-edit each other's work, which is very useful as inevitably students will ask for clarification about a content item or use of a vocabulary word and will find errors in mechanics, spelling, or grammar.

5. Finished projects can be presented to the whole class as a review of the material and to provide students with practice in giving oral presentations.

6. MakeBeliefsComix does not permit students to save their work online; they must either email or print it. As a result, students need to know that they

must finish the sequence of two, three, or four panels they are working on by the end of each class period.

7. ComicLife2 is only available for the Mac and iOS platforms; Version 1, however, is also compatible with Windows computers.

WEBSITES

MakeBeliefsComix (http://www.makebeliefscomix.com/): a free website for creating comic strips using templates for characters, speech bubbles, and objects.

ComicLife2 (http://plasq.com/products/comiclife2/): a downloadable program that allows students to create comic strip-like panels, but with more variety in templates and features than MakeBeliefsComix. It must be purchased after a free 30-day trial.

Glogster (http://edu.glogster.com/): a website to create online posters that can incorporate audio and video as well as text and images; a free version for educators is available, whereas the paid version has more features.

APPENDIX A: *Sample Project Handout*

Glogster Project: East Asian Geography

Objectives

1. to demonstrate your knowledge of one aspect of East Asian physical and human geography by creating an online poster

2. to use two vocabulary words from a chapter section correctly

3. to use correct capitalization, punctuation, spelling, and grammar in writing captions to images

Procedure

1. Read the section in the chapter that was assigned to you.

2. Use Glogster to create a poster.

   • Include a title that explains what geographical feature you are talking about.

   • Give at least two details for each subsection of your topic and label those subsections on your Glog.

- Give examples of the way that the environment has affected the region.

- Include at least one map and one other image that illustrate your section topic.

3. Design your Glog so that the information is clear and easy to read.

4. Check the language on your Glog for accuracy.

5. Make sure that two vocabulary words are included and used correctly.

   NOTE: Evaluation will be according to the *Glogster* rubric on the other side of this paper.

   Due date: _____

APPENDIX B: *ComicLife2 Checklist*

For a 2-Page Project

_____ Four selected facts are accurately explained in the students' own words. (20 points)

_____ Four images appropriately illustrated each selected fact. (20 points)

_____ At least two images are captioned accurately. (20 points)

_____ At least one thought/speech balloon is included. (10 points)

_____ At least two vocabulary words are included and used correctly. (10 points)

_____ Title and subtitle fonts are sized appropriately and are in color. (10 points)

_____ Spelling, grammar, capitalization, and punctuation are correct. (10 points)

_____ Total points

   Grade = _____

Comments: _____

_____

_____

APPENDIX C: *Glogster Rubric*

Category	5 points	4 points	3 points	2–1 points
Factual information	Four required facts are included and all are correct, plus at least one more additional, correct fact is included.	Four required facts are included and all are correct.	Three out of four facts are included and all are correct.	Only two facts are included and may or may not be all correct.
Graphics relevance	All graphics are related to the topic and make the Glog easier to read and understand.	All but one of the graphics are related to the topic, but those make the Glog easier to read and understand.	All but two graphics are related to the topic, but those make the Glog easier to read and understand.	Less than two graphics are related to the topic but those make the Glog easier to read and understand.
Attractiveness	The design, layout, and neatness of the Glog is exceptionally attractive.	The design, layout, and neatness of the Glog is very attractive.	The Glog's design is fairly attractive, but it is a bit messy and not so neat.	The Glog is not very attractive or well-designed, and it is messy and/or not very neat.
Vocabulary	Two vocabulary words are included and used correctly.	Two vocabulary words are included, but only one is used correctly.	Only one vocabulary word is included, but it is used correctly.	One vocabulary word is included, but it is not used correctly /OR/ no vocabulary words are included at all.
Language used	There are 0-3 language mistakes on the Glog.	There are 4–7 language mistakes on the Glog.	There are 8–12 language mistakes on the Glog.	There are more than 12 language mistakes on the Glog.

APPENDIX D: *Checklist for MakeBeliefsComix*

Your comic strip will be evaluated according to the features below. Both content information and use of language will count towards your grade. The total number of points for each item is given in parentheses.

Content	Comments
Information is accurate. (4 points)	_____
Includes introduction frame. (1 point)	_____
Includes required number of content frames. (2 points)	_____
Includes conclusion frame (1 point)	_____
Includes target vocabulary (2 points)	_____
Total points for Content =	_____

Language	
Spelling is correct. (2 points)	_____
Grammar is correct. (2 points)	_____
Punctuation is correct. (2 points)	_____
Capitalization is correct. (2 points)	_____
Target vocabulary is used correctly. (2 points)	_____
Total points for Language = _____	

Grand Total =   _____ x 5 = _____

Letter Grade =   _____

Speed in Processing Words: Antonyms or Synonyms?

F. Han

Levels	Advanced beginner +
Aims	Test ESL/EFL learners' speed in processing words
	Determine if processing speed needs improvement
Class Time	10 minutes
Preparation Time	5 minutes plus advance set-up time
Resources	Laptops, or a language laboratory with computers installed with **Windows**
	DMDX software

In this activity, *word processing* refers to the ability to recognize the forms and retrieve the meanings of words (Grabe, 2009). According to Perfetti's (1988) verbal efficiency model, inefficient word processing skills often inhibit readers from processing the concepts in texts and building a coherent interpretation of text content. This computer-based testing activity is adapted from Haynes and Carr's (1990) paper-based test and uses DMDX software, a free downloadable program which records both accuracy and reaction time in milliseconds (Forster & Forster, 2003). The assessment activity requires learners to decide as quickly as possible if a pair of words has a similar meaning (i.e., a synonym) or opposite meaning (i.e., an antonym).

PROCEDURE

1. This assessment activity requires installing software and setting up computers in advance. The teacher needs to download and run TimeDX.exe on each computer. Instructions are available at DMDX Experiment Software (http://www.indiana.edu/~clcl/Q550_WWW/DMDX.htm). Each computer only needs to be set up once; multiple students can then continue without repeating the set-up procedure.

2. Give students test instructions either on a computer screen or on a sheet of paper. Students will have 10 minutes to judge 50 pairs of words as synonyms or antonyms by pressing a specific key if a pair of words are synonyms (e.g., the *S* key), and a different key if a pair of words are antonyms (e.g., the *A* key). (NOTE: Teachers can decide which keys represent synonyms and antonyms and mark those keys when they set up the program.)

3. Include a practice session if the students are not familiar with the format of this assessment activity. The items in the practice session need not be scored.

4. Allow learners to ask questions after the practice session.

5. Answer their questions and proceed to the assessment session.

FEEDBACK AND SCORING

Although the activity measures both the accuracy and reaction time or how quickly learners can retrieve the meaning of a word, the focus is on speed. Speed can be calculated by looking at the computer output and averaging the reaction time for all the items. The reason for focusing on speed is that accuracy reflects learners' vocabulary knowledge. It is therefore suggested that the activity be based on a selection of high-frequency words, familiar to the learners. The accuracy scores can also be checked to ensure that the answers from the learners are valid and reliable.

CAVEATS AND OPTIONS

1. This assessment procedure can be administered to learners one by one or in groups of learners depending on the number of available computers.

2. If a single computer or laptop is used to administer the assessment to multiple students, make sure to rename the file generated with each student's results. Otherwise, *DMDX* will write over the previous student's file.

REFERENCES AND FURTHER READING

Forster, K. I., & Forster, J. C. (2003). DMDX: A windows display program with millisecond accuracy. *Behavior Research Methods, Instruments, and Computers, 35*(1), 116–124.

Grabe, W. (2009). *Reading in a second language: Moving from theory to practice.* New York, NY: Cambridge University.

Haynes, M., & Carr, T. H. (1990). Writing system background and second language reading: A component skills analysis of English reading by native speaker–readers of Chinese. In T. H. Levy & B. A. Levy (Eds.), *Reading and its development: Component skills approaches* (pp. 375–421). San Diego, CA: Academic.

Perfetti, C. A. (1988). Verbal efficiency theory in reading ability. In M. Daneman, G. E. MacKinnon, & T .G. Waller (Eds.), *Reading research: Advances in theory and practice* (pp. 109–143). New York, NY: Academic.

APPENDIX: *Example Synonym and Antonym Word Pairs*

Item	Synonym Word Pair		Part of Speech
1	fortunate	lucky	adj.
2	request	ask	v.
3	nation	country	n.
4	often	frequently	adv.
Item	Antonym Word Pair		Part of Speech
1	war	peace	n.
2	hot	cold	adj.
3	cry	laugh	v.
4	outside	inside	adv.

Interventionist Dynamic Assessment: Feedback on a Timed Reading

Mami Orikasa

Levels	*Beginner to intermediate*
Aims	*Investigate students' problem areas in reading*
	Check student comprehension levels
Class Time	*10–15 minutes*
Preparation Time	*10 minutes*
Resources	*Timed-reading materials*
	Score report

There are many commercial materials for timed reading. Those materials are useful for students to practice reading fast and to track their progress by self-scoring. For teachers, those materials can also be instrumental in helping them further pinpoint students' weaknesses in reading through interventions in one-on-one sessions. This activity aims to help teachers determine students' understanding levels and overcome problem areas with reading.

Interventionist dynamic assessment, was coined by Lantolf and Poehner (2004), along with *interactionist dynamic assessment*. Dynamic assessment, based on Vygotsky's zone of proximal development, is "a framework for conceptualizing teaching and assessment as an integrated activity of understanding learner abilities by actively supporting their development" (Lantolf & Poehner, 2011, p. 11). In interventionist dynamic assessment approaches, "tasks are selected and analysed with the goal of predicting the kinds of problems learners are likely to encounter" (Lantolf & Poehner, 2011, p. 15). Mediation, including hints and prompts, is pre-arranged in order from most implicit to most explicit, and the mediator follows this order until the learner answers correctly, or if the final mediation fails to work, the mediator provides the solution and explanation (Lantolf & Poehner, 2011).

PROCEDURE

1. Administer a timed-reading activity in class. Collect students' answer sheets.

2. Score individual answer sheets after class, and check for incorrect items.

3. Have a one-on-one feedback session with each student and inform them of their score and the number of wrong answers. Go over the wrong answers one by one. Pick the first wrong item and ask the student to choose an alternative answer (see Appendix A).

FEEDBACK AND SCORING

1. If the student picked only wrong answers, provide the correct answers and explain why they are correct. Investigate what the problem is. Describe the problem in the Reading Assessment Form, as well as the result of interactions (Appendix B). If the problem is fixed, check the Result box. If not, make a circle in that box.

2. If the student picked the correct answer but could not explain the reason well, he may not understand it properly. Record that on the Reading Assessment Form and explain the problem to the student.

3. At the end of the session, brief the student on problems he needs to overcome next time. If there is consistency in the student's problems, provide appropriate scaffolding for him to solve his problems.

4. Mid-semester, repeat the session. Brief the student on both progress and problem areas. Go over the student's score report sheet, which comes with the materials, to discuss scores as well as reading speed. Provide appropriate feedback for the student to improve his performance.

5. At the end of the semester, provide overall feedback to the student in written form. For the next semester, provide recommended additional readings.

CAVEATS AND OPTIONS

1. If there are too many students to deal with, the teacher may schedule one-on-one sessions on separate dates.

2. If some students receive a perfect score, the teacher may assign them to play the role of the teacher, as well.

3. If many students receive a low score on a particular reading unit, it may be more effective to bring up the problems in class, instead of having a one-on-one session with each individual student.

REFERENCES AND FURTHER READING

Lantolf, J. P., & Poehner, M. E. (2004). Dynamic assessment of L2 development: Bringing the past into the future. *Journal of Applied Linguistics, 1*, 49–72.

Lantolf, J. P., & Poehner, M. E. (2011). Dynamic assessment in the classroom: Vygotskian praxis for second language development. *Language Teaching Research, 1*, 11–33.

Poehner, M. E. (2008). *Dynamic assessment: A Vygotskian approach to understanding and promoting second language development*. Berlin, Germany: Springer.

APPENDIX A: *Feedback Inventory*

	Feedback Inventory
1	Start with the first incorrect answer; ask the student to choose an alternative.
2	Ask why the student picked that answer.
3	If the student picks a wrong answer again, let him choose another alternative. (Go back to #2)
4	If the student picked only wrong answers, provide the correct answer, and explain why it is correct.
5	Record the problem on the Reading Assessment Form.

Source: Adapted from Lantolf and Poehner (2011).

APPENDIX B: *Reading Assessment Form*

Semester _____ Name_____

Reading Assessment			
Date	Unit #	Problem	Result

Interactionist Dynamic Assessment: Feedback on Essay-Writing Assignment

Mami Orikasa

Levels	Any
Aims	Investigate problem areas in writing
	Learn to overcome the problems
	Determine understanding level for grammar and writing
Class Time	30 minutes
Preparation Time	15 minutes
Resources	Nothing additional

Using essay writing is a good way to understand the strengths and weaknesses of students' English abilities. Through interactions with students in this assessment activity, the teacher can help not only identify their real problem areas but also solve them. Teacher's individualized mediations are very effective, because students can recognize and overcome their problems through interactions with the teacher. When new problems emerge through interactions, the teacher can help students solve them and advance further through mediations.

Interactionist dynamic assessment was coined by Lantolf and Poehner (2004). Unlike interventionist approaches (see previous activity), interactionist approaches impose no restriction on mediation and require every possible mediation move in order to help the learner go beyond her current independent performance (Lantolf & Poehner, 2011).

PROCEDURE

1. Provide an essay writing assignment to the students. Collect, read, and grade them. Identify their problem areas in writing and select some of the main problems to focus on during one-on-one sessions with individual students.

2. In the one-on-one session, go over the main problems one by one.

    Point out the first problem sentence to the student and ask her what the problem might be. Keep in mind that mediations with the student should be gradual, appropriate, and timely (e.g., start by saying *There is something wrong with this sentence.*)

3. Ask the student to try an alternative answer if she does not understand. Provide hints, clues, and suggestions that are appropriate in this particular situation (see Appendix A).

4. Give the correct answer if the student cannot produce the correct answer after several interactions. Provide examples, explanations, and confirmation, where appropriate.

5. (Don't rush to give the right answer.)

6. Record the student's problem as well as the result of interactions on the student's assessment form (Appendix B). If the problem is fixed, check the Result box. If not, make a circle in the box.

7. If new problems emerge through the interactions, also record them on the Essay Writing Assessment Form. Fix these problems by following Numbers 3, 4, 5, 6 and providing appropriate mediations.

8. Move on to the next problem.

FEEDBACK AND SCORING

1. At the end of the session, remind the students of their problems in essay writing. If there is consistency in their problems, provide appropriate scaffolding for each student to solve them.

2. Mid-semester, have a session again. Brief the students on their progress and remaining problem areas. Go over each student's Essay Writing Assessment Form to discuss their grade. Provide appropriate feedback for the students to improve their performance.

3. At the end of the semester, provide overall feedback to the students in a written form. Point out each student's improvements as well as a few specific areas to overcome in the next semester.

CAVEATS AND OPTIONS

1. This type of assessment is time consuming, however, it is effective for helping understand the students' problem areas and enabling them to understand those problems.

2. Mediation is most often effective if it moves from implicit to explicit with the goal of confirming an understanding of problems. The Mediation Techniques in Appendix A are examples. Teachers should also try additional

mediation techniques which they think are effective with students. As it is almost impossible to go over all the problem areas in a short time, it is best to focus on a few of them which are the most important to address immediately. Furthermore, note that new problems often emerge through interactions with students, and those problems can be addressed if time permits.

APPENDIX A: *Mediation Techniques*

Source: Adapted from Poehner (2005)

- Elicitation
- Request for repetition
- Nonverbal cues (e.g., gestures, drawing)
- Metalinguistic clues
- Locating the error
- Giving the correct answer
- Code-switching
- Explanation
- Examples
- Confirmation

APPENDIX B: *Essay-Writing Assessment Form*

Semester _____ Name_____

Essay-Writing Assessment					
Date	Assignment	Grade	Problem	Result	New problem

REFERENCES AND FURTHER READING

Lantolf, J. P., & Poehner, M. E. (2004). Dynamic assessment of L2 development: Bringing the past into the future. *Journal of Applied Linguistics, 1*, 49–72.

Lantolf, J. P., & Poehner, M. E. (2011). Dynamic assessment in the classroom: Vygotskian praxis for second language development. *Language Teaching Research, 1*, 11–33.

Poehner, M. E. (2005). Dynamic assessment of oral proficiency among advanced L2 learners of French. Unpublished doctoral dissertation, Pennsylvania State University, University Park.

Continuous Reflection on Business Simulations

Clarice S. C. Chan

Levels	*High intermediate +*
Aims	*Identify strengths and weaknesses in business communication*
	Reflect on progress over the course
	Learn to identify solutions to problems encountered
Class Time	*10–15 minutes after each simulation*
Preparation Time	*20–30 minutes*
Resources	*Reflection forms (in hard copy or online)*

In business English, communicative tasks in the form of role-play simulations are often used to help learners develop and practice their language and communication skills (Chan, 2009). In courses where simulations are used throughout, continuous reflection may be adopted to help learners identify their strengths and weaknesses, the areas in which they have made progress, as well as those areas requiring improvement. In a business communication course, there is typically an activity on business meetings in which learners work on some business meeting simulations over several weeks. Learners can use the reflection forms in this activity to record their reflections after each simulation (Appendix A) and to write up their overall reflections at the end of the business meetings activity (Appendix B).

PROCEDURE

1. At the outset, explain to the learners the benefits of continuous reflection (e.g., that they can become more critical and can also estimate their progress), and tell them how they will be assessed.

2. After conducting each simulation, give the learners time to write down their immediate reflections. A record form showing different areas for reflection may be used to provide guidance (see Appendix A for a sample).

3. At the end of the course, ask the learners to reflect on the whole learning process and write their overall reflections, possibly in the form of an essay. Alternatively, give an assignment with several questions (see Appendix B).

FEEDBACK AND SCORING

1. Provide feedback as appropriate during the course to address the problems you have observed and those mentioned by the learners in their reflections.

2. The following areas may be addressed in the assessment criteria:

    • the learners' ability to give a clear, concise, and insightful account of what they have learned

    • the learners' ability to identify their strengths and weaknesses, with examples and elaboration as appropriate

    • whether or not the learner has taken or suggested sensible actions to improve future performance in similar situations

    • whether or not the reflections are written in clear and accurate language

3. Provide feedback at the end of the course and suggest ways that the learners can remedy their weaknesses through self-study and continuous learning.

CAVEATS AND OPTIONS

1. This type of assessment can be applied to other types of business English simulation (e.g., telephoning, negotiating).

2. With some adaptations, the procedure may also be used for nonbusiness English tasks (e.g., group discussions, oral presentations).

3. Depending on the practice opportunities available, it may be preferable not to give suggestions for improvement too soon; instead, let the learners first learn from their mistakes and experiment with different communication strategies.

4. Depending on the teaching context, the assessment of the reflections can be optional. Ask the learners to attach their reflections to the final assessments.

5. To facilitate the learners' reflection, encourage them to make an audio or video recording of some or all of the simulations.

REFERENCES AND FURTHER READING

Chan, C. S. C. (2009). Forging a link between research and pedagogy: A holistic framework for evaluating business English materials. *English for Specific Purposes, 28*(2), 125–136.

APPENDIX A: *Sample Record Form for Reflections*

1. I think I did well on: _____

2. I think I didn't do so well on: _____

3. If I encounter similar difficulties in the future, I should: _____

4. I think I need to work on:_____

5. Things I can do or actions I can take:_____

6. I think I've learned: _____

APPENDIX B: *Sample Guiding Questions for Overall Reflection*

1. From the experience you gained from working on the simulations, what can you say are your strengths?

2. From the experience you gained from working on the simulations, what can you say are your weaknesses?

3. What actions have you taken and/or do you plan to take to overcome your weaknesses?

4. Critically evaluate your performance in each simulation and analyze what made each of them difficult or easy for you.

5. Think about the difficulties you and your fellow students encountered during the simulations. Do you think you may encounter similar difficulties in the future in real-life business situations? If yes, what would you do to do a better job?

6. Overall, what have you learned about business meetings by doing the simulations?

7. If you have learned other useful things not covered in your answers above, please list them here:

8. Overall, how has this assessment activity helped you learn?

Continuous Audio Journaling for Self-Assessment

Mira Malupa-Kim

Levels	*Intermediate to advanced*
Aims	*To use audio journal recordings as a means to self-assess and repair patterns of errors*
Class Time	*50 minutes +*
Preparation Time	*60 minutes*
Resources	*Any audio recording device, or language lab*

Instead of implementing the more typically used written journals, students may also record audio journals to document their progress in speaking. With the help of the teacher, students are guided on assessing their own accuracy, focusing on the many features of discourse.

PROCEDURE

NOTE: This activity requires minimal preparation from the teacher at the beginning. The teacher may specify the time limit (start with 1-minute recordings) and topics. From there, the teacher may focus on any aspect of speaking that students need to work on.

1. Instruct the students on how to record audio journals and describe the expected end-product. Also tell students how frequently they should record a journal.

2. Assign the students topics, which may be content-related or focused on particular grammar structures and functions.

3. Have students save their audio files in the language lab, or save the files on a flash drive. If there is a shared platform (e.g., Sharepoint or Moodle), the students may save the files there.

FEEDBACK AND SCORING

1. Listen to the journals and present feedback in *audio* format within a week's time. Possibly use a rubric as support to the audio feedback.

2. While waiting for teacher feedback, the students can report on their own reflections about their speaking and their progress. Also, the teacher may prompt students on what to look for by giving the same rubric or a series of questions for self-assessment.

CAVEATS AND OPTIONS

1. This activity works best in small group classes.

2. In large classes, the teacher encourages students to record audio journals, and occasionally asks students to listen to their own files and report/reflect.

REFERENCES AND FURTHER READING

Celce-Murcia, M., & Olshtain, E. (2000). *Discourse and context in language teaching.* Cambridge, England: Cambridge University Press.

Lunt, T., & Curran, J. (2010). "Are you listening, please?" The advantages of electronic audio feedback compared to written feedback. *Assessment & Evaluation in Higher Education, (35)*7, 759–769.

Malupa-Kim, M. F. (2009, March). *Enhancing speaking and pronunciation classes using the sound recorder.* Presented at TESOL Convention, Denver, CO.

An A-maze-ing Assessment

Larry Davis

Levels	*Beginner*
Aims	*Assess comprehension of directions for moving in space*
Class Time	*10–15 minutes*
Preparation Time	*Minimal*
Resources	*Blindfolds made of fabric or paper*
	Chairs, tables, boxes, tape, or anything else that can be used to construct a maze

This assessment incorporates movement with the goal of playing to the strengths of kinesthetic-dominant learners. Movement can also be a useful way to assess younger learners, and it adds variety to the assessment process. As described here, the activity is intended for informal assessment of students' ability to give and understand directions, but the assessment can also be used for more formal grading purposes, as well (see **Caveats and Options**, below). Note that this assessment is inspired by the activity "A ship in a fog" from Chamberlin and Stenberg (1976, p. 50).

PROCEDURE

1. (Optional) Review words and phrases for giving directions, such as *go left, take a small step forward,* and *turn right.*

2. Divide the class in half; ask half to wait outside the classroom.

3. With the other half of the students, prepare a maze in the classroom using desks, chairs, or other obstacles, or by using tape to mark a path on the floor. It is usually best to leave plenty of space for maneuvering.

4. Give a blindfold to each of the students inside the classroom and ask her to go outside, find a partner, and blindfold the partner.

5. Ask each pair of students to enter the classroom, with the blindfolded student being guided by verbal commands given by the other student. Allow

enough space between pairs to avoid traffic jams. Unless the room is quite large, probably no more than 2–3 pairs should be in the maze at one time.

6. As pairs work through the maze, monitor whether or not (a) correct instructions are being given by the sighted student and (b) the blindfolded student is correctly following the instructions given.

7. Have the students reverse roles, with the previously blindfolded students re-organizing the maze for the other half of the class, now waiting outside.

8. Ask pairs to walk through the maze as before.

FEEDBACK AND SCORING

1. See Step 6 of the Procedure. The teacher can circulate around the pairs and make suggestions if a student is struggling to provide appropriate directions, or if the blindfolded student is having difficulty following the directions. Common errors or problems should be noted for later attention if needed.

2. Record the time it takes students to successfully navigate the maze. Declare the pair with the shortest time the winner.

3. Count as one point each instance of an appropriate command followed by the correct movement. This will likely require assigning a helper to score each pair, or by allowing only one pair in the maze at a time.

CAVEATS AND OPTIONS

1. If the assessment is to be used more formally, then the teacher (or a helper) can set up the maze. Allow only one pair of students in the maze at a time to avoid students overhearing other pairs. Students may be assessed individually, with the teacher giving directions and awarding a point for each correct movement. In either case, ask students who have finished the maze to sit down and work quietly on another activity.

2. Additional vocabulary or phrases may be added to the assessment, as long as they involve some form of movement that can be done by the blindfolded student (e.g., *jump, kick the ball*). Also, any vocabulary item that has been associated with a movement can be included. Such additional items can be incorporated into the maze by placing word cards or pictures at different stations along the pathway. As pairs reach each station, the student giving directions should say the appropriate item.

3. The assessment will require a fair amount of open space and is best suited to large classrooms, exterior areas, or other large spaces.

REFERENCES AND FURTHER READING

Chamberlin, A., & Stenberg, K. (1976). *Play and practice! Graded games for English language teaching*. Skokie, IL: National Textbook.

Matching Scents

Benjamin Bailey

Levels	Beginner
Aims	Assess use of simple sentences with adjectives and perception verbs (i.e., feel, look, and smell)
Class Time	15 minutes
Preparation Time	20 minutes (and possibly a trip to the supermarket)
Resources	One nontransparent plastic container for each student

This activity will assess students' use of simple sentences with adjectives and perception verbs such as feel, look, and smell. Students are engaged with a sense seldom used in the classroom—smell. The presence of a scent can greatly increase student memory and attention (Akpinar, 2005; Medina, 2009).

PROCEDURE

1. In class the day before the activity, tell students to bring to the next class an item with their favorite scent and they should keep these items secret from their classmates. Show them one of the plastic containers and tell students the item must fit inside. (NOTE: Write a number on top of each container.)

2. On the day of the activity, pass out the plastic containers. Each students should put her item into a container, and leave it on her desk.

3. Give each student the worksheet. Ask them to walk around the room and smell each of the items —opening the lid without looking inside—then write a description along with their guess as to what the item is. For example, *It smells sweet. I think it is chocolate.* This will be the bulk of the activity, and time will vary depending on class size. To add an extra element of excitement, instructors can add a time limit.

4. After students finish filling out their sheets, have them return to their desks and take turns revealing their items.

FEEDBACK AND SCORING

1. A prize can be given for correct guesses. (Of course the instructor is not assessing the smelling prowess of the students.)

2. After the activity is finished, collect the worksheets and check for perception verbs and scent adjectives.

CAVEATS AND OPTIONS

1. Be sure to check for medical issues—such as peanut allergies—and make sure the classroom has windows or a good ventilation system.

2. Instructors with many students or small classrooms might wish to limit the number of scents used. This can be achieved by assigning a favorite scented item to a group of students rather than to one individual. Also, teachers can stagger the activity of numerous classes with a limited number of students bringing in items each week.

3. Instructors may wish to bring all the scented items, or request students bring in scented items of their own. Bringing in items allows for greater control by the instructor yet greatly increases preparation time and cost. Having students bring in items decreases preparation time and cost but results in less ownership by the students.

REFERENCES AND FURTHER READING

Akpinar, B. (2005). The role of sense of smell and learning and the effects of aroma in cognitive learning. *Pakistan Journal of Social Science, 3*(7), 952–960.

Medina, J. (2008). *Brain rules*. Seattle, WA: Pear Press.

APPENDIX A: *Sample Worksheet*

Name _____

Matching Scents

What is it? Describe the smell and guess what it is!
Example: *It smells bitter. I think it is coffee.*

1. _____
2. _____
3. _____
4. _____
5. _____
6. _____
7. _____
8. _____
9. _____
10. _____
11. _____
12. _____
13. _____
14. _____

APPENDIX B: *Examples of Scent Adjectives*

great	stinky	fragrant	smoky	fresh	rotten
sour	salty	sweet	bitter	spicy	minty
fishy	delicious	strong	weak	clean	medicinal

"Choose One" Activity Menus Using Multiple Intelligences

Hillary Gardner

Levels	*Any*
Aims	*Assess student comprehension through mini-presentations in a format of a student's choice*
	Promote engagement and build awareness of different ways to learn about a topic
Class Time	*60–90 minutes*
Preparation Time	*3 hours*
Resources	*Additional reading text (optional)*
	Songs or poems related to reading topic (optional)
	Play-Doh, rods, or craft sticks for building (optional)

In this activity, the teacher creates an activity menu with options for making a report on a unit of study in different formats (e.g., skit, drawing, song, survey, list, writing, or further reading). Students choose how to represent what they have learned and create mini-presentations to share with the class.

PROCEDURE

1. At the end of a unit of study when students are ready to review what they have read, prepare an activity menu that provides students with different options for reporting on what they learned. Choices are based on activities that reflect Howard Gardner's theory of multiple intelligences (see Appendix).

2. Tell students they will choose one activity to review what they have learned. Distribute the activity menu and read it together. Make sure students understand they will choose one activity from the list of options.

3. Ask students which activity they want to work on. Note on your copy of the activity menu which option each student chooses so you can be sure students stay on task.

4. Assign one area of the room for each activity. Ask students to move to the

area that matches their choice. Distribute supplemental materials as needed to help students complete their chosen task.

5. Assign students a reasonable amount of time to prepare their work (e.g., 20–30 minutes). Start with a shorter amount of time at first. Extend it as needed as students become involved in their work.

6. Allow students to choose to work alone or in a small group. If there are more than five students choosing the same activity, break the group into two smaller groups to foster greater involvement and participation.

7. Students who finish early can make another choice from the activity menu. For example, students who have chosen to draw can be encouraged to write a description of their drawing to share with the class later.

8. Bring students back together and allow the students (or groups) to present their work. If possible, hang posters, lists, or writing samples on the wall to enhance student mini-presentations.

9. Acknowledge each student presentation with applause and and provide feedback on errors as appropriate.

FEEDBACK AND SCORING

1. Rather than scoring student presentations, have students reflect on how this approach helps their learning.

2. Point out there are many ways to learn about a topic and ask if it helped them to see the same topic presented in different ways.

3. Discuss with students what they might do differently next time and whether or not they liked making a choice, rather than being assigned a task.

CAVEATS AND OPTIONS

1. The more regularly this assessment is used in class, the more students will be comfortable with making choices and exploring different options from the activity menu. To promote engagement and encourage them to take responsibility for their own learning, avoid assigning students to a group or a particular task.

2. For beginning-level classes, reduce the number of options on the activity menu. Add one new option at a time until students build familiarity with the approach.

3. Activity menus can incorporate any favorite class activity. For example, teachers have found that a popular option is allowing students to re-read a

passage and list examples of -ed words in the reading, sorted into the three pronunciations unvoiced /t/ as in talked, voiced /d/ as in jogged, and fully pronounced -ed as in loaded.

4. Use activity menus to enhance student engagement in homework. Students can choose what kind of activity to complete for homework. Teachers have found that beginning-level students in particular do more homework using this approach.

REFERENCES AND FURTHER READING

Gardner, H. (2011). Promoting learner engagement using multiple intelligences and choice-based instruction. *Adult Basic Education and Literacy Journal, 5*(2), 97–101.

Kallenbach, S., & Viens, J. (2004). *Multiple intelligences and adult literacy: A sourcebook for practitioners.* New York, NY: Teachers College.

APPENDIX: *Sample Activity Menu for Unit on Industrialization*

Choose one of the activities below to summarize what you learned about industrialization in the United States.

1. Reflect on the ways that industrialization has changed life. Write in your journal or speak with another person. How has it changed the food we eat, the houses we live in, and the clothes we wear? Has it changed other things, too?

2. Draw a picture that shows the advantages and disadvantages of industrialization.

3. Write a story, poem, or journal entry that says something about the experience of industrialization.

4. Write a song that says something about industrialization. You can use a melody you know.

5. Create a movement, dance, or body sculpture that shows something about industrialization.

6. Create a survey for your classmates about some aspect of industrialization. Ask your classmates your questions and present the results.

7. Go outside and make a list of all the signs of industrialization you can find. What can you find that would have been the same in 1850?

8. Teach the class some things you know about industrialization. Write questions for the class or make a list of all the people, places, and dates you read about.

Assessing and Placing the Preliterate ESL Learner

D. Magrath

Levels	*Pre-beginning/preliterate*
Aims	*Assess pre-reading skills before starting instruction*
Class Time	*20–30 minutes*
Preparation Time	*60 minutes*
Resources	*Nothing additional*

Pre-beginning or preliterate learners present a unique challenge for assessment. Students may speak a language that uses a non-Latin alphabet such as Arabic, Chinese, or Japanese. Some learners may speak a language with no written alphabet, or they may be nonliterate in their own language. An oral interview can determine speaking proficiency, but how can literacy readiness be assessed? Student levels of proficiency may range from none, to some word and letter recognition skills.

Basic literacy is essential to the learning process. Both reading and writing are active skills that aid language acquisition and reinforce speaking skills. Preliterate students will vary in their ability to use and recognize the written word. The following suggestions will help ESL instructors find a starting point for ESL literacy instruction. Can the reader see the differences between symbols and recognize the concepts of same-and-different and left-to-right visual sequencing? Does the reader look to the number on the left and track to the right?

PROCEDURE

1. Because of the nature of this diagnostics assessment, it should be done individually, giving instructions orally in language the student can understand.

2. Give students a copy of the assessment activities in the Appendix.

3. Walk each student through the tasks.

4. If a student gets 2 of the 4 nonexample items correct in a task, continue to

the next task until the student falls below that score. Note the last letter the student successfully identified.

5. When the student is finished, thank him, and tell him when you will provide feedback.

FEEDBACK AND SCORING

1. Each subtest in the sequenced assessment activities indicates a higher level of pre-reading ability. From symbols, the test moves on to letters, and then to words. Some students may recognize familiar words.

2. Use this information diagnostically to form groups of students or to place students into levels of literacy study as follows:

    - A and B = Beginning

    - C and D = Letter recognition

    - E and F = Word recognition

    - G = Basic word knowledge

CAVEATS AND OPTIONS

1. This test assumes that students have mastered left–right visual sequencing. If they have not, then the instruction can begin at the level of left–right orientation. Some students will recognize sight words, especially if they have lived in an English-speaking country for a while.

2. Content and background knowledge or content schemata are an important consideration (Grabe, 1991, p. 381). For example, one would not use tropical words (e.g., frog, palm) in a program based in Alaska. Cultural knowledge is another factor that must be considered; pig or pork would not be good words for an ESOL program with Middle Eastern students. A phone icon would not work with a learner only familiar with cell phones.

REFERENCES AND FURTHER READING

Grabe, W. (1991). Current developments in second language reading research. *TESOL Quarterly, 25*(3), 375–406.

Magrath, D. (1988). Teaching non-Latin alphabets through communication. *International Review of Applied Linguistics, 26*(3), 244–247.

APPENDIX: *Sequenced Literacy Assessment Activities*

A. Mark the symbol that is different in each row:

1.	<u>O</u>	q	q	q
2.	❏	◆	❏	❏
3.	O	O	7	O
4.	7	'	7	7
5.	⊁	❏	⊁	⊁

B. Mark the symbols that are the same in each row:

1.	⊠	m	<u>❖</u>	<u>❖</u>
2.	♐	7	7	♌
3.	m	♍	m	&c
4.	q	◆	⚳	q
5.	❖	❏	⊁	⊁

C. Mark the letter that is different in each row:

1.	A	<u>S</u>	A	A
2.	F	D	D	D
3.	T	T	T	Y
4.	O	P	O	O
5.	Q	Q	Q	X

D. Mark the letters that are the same in each row:

1.	<u>A</u>	<u>A</u>	S	P
2.	B	C	J	B
3.	R	T	R	Y
4.	T	Y	O	Y
5.	M	N	N	W

E. Mark the word that is different in each row:

1. name   **lame**   name   name

2. run   sun   sun   sun

3. Monday   Monday   Sunday   Monday

4. go   so   go   go

5. July   June   July   July

F. Mark the words that are the same in each row:

1. **June**   July   June   soon

2. cat   hat   mat   cat

3. call   call   ball   tall

4. is   his   his   it

5. one   one   two   too

G. Match each word to a picture:

1. paper _____

2. _____

3. _____

4. _____

5. _____

mailbox
hand
paper
bell
letter

Do You See What I See? Using Works of Art in Oral Assessment

Christine Goldstein

Levels	Intermediate +
Aims	*Develop vocabulary, grammar, and fluency*
	Learn to engage an audience
Class Time	*10–15 minutes whole-class preparation;*
	then 5 minutes per student
Preparation Time	*1–2 hours*
Resources	*Pictures of works of art*
	Index cards

his assessment activity uses works of art to facilitate conversation and allows the teacher to assess speaking skills. Works of art provide a pathway for students to explore cultural history around the world. Depending upon the work of art, students make connections to their own culture or make inroads into new cultures. The richness of authentic art allows students to utilize concrete as well as abstract vocabulary.

PROCEDURE

Preparation

1. Find pictures of works of art. A good rule of thumb is to find twice as many pictures as there are students so students will have a choice. Color samples have the greatest impact. Good places to look include Google Images, websites of art galleries and museums, and gift shops in art galleries and museums (particularly postcards). Label each picture with the name of the artist and the title of the painting, if not provided.

2. Prepare a list of words that is relevant to each picture. Categorize these words into parts of speech and attach them to the back of the picture. An index card works well.

3. To provide more scaffolding, provide picture-specific questions on the back of each picture. Questions should be designed to facilitate students' thinking about art. Examples include

    - What is happening in the picture?

    - How do the people feel?

    - How would you feel if you were there?

    - Why do you think _____ is happening?

    - Why do you think the artist chose these colors?

    - How does this picture make you feel?

    - What story can you imagine based on this picture?

Implementation

1. Have each student select a picture. Give students time (as needed) to review the supplied words. On a separate index card, students may generate more picture-relevant words.

2. Inform students that they will describe their picture to the class. Tell students they may use the words supplied on the back of the pictures to structure their thoughts. They may also consider the questions on the back of the picture to guide their thinking.

3. Have each student present his work of art to the class.

FEEDBACK AND SCORING

1. Assess each student's oral language using the rubric provided in the Appendix (or a version that you have adapted).

2. You may wish to share your rubric with the students.

CAVEATS AND OPTIONS

1. Over time, build your resources by saving postcards and greeting cards that portray works of art.

2. Preparing the lists of words ahead of time provides scaffolding for newer language learners. Encourage more advanced learners to prepare their own word lists and categories.

3. Although this is an oral assessment and not a writing assessment, this activity can also be used to assess writing skills. To do this, instruct students to write a paragraph about the selected work of art and then share it with the class.

4. Guide more advanced students to research the work of art. Encourage them to analyse how their interpretation of the work of art was similar to or different from conventional interpretations.

WEBSITES

National Gallery of Art (http://www.nga.gov)

The Museum of Modern Art (http://www.moma.org)

Museum of Fine Arts Boston (http://www.mfa.org)

APPENDIX: *Scoring Rubric*

Name _____

Student performance	Approaching	Meets	Exceeds
Student uses vocabulary relevant to the work of art.			
Student consistently uses appropriate sentence structures.			
Student's pronunciation ensures intelligibility.			
Student shares with fluency.			
Student engages the audience and conveys artistic meaning.			

Alternative Feedback Perspectives

- **Self-Assessment**

- **Peer Assessment**

- **Self-Assessment Combined with Peer Assessment**

Part II: Alternative Feedback Perspectives

EDITOR'S NOTE

Traditionally, tests have been scored by teachers or by machines. Recently in language classrooms, some teachers have given over part of the responsibility for scoring to students. As you will see below, these student scoring methods take the form of self-assessments (in which students assess their own abilities, language production, or other aspects of their progress), peer assessments (in which students or groups of students rate or give feedback on each other's language performance, effort, or other aspects of their progress), or combinations of self-assessment and peer assessment. Note that in most of the contributions in this section, the teacher also assesses the students in order to satisfy students' demand for the teacher's reactions and feedback. Below I consider each of these scoring methods in more detail.

SELF-ASSESSMENT

Self-assessments are any assessments that require students to judge their own language abilities or language performances. Thus self-assessments provide some idea of how students see their own language development. Some of the advantages for using self-assessments are that they

- can be directly integrated into the language teaching and learning processes
- provide personalized assessments for each student
- are suitable for assessing learning processes while those processes are occurring
- require little extra time or resources
- involve students in the assessment process
- foster students' reflection on their own learning processes
- encourage student autonomy
- possibly increase students' motivation

The primary disadvantages of self-assessments are that

- the scoring is relatively subjective
- the accuracy of the scores may vary depending on skill levels (apparently, at least in some cultures, higher-level students tend to underestimate their abilities)

- the scores may be particularly unreliable in high-stakes situations (e.g., final exams or placement tests)

This last issue should be less of a problem in the relatively low-stakes assessment situations typical in the classroom (where many sources of information will typically be combined in making decisions about students' placement, progress, and promotion). The disadvantages can also be minimized by using a variety of other types of information (e.g., teacher assessments, peer assessments) in making such decisions.

The section on self-assessments begins with four contributions: having students assess themselves, their participation, and other aspects of their classroom performance ("Assess It Yourself"); integrating learner and teacher assessment ("Learner Access to Assessment"); getting students to regularly assess their own oral language progress on video ("Self-Evaluated Video"); and involving students in developing their own rubrics ("Building Rubrics Democratically").

PEER ASSESSMENT

Peer assessments are any assessments that require students to judge the language or language performance of one or more other students (or peers). Peer assessments thus give students some idea of the way other students perceive their language performance—providing an external, yet relatively unthreatening, perspective. Some of the advantages that advocates claim for using peer assessments are that they

- can be directly integrated into the language curriculum
- provide personal feedback for each student
- require little extra time or resources
- involve students in the assessment process
- foster students' reflection on the learning processes
- encourage student cooperation

The primary disadvantages in using peer assessments are that

- the scoring is relatively subjective
- the scores may be particularly unreliable in high-stakes situations (e.g., final exams or placement tests)
- interpersonal problems may develop among the students over the ratings

As with self-assessment, the problem of subjectivity can be minimized by using information from a variety of sources in making any important decisions about the students. Also like self-assessment, the problem of the unreliability of peer assessments in high-stakes decision making is probably less serious in the relatively low-stakes assessment situations typical of the classroom. The potential for interpersonal problems to develop out of peer assessments, however, is very real. The authors of the various contributions seem to favour two strategies for dealing with this issue: either keep the peer assessors anonymous (which is often difficult) or train them to provide only positive and constructive feedback (a skill that might also be useful in other parts of their lives).

The section on peer assessment offers six contributions: showing how to give students a chance to assess their peers' voice and body language in a public speaking situation ("So, How Did You Like My Presentation?"), helping students take an active role in constructively and positively evaluating the classroom presentations of other students ("Teachers and Students Assessing Oral Presentations"), encouraging students to use all four skills in doing a book report ("Active Book Report"), encouraging students to compare their own work with that of other students ("Benchmarking: Situational Autonomous Reviews"), involving students in being assessed while they are assessing other students ("Assess the Assessors"), and helping create an atmosphere in which students and teachers evaluate spoken English together ("Test Your Talk").

SELF-ASSESSMENT COMBINED WITH PEER ASSESSMENT

Combining self-assessments and peer assessments is yet another strategy that contributors describe in this part of the book. Using both types of assessment has the advantage of providing two types of information to the students and the teacher: the students' view of themselves and the way their classmates perceive their language performance. In addition, these two sources of information are most often combined with the teacher's feedback, which provides a third perspective. As mentioned above, combining information sources in this way is a good idea because it tends to minimize some of the disadvantages of assessments done by the students themselves or their peers.

The section on combining self- and peer assessments has six contributions designed for a variety of purposes: providing students with three-way feedback— self, peers, and teacher—on oral presentations ("Oral Presentations: How Did I Do?"), practicing key skills for effective presentations ("Gradually Growing Presentation Assessment"), reflecting on individual contributions to a group project ("Self-/Peer/Teacher Assessment of Group Performance"), encouraging the use of English outside the classroom ("Walk-Talk Oral Tests"), learning what types of public speaking will be important in their future and developing criteria for those presentations ("Interviews and Presentations for Clarifying Authentic Public Speaking Needs"), and identifying criteria for effective writing and applying those criteria to their own writing ("Activating Self-Assessment").

REFERENCES AND FURTHER READING

Ekbatani, G., & Pierson, H. (2000). *Learner-directed assessment in ESL.* Mahwah, NJ: Lawrence Erlbaum Associates.

Kollar, I., & Fischer, F. (2010). Peer assessment as collaborative learning: A cognitive perspective. *Learning and Instruction, 20*(4), 344–348.

Kuhn, B., & Perez Cavana, M. L. (2012). *Perspectives from the European Language Portfolio: Learner autonomy and self-assessment.* New York, NY: Routledge.

Roberts, T. S. (2006). *Self, peer and group assessment in e-learning.* Hershey, PA: Information Science Publishing.

Assess It Yourself

Doug Tomlinson

Levels	*Intermediate +*
Aims	*Get involved in the assessment process*
Class Time	*5–10 minutes*
Preparation Time	*2 hours*
Resources	*Nothing additional*

This activity is designed to involve students in assessing themselves, their classroom participation, and other aspects of their learning. Traditionally, teachers have jealously guarded their prerogative to assess student performance. This right can be shared if teachers are willing to trust their students to responsibly assess themselves. This assessment activity takes only a few minutes at the end of an instructional unit, course, project, semester, or academic year.

PROCEDURE

1. Prepare a handout containing the criteria for self-assessment (ideally with input from the students).

2. Share the criteria with each class at the beginning of instructional units, the course, the project, the semester, or the academic year.

3. Have the students assess themselves at the end of the period based on the criteria.

4. Incorporate these self-assessments in the overall teacher evaluation.

CAVEATS AND OPTIONS

1. Have adult learners commit to self-assessment based on a learning contract (see Renner, 1993).

2. For beginners, make the guidelines available and discuss them in their L1(s).

3. Apply the self-assessment to such areas as class participation, project completion, perceived progress, and skill acquisition.

REFERENCES AND FURTHER READING

Genesee, F., & Upshur, J. A. (1996). *Alternatives in second language assessment.* Cambridge, England: Cambridge University Press.

Renner, P. (1993). *The art of teaching adults: How to become an exceptional instructor and facilitator.* Vancouver, Canada: Training Associates.

Learner Access to Assessment

Magali de Moaes Menti

Levels	*Any*
Aims	*Become aware of own development*
	Perform an integrated teacher–learner assessment
	Produce a record of progress
	Be assessed during classroom tasks
Class Time	*40 minutes*
Preparation Time	*20 minutes*
Resources	*Listening, reading, speaking, or writing task*

Assessment should not be separate from teaching but rather a natural step within the teaching and learning process. In fact, assessment can give teachers one more opportunity to recycle input on content and have learners put that content into practice. The difference between this kind of assessment and any other practice task is that the learners have already worked with the content and will be asked to assess their performance after carrying out the task; teachers will do the same. The advantages of this type of assessment are that it is ongoing, is built into classroom tasks, provides a record of progress for learners and teachers, and allows learners to be aware of their development.

PROCEDURE

Listening or Reading Assessment

1. Follow the usual steps for prelistening and prereading exercises.

   - Use visual aids to help the learners forecast what the content of the task will be.

   - Guide the learners to create a hypothesis about the content by using headings, subheadings, and illustrations.

   - Elicit from the students what they predict they will have to find out about the material.

- List the questions the students will have to answer on the blackboard. At this stage, ask questions that concern a general understanding of the content.

- Make sure the learners understand the prelistening or prereading questions.

2. Expose the learners to the material.

3. Give the learners time to answer the questions individually.

4. Check the answers with the whole group; motivate peer correction and justification of responses.

5. Elicit from the students some detailed information presented in the task. Have the students do a second listening or reading to look for these details.

6. Repeat Steps 3 and 4.

SPEAKING OR WRITING ASSESSMENT

1. Follow the usual steps for prespeaking and prewriting exercises.

2. Use audiovisual aids to help the learners get ideas for carrying out the task.

3. Guide the learners to elicit topics for discussion or writing. List these topics on the blackboard.

4. Elicit from the learners the kinds of structures and vocabulary they will need to carry out the task.

5. Review any language items necessary.

6. Give clear instructions on what the students are to do and how they are to do it.

In a speaking assessment

- give the learners time to think about what they are going to say
- place them either in pairs or small groups
- be available to help the learners with any vocabulary or structures they need during the task
- have the learners discuss their performance with their peers

In a writing assessment

- have the learners do the writing assignment
- have the learners exchange papers and check the use of structures and

vocabulary as well as the understanding of content (instruct them to give only constructive or positive feedback)

- help them if necessary

FEEDBACK AND SCORING

Pass out the assessment sheet (see Appendix). Explain how to fill it out. For example, if the assessment is based on a listening task involving two people talking about the advantages and disadvantages of living in New York and Los Angeles, the students might fill in the Content space in the assessment sheet with *Comparing cities* and the Skill space with *Listening*.

Discuss with the students how they should assess themselves, how much of the activity they think they should have understood, and what they believe should be considered an *excellent, very good, good,* and *fair* performance. For example, for the listening task in Step 1, the following rubric might work: *Consider your performance* excellent *if you were able to list all the advantages and disadvantages mentioned. Consider your performance* very good *if you were able to list more than half of the advantages and disadvantages. Consider your performance* good *if you were able to list half of them.*

Give the students several minutes to grade themselves and write about their development.

Collect the assessment sheets. After class, go over the learners' self-assessments. Write down your opinion of their performance and ways they can improve (e.g., what they need to review or practice more).

Return the assessment sheets to the learners in the next class. Be available to the students during and after class to discuss their assessments.

CAVEATS AND OPTIONS

1. Integrate the use of two or more skills in the same task and assessment (e.g., listening *and* speaking, reading *and* speaking, listening *and* writing).

2. A suggested schedule for doing this assessment is after every 10 hours of class.

3. Some students may resist assessing themselves, believing that assessment is only valid if it comes from the teacher. Explain that you will assess their performance but that it is essential for them to know how they themselves feel about their progress.

REFERENCES AND FURTHER READING

Lewis, J. (1990). Self-assessment in the classroom: A case study. In G. Brindley (Ed.), *The second language curriculum in action* (pp. 187–213). Sydney, Australia: National Centre for English Language Teaching and Research.

APPENDIX: *Assessment Sheet*

NOTE: Fit multiple copies of the assessment on one piece of paper to hand out to the students.

Student's name _____ Group _____

Teacher's name _____ Date_____

Skill _____

Content _____

_____

_____

Student's assessment _____

_____

_____

Teacher's comments _____

_____

_____

Self-Evaluated Video

Tim Murphey

Levels	*Any*
Aims	*Use video recordings to assess conversational progress*
Class Time	*Variable*
Preparation Time	*10–15 minutes*
Resources	*Video camera(s) or video recording device(s)*
	Video recordings
	Timer (optional)

In this activity, students regularly view their own conversations on video to assess themselves in the short and long term. Each week, students practice certain conversational strategies with the intention of using them in a weekly video recorded conversation. The use of technology means that the teacher can provide students with a video recording of themselves to watch at home, and evaluate immediately. The teacher keeps a master video recording of all conversations or downloads videos recorded on students' mobile devices that can be used to assess the students' progress later in the course.

PROCEDURE

1. If you are using video cassettes, connect two video cassette recorders to each video camera 10–15 minutes before class. Make sure the students each have a video recording device.

2. Allow the students to do a warm-up conversation with their partners before anyone is video recorded.

3. Select two students' names at random. Have the students give their video recording device to the camera man as Camera 1. Have the two students sit or stand in front of Camera 1.

4. Repeat Step 3 for the remaining cameras and recorders.

5. Instruct the other students to find partners to practice conversing with while

they are not being video recorded and to change partners every 5 minutes. In this way, they can have 6–7 partners in one class.

6. Start the cameras and recorders, and tell the students to begin. If available, set a timer for 5 minutes.

7. After 5 minutes, stop the cameras and recorders, and give the students who have just been filmed their video recordings to view at home.

8. Repeat Steps 4, 5, 7, and 8 until all the student pairs have been video recorded.

9. Have the students view their video recordings at home.

FEEDBACK AND SCORING

1. Typically in a class that meets three times a week for 45 minutes, the teacher instructs the class on certain material the first two classes, video records the students the third class, and then has the students take their video recordings home to evaluate at the end of the week. They then bring back the video recordings the beginning of the next week.

2. Give the students a focus for viewing their videos at home that encourages them to notice what they are actually doing. For example, ask them to write a short summary and answer the following questions:

    • What did you do well?

    • What strategies did you use?

    • What did your partners do or say that you could use?

    • What mistakes did you make, and what are the corrections?

    • What specific things do you want to do differently next week?

3. In the next class, have the students share their impressions in pairs with their partners, or in groups with their partners and others.

CAVEATS AND OPTIONS

1. Note that the procedure will vary depending on the syllabus, the number of students, and other factors. With two video recorders, the third class meeting of each week will be similar to the one described above. It usually takes about 45 minutes to go through a class of 20 students.

2. At the end of the semester, the students typically have 10 segments of their conversations on one video recording device. Ask them to look at all the segments and write a self-assessment. Look at the first week's master video recordings, and compare them with those of the last week to assess the changes in the students' performance.

3. Suggest that the students view their videos with classmates, friends, or family, which seems to give the students a more objective, third-person perspective on themselves.

REFERENCES AND FURTHER READING

Murphey, T., Kenny, T., & Wright, M. (1995). Learner self-evaluated video. *Academia Literature and Language, 59*, 163–201.

Building Rubrics Democratically

Larry Davis

Levels	*High-intermediate to advanced*
Aims	*Have a voice in the assessment process*
	Think about what successful performance should look like
Class Time	*60 minutes*
Preparation Time	*10–15 minutes*
Resources	*Nothing additional*

Rubrics are useful tools for grading student performance, but each rubric also encodes a specific value system. In classrooms with a focus on "democratic learning" —where student input is key—the selection of the values represented in the rubric is an important area for discussion and collaborative decision making. Student participation in rubric creation also helps them think more carefully about what characterizes successful performance, which can then guide learning. This assessment activity describes one such process by which students take the lead in developing a scoring rubric. This activity is based on the "4x4" activity described in Stevens and Levi (2005, pp. 63–64).

PROCEDURE

1. Describe the assessment to the students. The nature of the assessment should be made clear, including (a) the instructional goal(s) that the assessment targets, (b) the assessment task, and (c) the purpose of the assessment (e.g., check mastery, provide feedback, encourage good study habits). It may also be necessary to briefly describe what a rubric is to students (see **Caveats and Options**, below).

2. Divide students into groups of 3–4. Have the groups discuss four features that they believe best represent a quality performance on the assessment task. These features will eventually form the scoring categories for the rubric, such as *content, pronunciation,* and *task completion.* It will also be helpful to provide guidance regarding the level of detail to be used in generating the rubric. For example, the assessment might target generalized language

skills (e.g., pronunciation, fluency, grammatical accuracy) or task-specific skills (e.g., salutation for a business letter). Finally, more or fewer features might be used depending on the nature of the assessment and time available for discussion. Fewer features will speed grading, while more features will provide greater feedback.

3. Each group presents their four features to the class, writing their list on the board. The teacher may facilitate this process by asking questions and comparing results among groups but should avoid making judgments.

4. The class selects the four features that best describe good performance through a vote or by consensus.

5. Back in groups, students discuss what different levels of performance would look like for each of the four features. Four levels of performance labelled 1–4 (1 being low, 4 being high) are described for each feature. Each group fills out its own rubric grid for presentation to the class (Appendix A). Alternatively, three levels of performance may be used, which may make writing descriptions easier and save time.

6. For each feature, each group presents their descriptions. Discussion may follow, with the top four descriptions chosen by vote or consensus.

7. The features and descriptions then become the rubric used for the assessment.

CAVEATS AND OPTIONS

1. This process requires a degree of sophistication on the part of the learners and is probably best used with students who have experience with the assessment task. Construction of rubrics in this manner also takes a fair amount of class time and so might be reserved for a more important assessment or a recurring assessment such as *participation*.

2. This activity will require students to understand what a rubric is. This knowledge might come from experience with rubrics in prior assessments, or from a brief teacher presentation describing them.

3. The teacher may reserve the authority to alter the final rubric as needed to ensure that it adequately addresses the target of the assessment. To maintain the collaborative nature of the process, however, it is advised that such alterations be kept to a minimum.

4. If there are doubts about the feasibility of having students produce a full rubric, then other less intensive approaches exist, such as asking students to write down the characteristics of good performance on slips of paper, which are then used by the teacher when constructing the rubric (see Stevens & Levi, 2005, pp. 58–65).

REFERENCES AND FURTHER READING

Stevens, D., & Levi, A. J. (2005). *Introduction to rubrics: An assessment tool to save grading time, convey effective feedback, and promote student learning.* Sterling, VA: Stylus.

APPENDIX: *Rubric Grid*

		Features: What are the important parts of the assignment?			
		1. _____	2. _____	3. _____	4. _____
Levels: What does performance look like at different levels? (1 = low, 4 = high)	1				
	2				
	3				
	4				

So, How Did You Like My Presentation?

Jeff Johnson (Deceased May 27, 2010. Jeff is much missed.)

Levels	*Intermediate +*
Aims	*Evaluate peers on voice and body language skills in a public-speaking course*
Preparation Time	*Variable*
Resources	*Nothing additional*

Factors which contribute to quality speech presentation skills include speaking at an appropriate volume and rate, using pitch effectively, enunciating clearly, standing with a solid posture, using gestures carefully, and making good eye contact. Giving students the opportunity to evaluate their peers on each of these skills not only gives them an important sense of responsibility for their fellow students' progress but also forces them to concentrate on the skills during their own presentations.

PROCEDURE

1. In the first 1–2 classes, concentrate on voice and body language skills. Voice skills include voice, rate, pitch, and enunciation.

    - The voice should be just loud enough for those in the back of the room to hear without straining.

    - Too many learners feel that better fluency means speaking faster. Slow them down.

    - Show students that the pitch and tone of the voice can be very important in conveying meaning.

    - Tongue twisters are an enjoyable way to practice enunciation.

2. Body language skills include posture, gestures, and eye contact. Let students know these tips:

    - Feet should be spread shoulder-width apart, weight should be equally distributed, and students should not sway or lean.

- Gestures should be used only to make important points; students should beware of touching their hair and scratching.

- Establish eye contact with everyone (in a class of 30 or fewer it should be possible to do).

3. To save paper, fit more than one evaluation form (see Appendix) on each sheet of paper. Give each student enough evaluation forms for the day's presentations.

4. Tell the students to rate the seven voice and body language skills above on a scale of 1 (meaning *room for improvement*) to 5 (meaning *excellent*).

5. Urge the students to write critical comments on the skills—especially when they assign low scores—and general comments on the presentation as a whole (e.g., *Your voice was a little too soft. We made eye contact five times!* or *I couldn't understand some of the words.*).

6. Collect the evaluation forms at the end of class, first giving the students extra time to add comments if necessary.

FEEDBACK AND SCORING

1. Average the student-assigned scores for each of the seven skills to calculate peer scores for each speaker.

2. Combine all the peer comments about each speaker.

3. List the peer scores and peer comments, along with teacher scores and teacher comments, on 1–2 pages to give to the presenters at the next class meeting. Keep the peer scores and peer comments anonymous.

CAVEATS AND OPTIONS

1. Note that teacher preparation time may vary considerably. It may take as little as 10–15 minutes to prepare copies of the evaluation form but an additional 5–10 minutes per student to average the scores and collate the comments.

2. Add a third category to the evaluation form: *content*. Have the students evaluate their peers on their introduction, body, and conclusion as well as the general interest level of their presentation. This part of the evaluation will be more difficult for the students and perhaps should wait until they are more competent in these areas.

3. In a debate class, use the same technique, with the addition of another category: *persuasiveness*. As feedback, give the presenters their persuasiveness scores and those of their opponent so that they know who the winner was. Do not show debaters their opponent's voice or body language scores.

4. Use the evaluations to assess the evaluators themselves. Judge whether students really understand how to recognize effective speech skills and whether their comments show that they are adequately following the presentations.

APPENDIX: *Evaluation Form*

Evaluator _____

Presenter _____

Title _____

	Poor	Fair	Good	Very Good	Excellent	Comments
Voice:						
Volume	1	2	3	4	5	
Rate	1	2	3	4	5	
Pitch	1	2	3	4	5	
Enunciation	1	2	3	4	5	
Body:						
Posture	1	2	3	4	5	
Gesture	1	2	3	4	5	
Eye contact	1	2	3	4	5	
General Comments:						

Teachers and Students Assessing Oral Presentations

Kristy King

Levels	*Intermediate +*
Aims	*Become aware of how an audience perceives a presentation*
	Actively evaluate oral presentations
Class Time	*15–20 minutes; 5–10 minutes for each presentation*
Preparation Time	*20 minutes*
Resources	*Nothing additional*

In this assessment activity, students give oral presentations individually or in groups while the teacher and the students in the audience share equally in evaluating them. Students are encouraged to evaluate others constructively and positively.

PROCEDURE

1. Assign the students oral presentations of any kind (e.g., speeches, group presentations, role plays). Explain any requirements.

2. Before the presentations, talk with the students about the characteristics of a successful oral presentation. For example, explain the importance of content and organization, eye contact, body language, facial expression, enthusiasm, and clarity of speech. Clearly explain the rating system and its connection to these characteristics.

3. Give an oral presentation as a model.

4. On the day of the presentations, give students the evaluation form they will use to evaluate the presenter(s) (see Appendix). Explain the scoring system. Ask them to be careful in rating each presentation and in giving comments. Tell them to point out the positive aspects of each presentation as well as any aspects that need improvement. In addition, ask them to remember their highest compliment to each student or group presenter.

5. Ask a student or group to give the presentation, and rate the student or group on any scale you choose with a maximum possible score of 50 points (e.g., the scales found in Mendelsohn, 1991/1992), while the students in the audience rate the student or group using the evaluation form. Allocate portions of the 50 points to subsections in proportions that reflect the relative importance you attach to each.

6. After the presentation, give the students in the audience time to rate the presentation and write comments on the student evaluation forms. Collect the forms.

7. Repeat Steps 4–6 for additional students or groups giving oral presentations that day.

FEEDBACK AND SCORING

1. When all the presentations for the day are concluded, draw a table on the blackboard, making open spaces for each student or group that presented. Write the name of each student or group in a space. Ask all the students to come forward and write their highest compliment for each student or group presenter.

2. Go over the compliments, and praise both the presenters and the audience.

3. After class, tally the students' scores and take notes on the students' comments. (Use a scale such as *excellent* = 5; *very good* = 4; *good* = 3.5; *fair* = 3; *poor* = 2, using the 50-point scale, depending on the grading scale that has been adopted.) Average the scores for each student or group presenter. Multiply the average by 10 to compute the student rating out of a total of 50 possible points. Add that number to the teacher rating out of a total of 50 possible points. Write the total score on the evaluation form, and add those comments that provide the most substantive feedback.

4. The next class, return the students' evaluation forms and the teacher assessment (with the total score plus comments) to the students or groups that presented the day before. Praise all the positive aspects of the students' presentations and evaluations.

CAVEATS AND OPTIONS

1. If the class includes more than 25–30 students, the teacher may want to modify the activity to have the students work on their ratings in groups. Assign these groups to do one of the following: (a) send a representative to the blackboard to write either all the compliments from group members or a single, mutually chosen compliment, (b) give compliments to different presenters, or (c) take turns in groups in coming to the blackboard.

2. Use the notes taken on the students' comments as the basis of further discussion of exemplary oral presentations. If possible, assign the students additional presentations so that they can put the ideas into practice.

REFERENCES AND FURTHER READING

Mendelsohn, D. J. (1991/1992). Instruments for feedback in oral communication. *TESOL Journal, 1*(2), 25–30.

APPENDIX: *Evaluation Form for Students in the Audience*

Name of student or group _____

Please rate the student or group that presented by circling the word that describes their work best:

| Excellent | Very good | Good | Fair | Poor |

Please add your comments: _____

_____

_____

_____

Active Book Report

Janice Lee

Levels	*Intermediate +*
Aims	*Use all four modes of language in a book report*
Class Time	*2½ hours*
Preparation Time	*2 hours*
Resources	*Books selected by students*

People generally think of preparing a book report as a boring process involving a student writing a paper after reading a particular book. This activity, however, takes an innovative approach to book reports that encourages reading in class and assessing the reading. Rather than writing just one final paper for the book report, various activities encourage students to read and to enjoy what they reading. Students participate in the process of assessment by evaluating peers. This way, the final score that the students receive is a joint product. This practice encourages the students to perform in class to the best of their abilities.

PROCEDURE

1. Ask the students to choose a book they want to read. If necessary, have them visit the school library to find one.

2. Allow the students an appropriate amount of time to read the book; this time may vary from class to class.

3. Train the students to ask questions of other students about a book they have read.

4. Ask the students to keep a journal on their reading. Set up a schedule so that they write in their journal about their book at least three times before completing the book.

5. Ask the students to choose a book-share partner.

6. The day the students are to have completed their reading, have them get together with their partners and share their reading by asking each other questions.

7. Pass out the Peer Assessment Sheet (see Appendix A). Have the students fill it out for their book-share partner.

8. Hand out and go over the Book Review Write-Up Sheet (see Appendix B) to make sure the students understand the assignment. Assign a written book review for homework.

9. On the same day, hand out and go over the Book-Share Presentation Instructions (see Appendix C). Assign a book-share presentation for homework.

10. In the next class, have the students deliver their book-share presentations.

FEEDBACK AND SCORING

1. As the teacher evaluates each student's presentation, have two of the student's peers evaluate them as well, using the Book-Share Presentation Evaluation Sheet (see Appendix D).

2. Calculate the students' total scores with the Active Book Report Final Grade Sheet (see Appendix E).

CAVEATS AND OPTIONS

Be sure to train the students to be accurate raters. Instruct them to pay attention to the quality of the discussion or presentation and not to simply give the best possible score to their peers.

REFERENCES AND FURTHER READING

Freeman, Y. S., & Freeman, D. E. (1992). *Whole language for second language learners.* Portsmouth, NH: Heinemann.

APPENDIX A: *Peer Assessment Sheet*

Partner's name _____ Date _____

Title of book _____

Author _____

		No			Yes
1.	My partner knows the plot of the book.	0	1	2	3
2.	My partner knows the characters in the book.	0	1	2	3
3.	My partner knows the personalities of the characters.	0	1	2	3
4.	My partner knows the conflict of the book and how it got solved.	0	1	2	3
5.	My partner knows the theme of the book.	0	1	2	3
6.	My partner can tell me the events of the book sequentially (in correct time order).	0	1	2	3
7.	My partner can answer my questions about the book.	0	1	2	3
8.	My partner explains himself or herself clearly.	0	1	2	3
9.	My partner read and understood the book.	0	1	2	3
10.	Working with my partner was helpful to my understanding of the book.	0	1	2	3

Total points   _____ / 30

APPENDIX B: *Book Review Write-Up Sheet*

You have just finished reading a book of your choice. I hope you enjoyed your book! Now, it's time for you to put your enjoyment into writing. This book review, however, is a little different from other book reviews. I don't want you to tell me what the plot, characters, climax, or the theme of the book is. Rather, I want you to be creative.

You are presenting the book to the readers in a very different way. You can pretend to be the author trying to urge readers to buy the book, you can create a different character for your book, or you can write a totally different ending of the story to suit yourself! Your book review has to do with the book you read, but the way you present the book is up to you. Be creative! Have fun with it!

APPENDIX C: *Book-Share Presentation Instruction Sheet*

Now that you have finished the book, share the story with the rest of the class through a Book-Share Presentation. The object of the presentation is to encourage your classmates to want to read the book you read. You can accomplish this by acting out your favorite part of the book or making the class really curious by telling them just a little bit about your book. You can even turn yourself into a book and tell the class what fun you (the book) can be! Be creative! Have fun with it!

APPENDIX D: *Book-Share Presentation Evaluation Sheet*

Presenter's name _____

		No			Yes
1.	The presenter got the audience's attention.	0	1	2	3
2.	I could hear the presenter.	0	1	2	3
3.	I could understand the presenter.	0	1	2	3
4.	The presenter used appropriate gestures.	0	1	2	3
5.	The presenter made good eye contact.	0	1	2	3
6.	The presenter did not move around unnecessarily.	0	1	2	3
7.	The presenter had all the necessary materials.	0	1	2	3
8.	The presentation was creative.	0	1	2	3
9.	The presentation held the audience's attention until the end.	0	1	2	3
10.	I think this book would be enjoyable to read.	0	1	2	3

Total points _____ / 30

APPENDIX E: *Active Book Report Final Grade Sheet*

Component		Points	
		Earned	**Possible**
1.	Journal (10 points for each of three entries): _____ + _____ + _____ =		30
2.	Peer Assessment Sheet (book-share with a partner): Total points _____ /2 =		15
3.	Book Review (write-up)		25
4.	Book-Share Presentation Evaluation: _____ + _____ + _____ /3 Peer 1 Peer 2 Teacher		30
Total points			**100**

Benchmarking: Situational Autonomous Reviews

Nathan Ducker

Level	Intermediate +
Aims	*Access and evaluate personal performance*
	Receive more tangible feedback of performance
Class Time	*1 class*
Preparation Time	*Varied*
Resources	*Copies of the work to be evaluated*

Subjective reviews can help students assess and evaluate their own performance because the immediacy of the assessment can lead to more tangible phenomena than an objective score (e.g., 1–10 points).

PROCEDURE

1. In the evaluation phase of an activity, set aside a lesson for a peer assessment.

2. Identify the criteria for evaluation with student input. With advanced students, there could be more negotiation, but with less advanced levels it might be better to have the teacher dictate which criteria should be used in evaluation.

3. Instruct students that they will compare their own work with that of another student's. This will be done anonymously.

4. Students will use the benchmarking assessment sheet (see Appendix) to decide whether or not their work is better than that of their counterparts.

5. Students must then write or video record advice to help themselves bring their work up to the level of the other students. In addition, students must also prepare advice to their anonymous counterparts to improve their work in areas where it is needed.

FEEDBACK AND SCORING

Teachers should collect all work at the end of the class and use judgment whether or not to pass on comments to the students whose work was reviewed.

CAVEATS AND OPTIONS

1. This is both a learning and an assessing activity. It can be used during the middle of the course to ensure students understand evaluation criteria.

2. The teacher could prepare a single example submission in order to avoid student discomfort in sensitive situations.

3. This activity makes an excellent basis for a group discussion activity.

4. This assessment activity works well for activities such as videos, presentations, posters, and essays with qualitative grading criteria (e.g., *Student effectively persuaded the audience.*)

REFERENCES AND FURTHER READING

Barfield, A., & Nix, M. (Eds.). (2003). *Learner and teacher autonomy in Japan 1: Autonomy you ask!* Tokyo, Japan: The Japan Association for Language Teaching Learner Development Special Interest Group.

Skier, E. M., & Kohyama, M. (Eds.). (2006). *Learner and teacher autonomy in Japan 2: More autonomy you ask!* Tokyo, Japan: The Japan Association for Language Teaching Learner Development Special Interest Group.

APPENDIX: *Example of a Benchmarking Assessment Sheet*

Group	Criteria	Comparison with our product						
		Much worse	Worse	A bit worse	Same as our product	A bit better	Better	Much better
Media								
	Used many	X						
	Used effectively						X	
	Used smoothly					X		
Message								
	Clear		X					
	Useful							X

Assess the Assessors

Selda Mansour and Wisam Mansour

Levels	*Intermediate +*
Aims	*Become aware of assessment procedures*
	Recognize the difference between written and spoken language
	Appreciate the importance of oral negotiation
Class Time	*Variable*
Preparation Time	*60 minutes*
Resources	*Nothing additional*

The whole class is involved in this activity. Students have a chance to practice evaluating others' performance, which has the added benefit of reinforcing their self-esteem.

PROCEDURE

1. Have the students each write a short essay, either in class or as homework, on a different topic that can be presented orally or in poster form. Then assign half the group to prepare their essays as 3–5 minute oral presentations, and assign the other half to prepare small poster presentations of their essays. Specify the date for the oral and poster presentations. If the class is small, hold both presentations on the same day.

2. Hand out one essay checklist (see Appendix A) to each student. Have each of the oral presentation students exchange essays with a poster student. Have them read and evaluate each other's essays using the criteria in the checklist. Tell the students that you will also be evaluating their evaluations.

3. Collect the essays and checklists that they have completed. After class, read the essays and complete your own essay checklist (Appendix A) for each student.

4. On the oral presentation day, follow these steps:

    •   Remind the evaluators that they are free to ask questions.

- Hand out a presentation checklist (see Appendix B) to each of the students in the poster group.

- Have the oral presentation students give their presentations. Tell the poster students to complete the checklist for the presentation of the student whose essay they read. During the presentations, complete your own presentation checklist (Appendix A) for each speaker.

- Hand out the essays and have the evaluators re-read the essay they previously evaluated. At the end of the activity, collect the essays and completed checklists.

5. On the poster presentation day, follow these steps:

- Hand out a poster checklist (see Appendix C) to each of the students in the oral presentation group.

- Have them evaluate the posters prepared by the students whose essay they read. Tell them to fill in the checklist. Meanwhile, go around and complete your own poster checklist (Appendix C) for each student's poster.

6. Have the presenters stand by their posters and answer questions from the evaluators. At the end of the activity, collect the completed checklists. After class, using the teacher's checklist (see Appendix D), evaluate the completed essay, oral, and poster presentation checklists that the students completed during the presentations. In all, there will be two checklists from each student (one for an essay and one for a presentation).

7. Hand all the checklists (including the teacher's checklist) back to the evaluators at the next class meeting.

8. Lead the class in a discussion of the evaluation process, the differences between assessing written and spoken work, the importance of being able to question the presenter, and any other relevant issues.

FEEDBACK AND SCORING

See Steps 3–5 of the **Procedure**.

CAVEATS AND OPTIONS

1. In small classes, have each student evaluate two or more presentations.

2. If desired, work with the students in preparing the checklists before starting the activity.

3. Use this activity to grade the performance of the students as writers and as presenters.

APPENDIX A: *Essay Checklist*

DIRECTIONS: Circle a number to score each item, and write your comments in the spaces provided.

		Excellent					Poor
1.	Is the *topic* clearly identified?	5	4	3	2	1	0

Comment: _____

| 2. | Is there a *unity* of ideas? | 5 | 4 | 3 | 2 | 1 | 0 |

Comment: _____

| 3. | Is there *coherence*? Are the ideas presented in a logical way? | 5 | 4 | 3 | 2 | 1 | 0 |

Comment: _____

| 4. | Is the *style* of writing interesting and attractive? | 5 | 4 | 3 | 2 | 1 | 0 |

Comment: _____

| 5. | Is *language* used correctly? | 5 | 4 | 3 | 2 | 1 | 0 |

Comment: _____

6. What did you like about this essay?_____

7. What did you dislike about this essay? _____

APPENDIX B: *Oral Presentation Checklist*

DIRECTIONS: Circle a number to score each item, and write your comments in the spaces provided.

		Excellent				Poor	

1. Was the *topic* clearly identified?   5   4   3   2   1   0

    Comment: _____

2. Was there a *unity* of ideas and *coherence*?
    Were the ideas presented in a logical and
    convincing way?   5   4   3   2   1   0

    Comment: _____

3. Were the speaker's *movements, gestures,*
    intonation, and use of *visual aids* (if any)
    appropriate? Was the speaker self-confident? 5   4   3   2   1   0

    Comment: _____

4. Did the speaker involve the *audience* in
    the presentation?   5   4   3   2   1   0

    Comment: _____

5. Was *language* used correctly?   5   4   3   2   1   0

    Comment: _____

6. What did you like about this presentation? _____

7. What did you dislike about this presentation? _____

8. Did the presentation help you understand the information given in the essay?

    _____

9. Why or why not? _____

APPENDIX C: *Poster Presentation Checklist*

DIRECTIONS: Circle a number to score each item, and write your comments in the spaces provided.

		Excellent					Poor
1.	Is the *topic* clearly identified?	5	4	3	2	1	0

Comment: _____

2. Is there a *unity* of ideas and *coherence*? Are the ideas presented in a logical and convincing way?　　　5　4　3　2　1　0

Comment: _____

3. Are the *graphical representations* appropriate?　　　5　4　3　2　1　0

Comment: _____

4. Is the *design* visually attractive?　　　5　4　3　2　1　0

Comment: _____

5. Is the poster *self-explanatory* (or did you have to ask questions?)　　　5　4　3　2　1　0

Comment: _____

6. What did you like about this poster?_____

7. What did you dislike about this poster? _____

8. Did the presentation help you understand the information given in the essay? Why or why not? _____

APPENDIX D: *Teacher's Checklist*

DIRECTIONS: Circle *Yes* or *No* for each question, and write your comments in the space provided.

Are all items answered appropriately and adequately?	Yes	No
Are the circled scores consistent with the comments?	Yes	No
Are the comments relatively consistent with your notes on the essay/presentation?	Yes	No
Do the comments show an understanding and appreciation of the essay/presentation?	Yes	No

Comments: _____

Test Your Talk

Clark A. Richardson

Levels	*Any*
Aims	*Evaluate spoken English with the teacher*
Class Time	*30–40 minutes to collect oral data*
	1–2 hours for checklist analysis
Preparation Time	*10–15 minutes*
Resources	*Audio recorders and video recorders*

etting the students choose what they want to talk about helps to motivate them. Limiting or extending the time students get to talk can have an impact on their production. Evaluating the changes as a class and, later, with independent assessors gives students an opportunity to participate in the assessment process. This type of assessment brings the student into the evaluation process.

PROCEDURE

1. Have the students pair up and sit in two facing rows, a comfortable distance apart. Place a desk or small table between each facing pair.

2. Most students have access to their own personal audio or video recording device. Make sure each pair has one, or give each pair one. Have them place it on the desk or table.

3. Assign a speaking role to the students in one row and a listening role to the students in the other. Ask the speakers to spend a few minutes first selecting a story topic and then thinking about what they would like to say. Tell them they have 4 minutes for their story.

4. Tell the listeners to turn on the audio (or video) recorders and tell the speakers to start speaking.

5. When 4 minutes have passed, have the listeners shut off the recorders.

6. Ask all the listeners to move over one seat to face a new speaker, leaving the recorders with the speakers.

7. Have the speakers tell their story again, but in 3 minutes. Then have the listeners shut off the recorders.

8. Again ask all the listeners to move over one seat to face a new speaker, again leaving the recorders with the speakers.

9. Tell the speakers to tell their story a third time to the new listener, this time in 2 minutes.

10. Ask the students to switch roles.

11. Tell the students to follow Steps 4–9 again as you time each round.

FEEDBACK AND SCORING

1. Give each student a copy of the assessment scale (see Appendix).

2. Have the students in groups of 6–8 listen to (or watch) the six conversations on each audio (or video) recording and evaluate them using the assessment scale.

3. After the first evaluation, collect the sheets and collate the results. Distribute more assessment scales, and give all the students the opportunity to evaluate each of the recordings produced.

CAVEATS AND OPTIONS

1. Use any number of different variations of the timed sequences (e.g., 4, 3, and 2 minutes).

2. Reverse the times: The first talk lasts 2 minutes; the second, 3 minutes; and the third, 4 minutes.

3. Use the completed assessment scales as the basis for individual interviews or group discussions.

4. Alter the assessment scale for various levels. For beginning level students, use a scale in their L1. (Note that the assessment scale acts as a listening task for the evaluators who are the first-place speakers.)

REFERENCES AND FURTHER READING

Brown, J. D. (2004). Promoting fluency in EFL classroom. In T. Newfield (Ed.), *Conversational fluency: Ideology or reality: Proceedings of the JALT Pan-SIG Conference, Kyoto, Japan, 2003*. Tokyo, Japan: Japan Association for Language Teaching. Retrieved from http://www.jalt.org/pansig/2003/HTML/Brown.htm

APPENDIX: *Sample Assessment Scale*

Student's name _____

Comprehensibility: Rate the speaker on a scale of 0–4. _____

0   Can't understand speaker's talk in English at all. Speaker reverts to native language.

1   Can't understand basic message. Some individual words are comprehensible.

2   Can understand basic idea. There are some pronunciation, grammar, and vocabulary problems.

3   Can understand all speech acts well. There are occasional grammatical and pronunciation errors.

4   Can understand all speech acts very well. There seem to be no errors in grammar or pronunciation.

Fluency and pronunciation: Rate the speaker on a scale of 0–3. _____

0   Speech is very halting. Message is not understandable.

1   Flow of words is slightly better; however, pronunciation is still very difficult to understand. There are many repetitions.

2   Flow is slow but smooth. Pauses between sentences and within sentences are still too numerous. Meaning is basically understandable. Mispronunciation is still marked.

3   Flow is smooth, and speed is adequate. There are only a few mispronunciations. Overall message is understandable.

Oral Presentations: How Did I Do?

Joan Blankmann

Levels	*High beginning +*
Aims	*Improve speaking skills*
	Become more attentive listeners
	Become involved in the evaluation procedure
Class Time	*10 minutes following each oral presentation*
Preparation Time	*20 minutes*
Resources	*Nothing additional*

A three-in-one assessment tool gives students complete feedback on their oral presentations while involving everyone in the class. The same simple form is used for self-assessment, peer assessment, and teacher assessment so no one is left out of the evaluation process.

PROCEDURE

1. Prepare an assessment form (see Appendix).

2. Introduce the form to the class on a day when no oral presentations are scheduled. First, emphasize that the purpose of the assessment form is not to criticize another student or give false praise, but to help each student improve. Point out that the presenter will fill out the form under the *Self* heading, the teacher will fill out the form under the *Teacher* heading, and the listeners will use the *Classmates* heading.

3. Explain the rating scale.

   • Make sure the students understand very clearly how each item is rated and how each rating is earned. This way, they have specific guidelines to follow when they are preparing a presentation or evaluating another student's presentation.

   • Show the students how to calculate the total score.

- If desired, have the students practice writing comments that will be helpful to the presenter. Encourage the students to state specifically what the presenter did well and what the presenter might work on for the next presentation.

4. At the next scheduled presentation, hand out the form in advance so that the students can make notes while they are listening. Give the students and the presenter enough time after the presentation to complete their assessment. Use this time to fill out the teacher assessment form.

5. Collect the forms to make sure the students are filling them out properly and to keep informed on what kind of evaluations the students are receiving.

FEEDBACK AND SCORING

1. See the **Procedure** (Steps 1–5) and the **Appendix** for scoring.

2. For feedback, give all the forms to the presenter at the next class.

3. If there is time, average the total scores of the peer reviews and keep a record of them along with the teacher score and the presenter's self-evaluation score. If desired, discuss this record in a conference with each student.

CAVEATS AND OPTIONS

Use an audio or video recording of a previously recorded oral presentation to teach the students how to use the assessment form. Make sure the recorded presenter is not a member of the class.

APPENDIX: *Three-in-One Assessment Tool*

Presenter's name _____ Date _____

Subject of oral presentation _____

Rating scale: 1 = poor, 2 = needs improvement, 3 = good, 4 = very good, 5 = excellent

Item	Evaluator		
	Self	**Classmates**	**Teacher**
1. Preparation			
2. Order of ideas			
3. Pronunciation			
4. Fluency			
5. Accuracy (correct vocabulary/grammar)			
Total (Add numbers in column)			
Score (divide Totals by 5)			
Comments:			

Gradually Growing Presentation Assessment

Patrick B. Gallo and George M. Jacobs

Levels	*Low intermediate +*
Aims	*Practice and identify key features of effective presentations*
Class Time	*Variable*
Preparation Time	*60 minutes*
Resources	*Video recording device*

In this activity, students do a series of four presentations of increasing length, each of a different type: narrative (2–3 minutes), demonstration (4–5 minutes), informational (5–7 minutes), and persuasive (6–8 minutes). Feedback from the presenters (sometimes using video), their peers, and the teacher follows each presentation, using a gradually growing list of criteria, which is also customized to the type of presentation. In this way, the students' skills grow from presentation to presentation.

PROCEDURE

1. Devise an assessment sheet for four types of presentations. Add one more criterion to each succeeding assessment sheet. The fourth feedback form (see Appendix), which evaluates the final presentation in the series, includes all the target skills. Examples of criteria for each presentation type include

   - narrative presentation: delivery

   - demonstration presentation: delivery and introduction

   - informational presentation: delivery, introduction, and conclusion

   - persuasive presentation: delivery, introduction, conclusion, and signposting

2. Explain the criteria before each presentation.

3. Video record the student presentations.

4. After each student presents, ask the presenter and peers to complete the feedback sheet for the type of presentation just given.

5. Play the video recording of each presentation. Have the students give positive and constructive feedback.

6. Ask the students to make a list of areas where they will try to make improvements for their next presentation.

FEEDBACK AND SCORING

As appropriate, view the video recorded presentations and rate them using the feedback form (see Appendix), or have the student presenters (or their peers) do so.

APPENDIX: *Oral Presentation Feedback Form*

This form is used to evaluate the final presentation in the series.

PRACTICE TASK 4: PERSUASIVE SPEECH

Speaker _____

Topic _____

Complete the questions according to the following scale and then give comments.

Excellent	Satisfactory	Weak	Unsatisfactory
3	2	1	0

Introduction
   Did the speaker attract the audience's attention?   _____
   Did the speaker state the purpose of the talk?   _____
   Did the speaker use blueprinting (previewing)?   _____

Main Points
   Were the main points clear and complete?   _____
   Did the speaker use signposting (emphasizing)?   _____

Conclusion
   Did the speaker summarize?   _____
   Did the speaker include a recommendation or concluding remarks? _____

Delivery
   Pronunciation   _____
   Language use (grammar and vocabulary)   _____
   Rate of speech/natural delivery   _____
   Eye contact with audience   _____
   Posture, gestures, energy   _____

Rated by _____

Self/Peer/Teacher Assessment of Group Performance

Genevieve Lau

Levels	*Intermediate +*
Aims	*Reflect on contributions to a group project*
	Master important communication skills
Class Time	*60 minutes*
Preparation Time	*60 minutes*
Resources	*Nothing additional*

The purpose of this assessment activity is to help students reflect on their contributions to a group project while they consider any areas that need improvement. The students also internalize important communication skills because they use these same skills as criteria for assessing their own performance and that of their peers. In addition, they receive teacher feedback on those skills.

PROCEDURE

1. Have the students read about a specific topic, then have a class discussion about it. Ask students to brainstorm related topics for a group project. Request them to select one topic and work with at most five others who have chosen the same one.

2. Tell the groups to plan a presentation to the class. Let the group decide on the mode of the presentation (e.g., individual speeches, a drama, a song and dance), but be sure all members of the group participate. Encourage visual aids such as photos or graphs, and tell the groups to produce a written script for the presentation.

3. Before the presentations, remind students of the ground rules for being in the audience (e.g., no talking during presentations).

4. As their turns come, ask each group to come up to the front of the class for their presentation.

FEEDBACK AND SCORING

1. Hand out a group score sheet (see Appendix A) to each group in the audience, and explain how to score the group that's presenting. Tell students that each group has to agree on one score.

2. After each group presentation, allow a few minutes for the other groups to discuss and score it.

3. After all the presentations, summarize the group scores on the blackboard (see Appendix B). To preserve the score givers' anonymity, ask the members of the group being scored to close their eyes. Point at the numbers on the blackboard, and have the other groups indicate their scores by raising their hands.

4. Hand out an individual score sheet (see Appendix C) to each group and explain the scoring system.

5. Ask one student in each group to write his name on the individual score sheet and pass the sheet to the person to the right. Tell the students to keep passing and entering scores until everyone in the group has entered a score and the sheet comes back to the originator.

6. Ask the students to add up the scores and divide by the number of scorers to get the individual's average score. Averaging to get the final score is important because each group may have a different number of scorers.

7. Collect the sheets.

8. Ask the students to write their thoughts about the group work and assessment experience in their journals. Either keep the journal entries entirely open-ended, or guide them by providing subtopics.

9. Collect the students' journals and group scripts.

10. Base the final group presentation feedback on the teacher and group scores, individual peer assessment scores, and scores for the scripts.

11. Give the students their total project score or grade.

12. Synthesize the findings from the journal entries and share them with the class in a discussion format. Usually the students make comments about the difficulties encountered or the benefits perceived.

CAVEATS AND OPTIONS

1. Do not do this peer assessment activity until the students have done some group work. This way they can appreciate that reflection and assessment are tools for internalizing and improving skills, rather than judgmental devices. The activity takes some degree of rapport and trust among the students.

2. Alert the students to the assessment procedure when introducing the project process so they know in advance the criteria by which they will be assessed and will assess others.

3. Use different assessment criteria according to the skill-building objectives for each project. Be explicit about what the students need to practice and link those areas to the assessment criteria. The criteria may be general (as in the example) or specific (i.e., *the effectiveness of eye contact*).

4. If desired, video record the group presentations, and play back 30-second segments of each one so that the students can see themselves in action and become aware of their own strengths and weaknesses.

5. Use an overhead projector to summarize the group scores instead of having to copy them off the blackboard.

6. Decide whether or not to keep the identities of group and individual scorers anonymous. (This decision depends on the dynamics of the class.)

7. Vary the range on the scoring scale (e.g., 1–3, 1–5). Give fewer choices to beginning-level scorers.

APPENDIX A: *Group Score Sheet*

Group number _____ Date of presentation _____

Project topic _____

Circle one score for content and one for presentation.

Content		Presentation	
Makes unrelated statements	0	Not understandable	0
States a consistent opinion	1	Barely understandable	1
Gives one kind of support	2	Clear	2
Gives different kinds of support	3	Expressive	3

Total group score: Content score _____ + Presentation score _____ = _____

APPENDIX B: *Sample Summary of Group Scores*

Group no.	Score							Total
	0	1	2	3	4	5	6	
1				///	/			13
2			//	//	/			14
3					////			16
4						///	/	21
5					/	//	/	20

APPENDIX C: *Individual Score Sheet*

Name _____ Date _____

DIRECTIONS: Sit in a circle with your group members and follow the steps below.

1. Write your name and the date on the sheet.

2. Pass the sheet to the person on your right.

3. When you receive another student's score sheet, write your score for that person in one of the squares below. Select a score of 1, 2, or 3 according to the Scoring Key.

4. Continue until you get back your own sheet.

5. Total the scores and divide the total by the number of scorers. The result is the average score.

Scoring Key
1 = Little participation in discussions and assignments
2 = Some participation in discussions and assignments
3 = A large contribution to the project

Total of all scores _____ Number of scorers _____

Your score: Total of scores ÷ Number of scorers = _____

Walk–Talk Oral Tests

Tim Murphey

Levels	*Any*
Aims	*Learn to assess own performance*
	Use English outside the classroom
	Be involved in kinaesthetic learning
Class Time	*25–40 minutes*
Preparation Time	*30 minutes*
Resources	*Nothing additional*

In this activity, students give each other oral tests while walking outside, and they learn to assess their own knowledge and ability in an alternate learning environment.

PROCEDURE

1. Prepare a test that reflects objectives that have been taught in class, subjects chosen by students, or both.

2. Pass out the test lists (see Appendix A). Tell the students to underline the items they don't know. Encourage the students to study them, use them every day in talking to friends, and teach them to others outside class until the day of the test. Hold a mock test once or twice before the real one so that the procedure is clear (see Appendix B). Ask the students to change partners once or twice to gain experience working with different people.

3. On test day, explain the test and grading procedure one more time. Tell the students the amount of time they have.

4. Send the students outside (if the weather is pleasant) to do the assessment activity.

5. Walk outside and be available in case anyone has a question.

FEEDBACK AND SCORING

The two ways of scoring that work with this assessment activity are Simple Protocol and Interactive Grading. Both are explained below.

Simple Protocol for Testing and Grading

1. Demonstrate the following procedure in front of the class because simply explaining it usually confuses the students.

   - Have the students exchange their lists. Tell them to take turns asking their partners a specific number of words and expressions on the list that have been underlined (i.e., the ones the student didn't know and has been studying).

   - Tell the students to circle the words they ask and, after the partner answers, to write down the number of points indicated by their partner for each word or expression. Make sure the students decide for themselves the points they think they deserve.

2. To stress conversational interaction, tell the students that they can score themselves as follows:

   - 1 point each for (a) speaking immediately, (b) speaking continuously for at least 4–5 sentences, and (c) being correct in their explanation of the item. (For 10 items, the maximum number of points possible is 30.)

   - 3 points if they speak only English.

   Someone who doesn't know the words can still get 20 points just by speaking a lot (e.g., *Strategy, umm, an interesting word, I can even remember studying it, and I'm sure it's an important word. I even remember Yuki telling me what it means. Let's see, I just can't seem to remember it right now. I guess I can only get 2 points for that one. Can you tell me what it means?*).

   Blackboard notes might look like this:

   > For each item:
   >
   > Speaking immediately = 1 point
   >
   > Speaking continuously = 1 point
   >
   > Giving a clear and correct explanation = 1 point
   >
   > Speaking English only = 3 points

3. Have students write their partner's total points at the bottom of the sheet and turn it in to you for recording.

Interactive Grading

Have the students use a more complex grading procedure, such as the one in Appendix B.

CAVEATS AND OPTIONS

1. A pleasant outdoor environment makes this assessment activity more enjoyable, but the activity also works if the students simply walk around the halls of the classroom building.

2. Vary the content, length of time, and number of points, depending on the teaching objectives.

3. For clarity, demonstrate the procedure in front of the class with a student.

REFERENCES AND FURTHER READING

Murphey, T. (1994/1995). Tests: Learning through negotiated interaction. *TESOL Journal, 4*(2), 12–16.

APPENDIX A: *Sample Student-Created Test List*

Source: Based on Murphey (1994/1995).

DIRECTIONS: The following are words and expressions chosen by the class for the conversation test. Underline only the ones you don't know and study them, use them every day in talking to friends, and teach them to others. In a few days, you will have to explain them orally (by talking).

a tip	my sight is poor	relative
he's all thumbs	follow the routine	rotate
let someone down	on my mind	squander
play around	commit suicide	slope
inspire	slam the door	get passionate about
clumsy	paste	strategy
rectangle	ban	inventory
impress	night owl	addiction
skim the headlines	no way	nicotine
artificial versus natural	turn (90, 180) degrees	kick the habit
potential	dawn is breaking	mumble
switch	sum up	get by
it is frowned upon	whisper	take a nap
enthusiastic	regress	numb
intensify	calculate	dormitory
fascinating	freckles	kidding
skip (two meanings)	daydream	piece of cake
flat (two meanings)	so far (e.g., *So far, you are*	decade
scary	*doing well.*)	in good shape
skim	jet lag	seldom
flexible	feel inhibited	keep one's word
illegal	I'm behind you (idiom)	be astounded
no kidding!	bored with	substitute
fabulous	guess	approximately
pot luck	the rest of ...	contagious
fade	dare to ...	a valid excuse
rag	extraterrestrial	weary
strum	interact with	competitive

APPENDIX B: *Sample of a Complex Interactive Grading Scheme*

English I Test

SECTION A: FILL THIS PART OUT YOURSELF.

English name _____

Grades: A+ (for English-only all the time)   A   B   C   F

- Based on what you think you know for the test, what grade would you give yourself now, before you take it?

  Grade/score:_____

- Based on how much time and effort you spent studying for the test, what grade would you give yourself now, before you take it?

  Grade/score:_____

Give your Vocabulary Study List to your partner, and take your partner's. Do the same with this sheet of paper.

SECTION B: HAVE YOUR PARTNER COMPLETE THIS PART.

Go outside (if the weather is pleasant) and take turns asking each other to explain the underlined words on your lists.

1. Call out every second word that is underlined on your partner's sheet, and ask your partner to explain it, use it in an example, or both. Do 10 words in this way.

2. Make sure your partner starts to answer immediately. If your partner doesn't start answering after 5 seconds, say *Time's up*. But give your partner all the time needed to answer completely.

3. Write here how many words out of 10 your partner could explain adequately.

   Grade/score:_____

4. When both of you have finished Step 3, ask your partner to describe an object at home (without naming it). Your partner should be able to tell you at least five things about it that describe what it is. Count the number of clues your partner tells you. Give your partner a score of 1–5 depending on the number of clues she gave you about the object. Then switch roles. (Make sure you and your partner do not choose the same object to describe.)

   Grade/score:_____

5. Ask your partner to choose one of the following topics and give at least three reasons why it is important. Write your partner's answers below, and give your partner a grade of 1 (poor) to 5 (excellent).

   • speaking English to nonnatives

   • shadowing/echoing

   • loving your mistakes

   Grade/score: _____

6. Ask your partner to name four ways to improve your oral English that the teacher has asked you to try outside class. Write your partner's answers below, and give your partner a score (maximum 4 points).

   Grade/score: _____

7. Ask your partner to name four songs and something he has learned from each song. Write these below and give your partner a score (maximum 4 points).

   Grade/score: _____

8. Give your partner 2 points if she has spoken only English since walking into the classroom this morning.

   Bonus points: + _____

9. Subtract points for every time your partner spoke in her native language

   Penalty points: – _____

   Total number of points: _____ (out of 26 possible points)

10. Return this paper to your partner.

SECTION C: FILL THIS PART OUT IF YOU COMPLETED SECTION A.

1. After having taken this test, what kind of grade do you think you should get?
   Grade/score: _____

2. Ask yourself the following questions: Do you think this test gave a fair picture of what you know? Was it easy, enjoyable, or difficult? Would you like to take other tests like this? Was it useful? Could it be improved in any way? Write your feedback below: _____

   _____

Thank you very much.

Interviews and Presentations for Clarifying Authentic Public-Speaking Needs

John M. Norris

Levels	*Advanced*
Aims	*Determine types of public speaking used in specific major fields*
	Develop individualized criteria for effective academic presentations
Class Time	*30 minutes (group work)*
	10 minutes per student (presentations)
Preparation Time	*30 minutes*
Resources	*Audio or video recorders*

Early in their academic careers, L2 university students often have little idea of what kinds of academic and public-speaking situations they will encounter over the course of their college education. Public-speaking expectations for undergraduate-level as well as graduate-level students can differ substantially in various L1 backgrounds. Students therefore often have a wide variety of ideas about the extent to which they will be expected to speak in the L2 college environment. This exercise enables students to gain insight into what kinds of public-speaking and academic presentations are in store for them. Students use their communication skills authentically and meaningfully as they develop interview questions, defend their ideas, conduct interviews, and present their findings. The results of interviewing expert informants provide the teacher and student with valuable, discipline-specific criteria to use in preparing, organizing, and evaluating presentations. Based on these criteria and on students' abilities in presenting them, teachers learn the kinds of public speaking that students in different majors need to focus on, and give evaluative feedback to students with the same majors. With the introduction of peer and self-review of the presentations, students engage in and are exposed to critical reflection based on criteria that they themselves have formulated.

PROCEDURE

1. Before class, prepare an interview questionnaire (see Appendix A). Design the questions and activities to prompt the students to think about the academic and public-speaking demands of their chosen field of study.

2. In class, have the students meet with a partner (preferably from a different discipline) to discuss the questionnaire. Stress that the students should describe their own perceptions of academic and public speaking. The students should not necessarily come to a consensus, as students in different academic disciplines are likely to be faced with different speaking contexts. Tell the students that they will work with these partners for the remainder of the project.

3. Have each student choose an interview informant based on the criteria found at the bottom of the interview questionnaire. Generally, the informant should be someone in the same discipline as the student, someone at a more advanced level of study than that of the student, and someone the student respects as a public speaker.

4. Have the students each generate a set of interview questions based on (a) their specific interests, (b) the person they have chosen to interview, and (c) their own ideas about public speaking in their majors, using the questions on the interview questionnaire as a guide. The idea is for the students to solicit relevant information about the public speaking they will face, the preparation that is involved, and the techniques that are effective in these public-speaking situations. Have the students finish this step (possibly as homework) before moving on to Step 5.

5. Schedule 10-minute conferences with the pairs of students. Tell the students to come prepared with a firm date and time for their projected interview sessions, a list of interview questions, and a rationale for their choices (of both informant and questions).

6. After commenting on and confirming the student' interview plans, make the following suggestions:

   - Work together during the interview. The student who is not asking questions should operate the recording device.

   - Have the student conducting the interview also note the informant's answers.

   - Estimate the amount of time required to answer each question, and realize that informants may speak with unexpected length or brevity. Thus, be prepared to adjust the interview to the informant's responsiveness.

7. Have the students conduct each of their interviews.

8. Schedule individual student presentations in class soon after the interviews have been conducted. Tell the students to organize their presentations around the interview questions, notes, and audio recordings (if available). Encourage them to incorporate into their own presentations anything they learned from their informants about academic and public speaking. Agree on time limits in advance; 5–10 minutes per student should be sufficient.

9. During the presentations,

   • Have all listeners (other than the teacher and the speaker's partner) take careful notes. Collect them directly following each presentation.

   • Along with the speaker's partner, respond to the rating scales found in the feedback scoring rubric (see Appendix B). Keep these response sheets with the collected notes.

10. Directly following each presentation, have the speakers each rate their own presentation using the feedback scoring rubric (see Appendix B).

FEEDBACK AND SCORING

1. Feedback on the interview presentations takes multiple forms.

   • Teacher ratings and comments on the feedback scoring rubric help the students understand the extent to which they have met the general criteria for academic presentations. In addition, they see how well they were able to apply knowledge that they acquired from the interview.

   • The partner's ratings provide the same kind of information with the added insight of someone who also witnessed the interview. Have the students compare their self-ratings with the teacher assessment as well as their partner's. This will help determine the extent to which the teacher, the students, and their peers have a common understanding of public-speaking needs within a given academic context.

   • Have the student speakers reflect on the notes taken by the other students in the class to determine how successfully they presented the findings of their interviews.

   • Have the students combine all of these sources of input and write a reflective piece on their strengths and weaknesses in making presentations. Then have the students further apply the criteria provided by their informants to suggest areas for improvement on future public-speaking occasions.

CAVEATS AND OPTIONS

1. Equipment availability and time permitting, make a video recording of the presentations.

2. Have the students review the audio recording individually before rating themselves on the feedback scoring rubric.

3. Review the audio recording in further conferences among the student, the partner, and the teacher. Each can comment on strengths and areas for improvement in the presentation.

REFERENCES AND FURTHER READING

Norris, J. M. (1996). *Performance and portfolio assessment (1985-1995): An extended bibliography of resources useful for language teachers* (Research Note). Honolulu, HI: University of Hawai'i, Second Language Teaching and Curriculum Center.

APPENDIX A: *Academic Speaking Interview*

1. Think about academic speaking in your major. Meet with a partner and discuss your ideas about the following questions. Try to discover differences as well as similarities in the kinds of academic speaking in which you engage.

   - What kinds of academic speaking do you currently have to do (e.g., presentations, article critiques, comments)?

   - How do you prepare yourself for speaking in public or in class (e.g., making notes or outlines, practicing in front of a mirror or with a partner, timing yourself)?

   - What techniques do you use in order to give effective academic presentations?

   - What would you like to change about your ability to give presentations in class or in public?

2. Think of someone from your field of study whom you would like to interview about academic speaking. Follow these guidelines:

   - Choose an informant from the academic area in which you study or from a related area that interests you.

   - Try to pick someone whom you respect as a public speaker. (Think about why you consider this person an effective speaker.)

   - Try to find someone who has been studying in your field for longer than you have (e.g., if you are an undergraduate in business, consider interviewing a graduate student from the MBA program).

   - Make sure the person you pick is willing and able to give you an interview. When you schedule the interview, estimate about how much time you will need (more than 30 minutes is probably too long), and adhere to that time block.

APPENDIX B: *Scoring Rubric for Academic Speaking Feedback*

Using the rating scales provided, score the following statements about the presentation. Please use the space below each statement to explain your rating.

	Disagree				Agree

1. The speaker seemed well-prepared for this presentation. 1 2 3 4 5

    Please explain: _____

    _____

2. The speaker used the techniques suggested by the informant. 1 2 3 4 5

    Please explain: _____

    _____

3. The presentation successfully conveyed interview findings. 1 2 3 4 5

    Please explain: _____

    _____

Activating Self-Assessment

Lorraine Valdez Pierce

Levels	*High beginning +*
Aims	*Apply criteria for effective writing*
Class Time	*45–60 minutes*
Preparation Time	*60–120 minutes*
Resources	*Several effective writing samples*
	Overhead projector and transparencies
	Chart paper and markers
	Index cards

This activity helps learners identify criteria for effective writing and apply them to their own work. By reflecting on their writing and comparing it with a standard, students become more aware of how to improve their own writing. This awareness enables them to become independent learners. The teacher's role is to scaffold the self-assessment process by guiding students through a series of steps. The process moves from a whole-class session, to partner work, and finally to self-assessment—a key element of effective learning essential to portfolio assessment.

PROCEDURE

1. To provide a model that is appropriate for the language proficiency and grade level of the students, select a one-page sample of quality writing produced either by a former student or by a student currently in the class. Obtain the student's permission to use the writing, and remove the name from the copies and the transparency you share with the class. Enlarge the writing sample if necessary to improve its legibility, then make a transparency of it.

2. Invite the class to generate criteria for quality writing. Put the transparency on the overhead projector, and ask the students, alone or with a partner, to read it and to write down as many characteristics as they can to describe what makes the writing good quality.

3. Make a criteria chart: After giving the students a few minutes to work, ask them to share with the whole class why they think the sample represents quality writing. If the students are reticent, guide them with questions that reflect what they have learned in your class about good-quality writing, such as *What do we know about the first letter of the first word in a sentence?* Using the overhead projector, chart paper, or wall chart, write their comments, rephrasing the language where needed to produce short sentences (5–10 words) and to model appropriate language. The result will be a criteria chart.

In the chart, express each phrase in the first-person singular (e.g., *I can, I put, I write with*) or in the imperative (e.g., *Put a period at the end of a sentence.*).

For older or more proficient learners, simply list the criteria in short phrases with bullets or check marks (e.g., main idea in paragraph, periods, capital letters, spelling).

4. Add to the criteria chart while going through the modeling process several times with the whole class. Ultimately, put the chart up on the wall. It can evolve into a writer's checklist (see Appendix).

5. Give the students a copy of a different writing sample. Have them work with a partner to compare it with the criteria on the wall chart and to identify additional elements of quality writing. Monitor the pairs to see that they understand the task.

6. After about 10 minutes, ask the whole class for feedback on how the second writing sample compares with the student-generated criteria chart. Engage the whole class in a discussion of the criteria, and add newly named elements to the chart.

7. Repeat Steps 1–6 at least twice more using different writing samples before proceeding to **Feedback and Scoring**. For the first few times, show the students models of effective writing so that they can identify the criteria for quality writing. After several sessions, use models of less-than-effective writing written by the students in the class as the basis for mini-lessons that meet the current needs of the students.

FEEDBACK AND SCORING

1. Teach the students what constructive feedback sounds like, perhaps by providing some key lead phrases such as *What I liked about this piece was . . . .* or *Your writing can be improved by . . . .* Teach the students to respect each other by listening to each other's feedback and using it to improve their work.

2. Have the students apply the criteria to a peer's work in a subsequent session, perhaps 1–2 days later. For example, if the students have been taught the various steps of process writing or writers' workshop, after the first or second draft ask the students to swap drafts with a partner for feedback based on the criteria chart. In many cases, the students respond much more positively to a peer's feedback than to a teacher's red ink.

3. Invite the students to apply the criteria to their own work. After a number of sessions during which the students provide feedback on a partner's work, they will be ready to apply the criteria for effective writing to their own work, the culminating step of the self-assessment process.

4. After a writing assignment, ask the students to take a few minutes to apply the criteria on the wall chart to their own work.

5. Ask the students to get feedback from a partner. Monitor the partners to see that they are on track, and engage all the students in a discussion of their readiness to apply the criteria to their own writing.

6. Ask the students to set learning goals for the benchmark or model sample. Begin by revisiting Step 2 of the **Procedure**. Returning to the original writing sample (on the transparency) used for generating criteria for quality writing, ask the students what writing goals the author of the sample might set for himself to work toward during a semester or quarter.

7. Have the students set learning goals for a peer. As in the process described above for setting criteria, first provide the students with several opportunities to set goals for writing models as a class. Then give the students opportunities to suggest writing goals for each other on several occasions.

8. Invite the students to set learning goals for their own work. This can occur in a writing conference with the teacher, through a learning log or writer's journal, or by writing their goals on an index card and attaching it to the writing draft. If students are keeping writing portfolios, they can include the various drafts of their writing and their goal cards to share during portfolio conferences with the teacher.

CAVEATS AND OPTIONS

1. Help weak writers by teaming them up with a partner who will support their efforts. Research has shown that when English language learners are shown the criteria for quality work along with samples of quality writing (called *benchmarks*), their writing improves (Kolls, 1992).

2. This activity can be used with high-beginning-level students after they have received at least 1–2 semesters or quarters of instruction and have acquired enough language to generate the criteria for the wall chart. Children as young as kindergartners can engage in this activity (Clemmons, Laase, Cooper, Areglado, & Dill, 1993).

3. Use the feedback from the students on their writing goals to develop minilessons aimed at helping them reach those goals.

REFERENCES AND FURTHER READING

Clemmons, J., Laase, L., Cooper, D., Areglado, N., & Dill, M. (1993). *Portfolios in the classroom, Grades 1–6*. New York, NY: Scholastic Professional Books.

Kolls, M. R. (March, 1992). *Portfolio assessment: A feasibility study*. Paper presented at the 26th Annual TESOL Convention, Vancouver, Canada.

O'Malley, J. M., & Valdez Pierce, L. (1996). *Authentic assessment for English language learners: Practical approaches for teachers*. Reading, MA: Addison-Wesley.

APPENDIX: *Sample Student-Generated Criteria*

I make a plan before I write.

I put a main idea in each paragraph.

I use words to make a picture.

I begin all sentences with a capital letter. I end all sentences with a period, question mark, or exclamation point.

I spell words correctly.

Alternative Ways of Doing Work-Based Assessment

- **Group Work**

- **Pair Work**

- **Group and Pair Work**

Part III: Alternative Ways of Doing Work-Based Assessment

EDITOR'S NOTE

Traditionally, tests have been administered to each student separately in paper-and-pencil format. That does not mean that one-by-one testing is the only way to do things, however. As language teaching practices around the world have begun to change in favor of communicative teaching organized around tasks, pair and group activities have become increasingly common in the classroom. Apparently, judging by the contributions in this section, many teachers are also experimenting with group work and pair work for doing assessments in their classrooms.

Group work assessment will be defined here as any observations or scoring done for the purpose of giving students feedback while those students are working in groups, whether the group work was specifically designed for assessment purposes or occurred naturally for other pedagogical purposes. Similarly, *pair work assessment* will be defined as any observations or scoring done for the purpose of giving students feedback while those students are working in pairs, whether those pairs were formed for assessment purposes or occurred naturally for other pedagogical reasons. These are very straightforward definitions, so no further explanation will be given.

Nevertheless, one question remains: Why would teachers want to use these two ways of grouping students for assessment purposes? Group work and pair work assessments are useful because (a) they provide opportunities to assess actual language production, (b) they match the pedagogical practices going on in the classroom, (c) students may feel more relaxed and less threatened when tested in groups or pairs, and (d) such assessment can be much more efficient timewise than other techniques (e.g., oral interviews conducted individually).

Group work or pair work assessment has some disadvantages as well. For instance, scoring and feedback tend to be subjective, a problem that can be minimized by getting multiple ratings for each student (as when several teachers rate each student), by getting ratings from multiple perspectives (e.g., from the viewpoints of the students themselves, their peers, and the teacher), by making the guidelines for scoring very clear to the scorers, by doing specific training and practice in the scoring method, or ideally by using some combination of these practices.

Another set of problems associated with group work and pair work assessment is that, by chance, some students may be relegated to weak partners or contentious groups, which alone could affect their language performances and thus their scores. Naturally, comparing such students with students who have had well-matched partners and cooperative groups would not be fair. One way to address this issue is to make sure that each student participates in multiple groups or multiple pairs so that the teacher observes all students in a variety of groupings or pairings.

In addition, group work and pair work assessments may favor the more vocal students in class. This issue can be minimized by structuring activities for equality, in the sense that you make clear from the outset that the whole group's scores will be lower if some members talk too much and others too little.

Still another problem that may arise is that, because of their personalities, cultural background, or other factors, some students may not speak up at all when paired or grouped with others. As a result, they will not produce enough language for you to score them or give them any kind of feedback. The solution described in the previous paragraph might help—that is, make it clear to students from the outset that their scores depend on their active participation. Or, try making the activity competitive so that all members want to chime in. Another possibility would be to appoint the shy students as group leaders so they have to participate. In addition to the above solutions, consider having a backup assessment option for any students who truly cannot participate actively because they are shy or otherwise unwilling to do so. For instance, consider holding individual assessment conferences with groups or pairs of such students or use other assessment techniques to draw them out.

Six of the contributions in this part of the book explain group work techniques for assessment, and as elsewhere in this book, the contributions have a variety of purposes: to develop an increased awareness of the structure, style, and other aspects of text while encouraging students to revise and edit their own writing ("Author, Author! Guided Reader Response"); to assess students' oral skills without using time-consuming one-on-one interviews ("Group Oral Tests"); to foster turn-taking and conversational repair strategies ("Putting It Together: A Jigsaw Task"); to give students an opportunity to demonstrate their fluency skills while explaining a process ("Let Me Explain"); to apply reading comprehension strategies to unfamiliar texts ("Reciprocal Teaching: Reading Strategies at Work"); and to demonstrate the pragmatic skill of turn-taking in natural environments ("Assessing Topic Maintenance and Turn Taking").

Five other contributions explain pair work techniques: assessing students' oral communication ability ("Face to Face"); helping students logically connect oral sentences ("Three-Sentence-Speech Speaking Test [TSSST]"); helping both students and teachers recognize differences in their views of speaking ability ("The Audio Mirror: Reflecting on Students' Speaking Ability"); encouraging students to predict, negotiate, and experiment in finding answers about colors ("Using the Science and Art of Colors to Teach ESL"); and helping students organize and describe sequential events in the past ("Organizing Ideas With Pictures").

Three contributions in this section combine group work and pair work, again with a variety of purposes: to identify students' strengths and weaknesses and set learning goals for their spoken English ("Observation, Feedback, and Individual Goal Setting"); to encourage and assess conversational English directly related to course objectives ("Consolidate Yourself"); and to help students understand the function of pronouns ("Whose Shoes Do You Use?").

REFERENCES AND FURTHER READING

Brown, H. D. (2002). English language teaching in the "post-method" era: Toward better diagnosis, treatment, and assessment. In J. C. Richards & W. A. Renandya (Eds.), *Methodology in language teaching: An anthology of current practice* (pp. 9–18). Cambridge, England: Cambridge University Press.

Norris, J. M., Brown, J. D., Hudson, T. D., & Bonk, W. (2002). Examinee abilities and task difficulty in task-based second language performance assessment. *Language Testing, 19*(4), 396–418.

Roberts, T. S. (2006). *Self, peer and group assessment in e-learning.* Hershey, PA: Information Science Publishing.

Tolley, H., & Wood R. (2011). *How to succeed at an assessment centre: Essential preparation for psychometric tests, group and role-play exercises, panel interviews and presentations* (3rd ed.). London, England: Kogan Page.

Author, Author! Guided Reader Response

Kim Hughes Wilhem and Marilyn Rivers

Levels	*Any*
Aims	*Assess, revise, and edit own writing*
	Increase awareness of text structure and expected style
	Review and critique texts
Class Time	*1–2 hours*
Preparation Time	*20 minutes*
Resources	*Drafts of students' papers*

In this assessment activity, students perform a guided text review and critique their peers' writing efforts. The purpose is to encourage writers to assess their own work as well as revise and edit it. The activity should also help them to develop an increased awareness of the structure of text, style, and other elements of writing.

PROCEDURE

1. Put the students into mixed-proficiency groups of three. Make sure the students each have a completed draft of a composition and a response guide (see Appendix A).

2. Go over the instructions and the parts of the guide, then answer questions. Explain that the purpose of the activity is for the students to help each other find problems and improve their papers by seeing where more details are needed, support is inadequate, language is confusing, and any other issues. Confirm that the students understand the purpose of the activity and the instructions.

3. Explain that it's often easier to hear language problems when a text is read aloud. Ask one author at a time in each group to read her paper aloud once. Ask the other members of the group to listen and to suggest corrections in language use. Warn against overcorrecting, and ask the students to confer with the teacher if the group disagrees on an editing point.

4. Have another student in each group—the questioner—ask the questions in the response guide (see Appendix A) in sequential order, then ask the author to respond. Ask the third student in the group—the recorder—to write in the response guide the answers given and any problems identified.

5. After the groups have worked their way through the paper in this fashion, tell them to switch roles. Continue this process until all three papers have been reviewed and critiqued.

FEEDBACK AND SCORING

In addition to the feedback that is integrated into the **Procedure**, use the grade sheet (see Appendix B) to score the final revised version of the writing assignment.

CAVEATS AND OPTIONS

1. As an extension activity, consider asking the students to select the best paper from their group, and have each group member rate it according to the grade sheet (see Appendix B). Ask them to compare the grades given and negotiate to agree upon a grade. This activity helps students understand what the teacher looks for in a paper.

2. If desired, collect the response guides and review them while examining the revised draft of the paper to see if the writer followed the suggestions given.

3. Consider giving each group a grade on the basis of effort and the quality of feedback noted on the activity. If you let the students know ahead of time that they will be receiving a grade, the feedback will likely be better.

APPENDIX A: *Reader Response Guide*

This guide is designed for an argumentative paper.

DIRECTIONS: You will work in groups of three. One of you is the author, one a questioner, and the third a recorder. You will trade roles after going over each paper so that each of you has a turn in each role. Each of you will have a turn reading your paper aloud, while the other members of your group help correct and improve the language use in it (e.g., grammar, vocabulary, sentence structure). Also listen to the content. When you've finished this *surface editing* of the paper, the questioner will ask (aloud) the questions below, and the author will respond. The questioner should ask follow-up questions when necessary to get the author to clarify or better explain his or her answers. The recorder will take notes and list the main answers given by the author. Even more important, the recorder should make notes to help the author improve the paper, listing weak areas and making suggestions for improving the paper. Note: Ask your teacher now if your group has any questions.

A. Ask and answer these questions, focusing on the introduction:

1. What is the topic of your paper?

2. What are the issues presented? (Include both sides of the argument.)

3. Why is this an important or interesting issue?

4. Have you provided details to convince the reader that it is important? What are some details or examples?

5. What do you think about this issue? What is your position or thesis? What would the opposite side say?

B. Ask and answer these questions, focusing on the body of the paper:

1. What reasons or ideas have you given to support your position? Summarize your main points. Do these reasons make sense? Can you think of any more that you could or should include?

2. What do you want me to believe? Why should I believe that (i.e., what is the first main point you use to support your position)? Does it make sense to the reader?

3. How does that first main point relate to the thesis?

4. What examples, anecdotes, and quotes from experts, statistics, and other support have you given to convince me that I should believe you?

5. Have you given me more than one type of support (e.g., statistics and expert opinion)? One is usually not enough.

6. What is your thesis again? What is the second main point you give to make me believe or agree with you? Remember, I won't believe you if your idea is not logical.

7. Again, what evidence have you given to convince me that I should believe you? In other words, what examples, anecdotes, statistics, data, counter-arguments or refutation, and other support have you given?

8. Again, have you given me more than one type of support (e.g., statistics and expert opinion)? One is usually not enough.

9. What is your thesis again? Do you have a third main point to convince me that I should believe you?

10. How do you support your third main point (e.g., examples, anecdotes, statistics, data, counter arguments, and refutation)? Have you given enough support, and enough types of support?

11. Sounds good, but what main arguments would your opponents have? What have you done to attack their arguments? (In other words, what counter-arguments have you used to refute their position?)

C. Answer these questions, focusing on the conclusion of your paper:

1. What do you want to convince me to do? What action should I take?

2. What do you want me to remember (or change) after I finish reading this essay? How is this applicable or important in my life? (A summary of the ideas you stated earlier is not enough to convince me that I should change.)

III

APPENDIX B: *Sample Grade Sheet*

The following grade sheet is designed for a persuasive paper.

Writer's name and ID _____ Date _____

Content, Organization, Logic

____(10) The introduction clearly states the issue, its importance, and the writer's position on the issue.

____(10) The thesis statement is well-developed, clear, and appropriate.

____(10) The main reasons presented clearly support the thesis and make sense logically.

____(10) Appropriate explanations, examples, statistics, and details are given.

Composition Structure

____(10) Topic sentences and transitions communicate clearly, and effectively orient the reader.

____(5) The paragraphs are well-developed and unified. The information given is not redundant or irrelevant.

____(10) The arguments and positions move from general to specific, are supported clearly, and are in a logical sequence.

____(5) Logical, useful counterarguments (or refutations) are provided.

Grammar/Language Use/Mechanics

____(10) The paper shows mastery of simple sentence constructions with few grammar errors (agreement, verb tense and form, number, word order). Sentence variety is attempted with effective complex sentence constructions.

____(10) The vocabulary range is sophisticated, word and idiom choices and usage are effective, word forms are correct, and register and tone are appropriate.

____(5) The paper shows mastery of mechanics and form, spelling, and punctuation.

____(5) Use of quotation, paraphrase, and citation formats is correct.

____(100) Total (See comments on back.)

....

Group Oral Tests

Rex Berridge and Jenny Muzamhindo

Levels	Intermediate +
Aims	Gain familiarity with oral assessments other than direct teacher–learner interviews
Class Time	15–20 minutes per group
Preparation Time	Minimal
Resources	Nothing additional

The teacher–learner oral interview can be both intimidating to students and time-consuming for teachers, particularly when classes are large. One strategy for alleviating these problems is to have the students discuss a prepared topic in groups while the teacher observes and assesses.

PROCEDURE

1. Create discussion topics, perhaps with student input, and form groups (see Appendix A).

2. Give the students the topic(s) and the assessment criteria (see Appendix B) in advance, to allow planning time and to let the students know what they are aiming for.

3. Put the students into groups, or allow them to form groups themselves.

4. Have the students discuss the topics. Observe the students unobtrusively but make sure you can see and hear all students clearly.

FEEDBACK AND SCORING

1. Award grades according to the chosen criteria and the reason for testing (see Appendix B).

2. Optionally, have the students immediately reflect on their own performances, or give them immediate feedback.

CAVEATS AND OPTIONS

1. This approach normally depends on a cooperative attitude among the students such that they all participate in a significant way and support each other. If this attitude does not prevail, consider whether this will affect the execution and validity of the group test.

2. If desired, assess participation skills, including leadership of the group. This option might involve an element of competitiveness—making one's point strongly—alongside equitable chairing skills.

3. Give the students one topic or a range of topics to prepare. Either tell them the composition of their groups in advance, or put them in groups at the time of testing. Avoid giving the students an opportunity to script their discussions.

4. In some cases, (e.g., if the students are trainee teachers), consider content as one component of the assessment.

APPENDIX A: *Creating Topics and Groups*

Select from the following table.

Number of topics	Topic selection	Group formation
A. One	C. Random	E. Random
B. Several	D. Decided in advance	F. Decided in advance

Possible approaches:

A, D, E	B, D, E
A, D, F	B, D, F
A, C, E	B, C, E
A, C, F	B, C, F

APPENDIX B: *Sample Score Sheet*

This score sheet presupposes a set of criteria for assessing Levels 1–5 (e.g., Voice, Audibility: frequently too quiet or too loud, 1; consistently at a comfortable level, 5). Factors such as communicativeness have been omitted as being largely unmeasurable in this way. Participation is a very subjective area to assess unless frequency counts or similar devices are used.

Accuracy		1	2	3	4	5
Fluency		1	2	3	4	5
Lexis	Range	1	2	3	4	5
	Appropriateness	1	2	3	4	5
Voice	Audibility	1	2	3	4	5
	Pitch/tone	1	2	3	4	5
	Stress	1	2	3	4	5
Content	Relevance	1	2	3	4	5
	Supporting arguments	1	2	3	4	5
Participation	Amount	1	2	3	4	5
	Leadership	1	2	3	4	5
	Support for others	1	2	3	4	5

REFERENCES AND FURTHER READING

Bygate, M. (1987). *Speaking.* Oxford, England: Oxford University Press.

Fulcher, G. (2003). *Testing second language speaking.* New York, NY: Pearson ESL.

Luoma, S. (2004). *Assessing speaking.* Cambridge, England: Cambridge University Press.

Putting It Together: A Jigsaw Task

Michael Carroll

Levels	***Beginning***
Aims	***Demonstrate ability to arbitrate speaking turns in groups***
	Demonstrate use of conversational repair strategies
	Learn to share information
Class Time	***40–50 minutes***
Preparation Time	***60 minutes***
Resources	***Personal recording devices, language lab, or three audio recorders***

his activity is a jigsaw listening task that, consistent with task-based teaching and testing approaches, integrates the four language skills and places evaluative emphasis on completing the task. The **Procedure** assumes that the students have already done several similar tasks for practice. Information-gap activities done in pairs are a great improvement over the sorts of drills common in precommunicative teaching methods. They are all too predictable in some adverse ways, however. Because the information is often split evenly between the students, conversational turn-taking may become a matter of the two students simply alternating. In this way, opportunities to practice more natural turn-taking skills are limited. Jigsaw activities, on the other hand, allow several students to practice negotiating turns without any one student knowing exactly who has the necessary information. The tasks can be graded on difficulty of use. That way, even beginning-level students can learn the skills they will need to negotiate conversations in groups.

PROCEDURE

1. Before class, audio record the three scripts A, B, and C in Appendix A.

2. Hold the activity in the language lab or a similar space where three groups of students can each listen to a different audio recording at the same time. Explain to the students that they are going to draw a picture from information they get from a recording. Divide the students into three groups, and have the students in each group move their chairs together.

3. Provide each group with an audio recording of script A, B, or C.

4. Hand out the worksheet (see Appendix B).

5. Have the students listen to the audio recordings and take notes on (not transcribe) the content of their recordings on the worksheet. Provide an example on the blackboard:

   Recording   Notes
   The book is on the floor.   *book on floor*
                                     (or *book on the floor*
                                     or *a book on the floor*)

   Allow the students to listen to the recording as many times as they need to.

6. After they have finished taking notes from their recordings, have the students form new groups with one at least one A, B, and C student in each. Tell any extra students to double up in an existing group or work with a teaching assistant.

7. Tell the students they are going to share the information that they heard on the recordings and draw the objects (e.g., sofa, book, table) on the picture on their worksheets. Model a typical exchange in which one student advances an incomplete piece of information and asks a question, and another student responds:

   A: The book is on the table, but where is the table?
   B: The table is next to the door. Where is the door?
   C: It's on the right.

8. Remind the students of some techniques for solving conversational problems (e.g., *Excuse me? Could you say that again? On the right?*).

9. Make sure to set a clear time limit (about 20 minutes), and encourage the students to draw their pictures quickly rather than beautifully.

FEEDBACK AND SCORING

1. Circulate while the students are working. Take note of the groups' progress, their turn-taking skills, and their conversational repair strategies. Check that individuals are participating in English.

2. Use the checklist (see Appendix C) as part of the course's achievement testing or simply to provide feedback to the students on their strengths and weaknesses.

CAVEATS AND OPTIONS

Develop similar jigsaw listening activities with a variety of formats and requirements. See Ur (1984, pp. 152–160) for a discussion of jigsaw listening techniques and Anderson and Lynch (1988, pp. 80–96) for ways to grade listening tasks.

REFERENCES AND FURTHER READING

Anderson, A., & Lynch, T. (1988). *Listening.* Oxford, England: Oxford University Press.

Buck, G. (2001). *Assessing listening.* Cambridge, England: Cambridge University Press.

Ur, P. (1984). *Teaching listening comprehension.* Cambridge, England: Cambridge University Press.

APPENDIX A: *Scripts*

Script A

The bookshelf is under the picture.

The CDs are on the bottom shelf.

The cat is behind the chair.

The three cushions are on the sofa, on the left.

The coat is on the floor next to the coffee table, on the right.

Script B

The two dirty socks are next to the coat, on the right.

The coffee table is in front of the chair.

The glasses are on the bookshelf, on the top.

The clock is above the chair.

The sofa is under the window.

Script C

The pizza is on the table.

The light is on the ceiling.

The plant is between the bookshelf and the sofa.

The book is next to the glasses.

The big chair is next to the door, on the right.

APPENDIX B: *Where Is It?*

1. Divide into groups and listen to the recording. Don't write everything you hear. Write only the main ideas. For example, if you hear

   The book is on the floor.

   write

   book on floor

   _____

   _____

   _____

   _____

2. In groups of three, ask the other students about the items in the picture. Draw the objects on a blank sheet of paper.

APPENDIX C: *Evaluation Checklist*

Student's Name _____

Group	Yes				No
Is the picture finished?	5	4	3	2	1
Is the picture drawn correctly?	5	4	3	2	1
Did the students take turns smoothly and appropriately?	5	4	3	2	1
Did the students fix problems in the conversation?	5	4	3	2	1

Individual					
Did the student participate in the group?	5	4	3	2	1
Did the student use English?	5	4	3	2	1

Let Me Explain

Robin Russ

Levels	*Low intermediate +*
Aims	*Demonstrate fluency in explaining a process*
Class Time	*15–30 minutes to introduce*
	7–10 minutes per workshop
Preparation Time	*60 minutes*
Resources	*Stopwatch*

In this assessment activity, students give mini-workshops or short lessons to explain a hobby or teach a skill to a group of fellow students. The activity assumes that the students have studied how to give instructions, are familiar with the appropriate lexis and grammatical structures (e.g., *first, then, next, finally,* and imperatives), and are familiar with asking for repetition and repetition. The activity requires students to demonstrate their ability to give instructions logically and clearly, examines their control over appropriate vocabulary, and checks their fluency.

PROCEDURE

1. Explain the activity to the students.

   • Have the students each select a topic (e.g., how to play a sport, draw a picture, make pottery, play a musical instrument, arrange flowers) and prepare a mini-workshop in which they explain or teach some aspect of that topic. Encourage the students to bring realia (e.g., a golf club, a cutout of a piano keyboard) when possible so that the other students can actually practice what they are being taught.

   • Inform the students that some of them will be trainees who will act out the instructions while they are being given. Tell them to ask for clarification or repetition any time they are unsure of the instructions or confused about what to do.

2. The following week, have the students confirm their workshop topics. If necessary, help them with ideas for realia.

3. A week or so later, on the day of the workshops, divide the class into groups of 5–10 students. Have the students in each group arrange their chairs in a semicircle.

4. Designate 1–2 students from each group as trainees. To evaluate fluency as well as the ability to explain a process, encourage appropriate communication between the presenter and the trainees. Give the students useful prompts, for example,

   - *Sorry, would you repeat that?*

   - *I beg your pardon?*

   - *Did you say _____?*

   - [a brief reiteration of what the presenter says]

   Have the remaining group members write down the instructions as they are being explained using the target structures (e.g., *first, then*). Encourage the students to ask questions if they are unsure of the instructions.

5. Have the presenter and the trainees stand up and begin the workshops.

FEEDBACK AND SCORING

Using a scoring form (see Appendix), circulate among the groups, and quickly circle the appropriate number for each student's performance level in each category. Total the four scores.

CAVEATS AND OPTIONS

1. If the class is large, schedule the workshops over a few weeks.

2. Expect the students to give their workshops without notes. Depending on the complexity of the task, however, the students may be permitted to write down a short list of vocabulary items.

REFERENCES AND FURTHER READING

Liskin-Gasparro, J. (1987). *Testing and teaching for oral proficiency.* Boston, MA: Heinle & Heinle.

Weir, C. (1994). *Understanding and developing language tests.* Upper Saddle River, NJ: Prentice Hall.

APPENDIX: *Sample Scoring Form*

Student's name _____

	Low				High
Structures	1	2	3	4	5
Vocabulary	1	2	3	4	5
Strategic skills (repetition/reiteration, circumlocution, fielding and answering questions)	1	2	3	4	5
Communicative effectiveness (pronunciation, voice quality, intelligibility, paralinguistics)	1	2	3	4	5

Total _____

Reciprocal Teaching: Reading Strategies at Work

Lorraine Valdez Pierce

Levels	*Intermediate +*
Aims	*Apply reading comprehension strategies to unfamiliar texts*
Class Time	*30–60 minutes*
Preparation Time	*1–2 hours*
Resources	*Projector*
	Reading passages unfamiliar to students

This activity helps students routinely apply reading comprehension strategies (i.e., summarizing, predicting, and asking questions for clarification) to unfamiliar texts. English language students generally need a great deal of support in activating these strategies and using them consistently. Through effective teacher modeling and repeated opportunities for practice in small groups, students learn to formulate questions reflecting literal and inferential comprehension, analysis, and other critical thinking skills. The importance of modeling cannot be overstated. When the activity is used for instruction, the teacher can assess reciprocal teaching as students work in small groups with a Reading Strategies Group Record (see Appendix A) or an Anecdotal Record (see Appendix B).

PROCEDURE

1. Select several reading passages unfamiliar to the students. The passages should be at a challenging or instructional reading level (not too easy, not too hard), as well as of interest to them. The passages can be either excerpts or entire texts consisting of several paragraphs. Enlarge the first four paragraphs of each, and project them for the class..

2. Project the first passage, and model the activity several times with the whole class as follows:

   • Ask all the students to read the first paragraph silently. Give them three purposes for reading: (a) to summarize the paragraph, (b) to ask questions for clarification of something in the paragraph that is unclear or that provokes a personal response, and (c) to predict what will appear in the following paragraph of the text.

- When the students finish reading, (a) produce a one-sentence summary of the first paragraph; (b) ask yourself and the students one question for clarification posed by the first paragraph, perhaps a point that is difficult to understand; and (c) predict what the author(s) will likely say in the second paragraph. Discuss possible answers.

- Repeat the modeling process with the second paragraph.

- For the third paragraph, ask for student volunteers to do each step (one step per student). Restate each student's response in order to model appropriate language where necessary.

- Repeat the modeling process with the fourth paragraph.

3. At intervals of several days, repeat the entire modeling sequence (Step 2) with a different reading passage until the students appear comfortable with it. When the students begin to be comfortable with the process, name the three strategies (summarizing, predicting, and questioning) as they are being modeled, and encourage the students to name each strategy when they use it.

4. Give the students a printed copy of the three steps of reciprocal teaching, or display them using the projector.

5. Tell the students they will follow the three-step reciprocal teaching process in small groups as follows:

- A leader reads the first paragraph and applies the three reading strategies.

- The next student applies the strategies to the second paragraph, and so on.

- Each student in the group gets a turn at being the leader. In this way, each student has an opportunity to practice and get feedback from peers and is held accountable for using the strategies.

6. Form small groups of 4–5 students.

7. Ask each group to pick a leader and begin the reciprocal teaching process.

8. Monitor each group to see that the students are following the process appropriately. Use either of the records in Appendix A or B.

9. Encourage the students to use the three strategies in their independent reading and to report back on their successes, their difficulties, and the ways they overcame any obstacles to effective strategy use.

FEEDBACK AND SCORING

1. Use the information generated on the records (see Appendices A and B) to revisit this activity and to provide additional modeling or instruction in the application of reading strategies.

2. The Reading Strategies Group Record provides space for comments on each student's application of the reading strategies. Give feedback to groups or individual students in conferences or in a short write-up.

CAVEATS AND OPTIONS

1. Support weak readers in one of several ways:

    *   Form heterogeneous groups for the activity.

    *   Team up weak readers with partners who will support their efforts.

    *   Ask each team to assist students who need it.

    *   Allow weak readers to opt out of the activity if they do not feel comfortable. (Note: They will still be exposed to continuous modeling of both the reciprocal teaching process and the language involved.)

2. With large classes, monitor only a few groups—perhaps those with the weakest readers—each time this activity is conducted.

REFERENCES AND FURTHER READING

O'Malley, J. M., & Valdez Pierce, L. (1996). *Authentic assessment for English language learners: Practical approaches for teachers.* Reading, MA: Addison-Wesley.

Palincsar, A. S., & Brown, A. L. (1984). Reciprocal teaching of comprehension-fostering and comprehension-monitoring activities. *Cognition and Instruction, 1*, 117–175.

APPENDIX A: *Reading Strategies Group Record*

Date _____

Student	Reading strategy			Comment
	Summarizes effectively	Asks questions for clarification	Makes predictions based on text and prior knowledge	
1.				
2.				
3.				
4.				
5.				

APPENDIX B: *Anecdotal Record*

Student's name _____

Date	Use of reading strategies		
	Reading strategies applied effectively	Reading strategies not applied	Additional instruction needed

Assessing Topic Maintenance and Turn Taking

Kristin Jatkowski

Levels	*Beginning, preschool/early elementary school*
Aims	*Use the pragmatic skill of turn taking in natural environments*
	Maintain a particular topic for a short period of time
	Listen to the speaker and respond
Class Time	*5–7 minutes per student*
Preparation Time	*5–10 minutes*
Resources	*3–5 pictures of topics appropriate to cultural background, age, and experience of young children*

Young children should learn the English pragmatic skill of turn taking in natural environments, as they may differ from their native language. In addition, they should be able to maintain a particular topic for a short period of time, listen to the speaker, and respond to the speaker. This activity is designed to assess the learner's ability to maintain a topic for three turns and demonstrate appropriate turn-taking skills in a natural environment rather than teaching students isolated pragmatic rules.

PROCEDURE

1. Allow the learner to choose which picture they would like to discuss.

2. Ask the learner a question, such as *What do you see in this picture?* or *Why did you choose this picture?*

3. Allow the learner to respond.

4. Repeat the question and answer sequence two more times.

5. During the assessment, notice whether or not the student demonstrates appropriate turn-taking behavior, such as waiting for the teacher to finish the question before beginning their response.

SCORING AND FEEDBACK

After the conversation has finished, the assessment rubric (see Appendix) can be used to assess the learner's ability to maintain a topic and demonstrate turn-taking behavior.

CAVEATS AND OPTIONS

1. Turn taking is a skill that needs to be systematically taught to young children; however, it is recommended it be taught in a natural environment. They need to be aware of not interrupting speakers before they are finished talking.

2. Students from different cultural backgrounds may have a different concept of turn taking, and this should be taken into account when working with learners. Even students with high language proficiency may not be proficient in the pragmatics of English.

3. This activity may be expanded for older students by increasing the number of turns and the time the topic must be maintained. It could also be used with older students by using written topics rather than pictures. These topics could be related to the content area the learner is studying, so there can be separate assessments for language and content objectives.

REFERENCES AND FURTHER READING

Stockhall, N. (2011). Cooperative groups engaging elementary students with pragmatic language impairments. *Teaching Exceptional Children, 44*(2), 18–25.

APPENDIX: *Assessment Rubric*

	At Target (3/3)	Approaching Target (2/3)	Below Target (1/3)
Student maintains topic for three turns			
Student provides appropriate explanations for questions			
Student demonstrates appropriate turn taking			

Face to Face

Juergen J. Bulach

Levels	**Low beginning to high intermediate**
Aims	**Demonstrate ability to use descriptive adjectives orally**
Class Time	**10 minutes**
Preparation Time	**10 minutes**
Resources	**Watch or timer**

Tired of having to call on students to get them to answer a question? This assessment activity compels students to start speaking English right away, and the teacher hardly has to utter a word. It's enjoyable and competitive, and the teacher can concentrate on a number of areas (e.g., grammar points, vocabulary reviews, assessments of strengths and weaknesses).

PROCEDURE

1. Have the students count off by number. Break up the class into pairs of one odd- and one even-numbered student.

2. Have the odd-numbered students arrange their desks with their backs to the blackboard. Have the even-numbered students arrange their desks so that they face their partners' desks. Have all the students sit down.

3. Tell the students that one word at a time will be written on the blackboard and that they must describe the word on the blackboard to their partner within a certain time limit. Also instruct students that they (a) cannot use hand gestures and (b) must speak only English.

4. Model a word for the students. For example, write the word *apple* on the blackboard. Describe the word to a model partner whose back is to the blackboard: *It is a fruit. It is round. It is green or red . . . .* Continue until the student answers correctly or the time limit is called.

5. To begin the assessment, give the student pairs names or numbers for identification purposes. Write *A* and *B* on the blackboard to represent the students in each pair.

6. Write a word on the blackboard and instruct the students to begin. Tell the students when the time has expired. If the word is guessed correctly, award 1 point to the student who does the explaining.

7. Have the students switch seats (and roles) after several words have been played.

FEEDBACK AND SCORING

Tally the number of words each student has successfully described, as indicated by the other student's guessing it.

CAVEATS AND OPTIONS

1. In a class with varying levels, avoid pairing students with relatively strong English skills. Instead, form pairs made up of a strong student and a weaker one so that there are no overly dominant pairs.

2. If teaching a class with students of varying nationalities, avoid pairing people who speak the same language to minimize the students' temptation to speak their L1.

3. If any strong or weak pairs disturb the flow of the activity, give one of the students a list of words. Have that student come to the blackboard and take the teacher's role in writing the words. Have the other partner team up with another pair to make a threesome, or the teacher can take the student's vacated seat and join the students.

4. This activity can assess the students' listening comprehension skills, too, by simply awarding points to the student who has guessed the correct word.

Three-Sentence-Speech Speaking Test (TSSST)

Yuji Nakamura

Levels	*Beginning*
Aims	*Logically connect sentences orally*
Class Time	*20 minutes per class for every six students*
Preparation Time	*5 minutes*
Resources	*Nothing additional*

III

This activity gives quiet students something to talk about and encourages them to speak out as much as possible, with the positive washback effect of process assessment. The more students speak, the more logically they speak, the more natural they sound, and the more points they can earn.

PROCEDURE

1. Ask the students to arrange their chairs in a circle. Assign each student a number.

2. Have the students form a pair with the student beside them.

3. Have one partner ask the other partner a question (e.g., *What did you do last weekend?*).

4. Tell the partner to answer the question in at least three sentences.

5. When the first partner is finished with the three-sentence response, tell the answering partner to ask the same question of the other partner (e.g., *How about you? What did you do last weekend?*).

6. Choose one pair of students to do this dialog exchange aloud in front of the entire class while you assess the two students' speaking ability.

7. When the exchange is finished, ask the odd-numbered students to stand up and look for a new dialog partner to their left.

8. Have the new pairs repeat the dialogue exchange. Assess another pair's speaking ability while they are performing their dialog.

9. When the second exchange is finished, ask the students with odd numbers to stand up and look for a new dialog partner to their left.

10. Let the new pairs perform the same dialog. Assess another pair's speaking ability while they are performing their dialog.

11. When the third pair's exchange is finished, tell the students to go back to their original seats.

12. One by one, call on the six students assessed during the dialog exchange, and while the other students listen, have them attempt a narrative discourse on what their partners in the last pair did over the weekend.

FEEDBACK AND SCORING

Assess each student's narration ability (third-person narration using *he* or *she*). Try to focus evaluation on the students' efforts to make sentences, then on the quality of the sentences they make.

CAVEATS AND OPTIONS

1. Choose relevant topics for the dialog exchange (e.g., *What will you do during winter vacation? What do you usually do on weekends?*) so that the students will be motivated to speak out.

2. Be patient with the students' frequent pauses.

3. Advise the students to repeat the last sentence or the last word of the previous sentence several times when they cannot come up with a new sentence immediately.

The Audio Mirror: Reflecting on Students' Speaking Ability

John M. Norris

Levels	*Advanced*
Aims	*Reflect on content-specific speaking abilities*
	Demonstrate conceptions of language abilities
	Identify differences between students' and teachers' conceptions of speaking ability
Class Time	*2 hours*
Preparation Time	*30 minutes*
Resources	*Audio recorders or personal recording devices*
	Audio recordings or copies of audio files sent via email to the teacher

This assessment activity mirrors students' and teachers' attitudes toward the speaking process so that they can more clearly see and understand them. By listening to themselves speak on academic topics from their fields, students get to hear what they sound like when talking about subjects that interest them. By analyzing and critiquing their own speech, students reveal their ideas about their speaking ability and about what they think are their strengths and weaknesses. This exercise also reflects a teacher's impressions. By conducting the same kind of analysis as the students, teachers reveal their attitudes toward individual students' ability as well as what they think constitutes effective speaking. In comparing these points of view via conferences, both teacher and student can come to agreement on the student's goals for contextualized speaking needs. The entire reflective process generates an example of an effective academic speaker that enlightens both students and teachers.

PROCEDURE

1. Tell the students to come to the next class meeting prepared to give a brief (5–10 minute) explanation of a single concept that they consider essential in their major academic area. Give a sample explanation. (See **Caveats and Options**, No. 1.)

2. Before the next class, set up enough recording stations to allow the class—working in pairs—to record a conversation without disturbing the other groups. A language lab is ideal for this activity.

3. To encourage authentic explanation and questioning, pair students with different academic majors.

4. Make sure the students understand how to use the audio recorders, or have them record the assessment on their personal audio recording device. Tell the students to turn on their audio recorders and explain their chosen concept to their listening partner, assuming no previous understanding, as follows:

   • tell the students to give a definition of the concept, explain how it applies to their major field of academic interest, and give reasons why it is an important concept to know.

   • encourage the listening partners to question the speaker at any stage of the explanation (i.e., the students might request repetition of misunderstood speech, clarification of ideas, or definitions of words used

5. Give the students 30 minutes in which to record the concept explanations of both partners.

6. Collect the audio recordings or have the students email the audio file to the teacher.

7. For the next class, make sure there are enough listening stations for all students to individually listen to their audio recordings.

8. In class, redistribute the audio recordings to their owners, or have them access their recording on their personal audio recording device. Have the students begin by listening to their audio recordings once through to give them an idea of what they sound like while speaking on their areas of academic interest.

9. Pass out the handout (see Appendix). Have the students address the questions on it as they listen to their audio recordings again. Advise the students to be as specific as they can when answering the questions on the handout. Give them plenty of time (an entire class period), and tell them to listen to their audio recordings several times—rewinding, stopping, and analyzing as they go.

10. Collect the audio recordings and handout answers at the end of class. Do not read the students' answers until you have completed Step 11.

11. Listen to and reflect on the student's audio recordings. For each student, give sample answers to the questions on the listening handout.

12. Retain copies of both forms. Mark and return additional copies of both forms to the students.

FEEDBACK AND SCORING

1. Schedule individual conferences with the students to compare the teacher sample assessment with theirs.

2. In the conference, note similarities between both teacher and student responses. In particular,

   - Do both assessments agree on the student's strengths and weaknesses?

   - Do both assessments make similar suggestions with respect to improving the student's speaking abilities?

3. Move on to disagreements. Try to decide to what extent disagreements stem from field-specific knowledge that the students have (and to which the listening student or the teacher may not be privy) and to what extent preconceptions about speaking needs and speaking ability are operating (for both of the listening student and the teacher).

4. Probe the students for deeper information on their individual academic speaking needs.

   - Do they think their performance was representative of how they generally speak in academic situations?

   - Do they think the explaining function was typical of the academic speaking they are faced with?

   - Do they notice a difference between academic and everyday speaking requirements?

5. In class, address the range of comments and their similarities as well as differences across the different speakers.

CAVEATS AND OPTIONS

1. Give a sample explanation before Step 1 of the Procedure, but not on taping day. That way the students can get an idea of what kind of discourse is expected, even if the form of their explanations won't be the same. For example, give a 5-minute explanation of standardized testing—what it means and how it influences the student's work.

2. Use this assessment activity at the beginning of the semester. After holding conferences with all of the students, compile sets of field-specific speaking

criteria from any notes taken, and share them with the students. Or, form the students into groups by areas of academic similarity to create speaking standards based on contextualized speech, the students' individual reflections, and any teacher reflections. Building these student-teacher-negotiated criteria transfers ownership of the assessment process from class-external or top-down sources to the individuals involved in the assessment process.

3. Follow up this activity by giving the students the opportunity to re-record their concept explanations. This encourages the students to plan and revise.

REFERENCES AND FURTHER READING

Norris, J. M. (1996). *Performance and portfolio assessment (1985–1995): An extended annotated bibliography of sources useful for language teachers* (Research Note). Honolulu, HI: University of Hawai'i, Second Language Teaching and Curriculum Center.

APPENDIX: *Listening Handout*

Listen once to your audio recording. Then read the following questions and listen again. Try to give detailed responses to all of the questions. Feel free to replay and listen again as many times as you need to.

1. Do you think you gave a sufficient explanation of the concept to your partner? Why or why not?

2. Were you able to give reasonable and clear answers to your partner's questions?

3. On this occasion, what were your major strengths when speaking about your academic interests?

4. On this occasion, what were your major weaknesses when speaking about your academic interests?

5. Based on this exercise, what should you do to improve your academic speaking abilities?

Using the Science and Art of Colors to Teach ESL

Sharon F. Okano

Levels	*Intermediate; ages 7–11*
Aims	*Use English communicatively*
	Heighten consciousness of colors in the environment, in print, and in oral communication
	Use prediction, negotiation, and experimentation skills to find answers
	Work with primary and secondary colors
Class Time	*60 minutes*
Preparation Time	*20 minutes*
Resources	*Story, poem, or passage*
	Materials (see the list in Appendix A)

Color plays an important part in everyday life. It can alter moods, can express ideas and feelings, and is a key descriptor used in spoken, visual, and written communication. This introductory color assessment activity gives children hands-on experience with how colors are formed and how they are related.

PROCEDURE

Preparation

Before class, list the materials required for the activity on the chalkboard or chart paper (see Appendix A).

Introduction

1. Read the students a story, poem, or passage that includes color as a descriptor.

2. Conduct a short discussion with the students about how color is used in the text, and ask them for their own examples of where they see colors (e.g., in television commercials, clothing, makeup, cars).

3. Tell the students what primary colors are, and ask if anyone knows what *primary* means.

4. Group the students into pairs, designating one person as *Diamond* and the other person as *Heart*.

5. Ask the Diamonds to get the materials preceded by a diamond on the chart paper or blackboard, and ask the Hearts to get the materials preceded by a heart. Tell the students how much time they have to do this.

6. Inform the students that they will use newsprint to experiment with blending colors. Explain that the Diamonds will be responsible for spooning a small-sized glob of paint onto the newsprint and that the Hearts will be responsible for blending the paint on the newsprint with the paintbrush.

Tell the students to paint three small dots on the paper-plate color wheel as follows: red in Section 1, blue in Section 3, and yellow in Section 5.

Worksheet 1

1. Inform the students that they will work in pairs to complete Worksheet 1 (see Appendix B). Pass out a copy of Worksheet 1 to each student, read the directions aloud, and give an example for each activity. Ask the students if they have any questions.

2. Tell the students to fill in the remaining three of the six sections of the color wheel with a blend or secondary color made by mixing the two adjacent primary colors.

3. Have the students clean up their work areas and recycle the plastic spoons.

Worksheet 2

1. Pass out a copy of Worksheet 2 (see Appendix C) to each student, read the directions aloud, and give an example for each activity.

2. Tell the students to look at their color wheel (see Appendix D) for hints on the answers.

FEEDBACK AND SCORING

1. Collect Worksheets 1 and 2 and the color wheel from each pair. Comment on the accuracy of their observations about color.

2. If desired, comment on the accuracy of the language the students used in expressing their observations.

3. Return the materials to the students.

CAVEATS AND OPTIONS

1. As a follow-up game, divide the class into two groups (Diamonds and Hearts), and choose one student from each group. Ask such questions as: *What primary colors are used to make the color orange?* and *What is a complementary color of blue?*

2. In a variation of the follow-up game, have each student write down the answers and turn them in.

REFERENCES AND FURTHER READING

Blanton, L. L. (1992). A holistic approach to college ESL: Integrating language and content. *ELT Journal, 46,* 285–293.

Crandall, J. (1993). Content-centered learning in the United States. *Annual Review of Applied Linguistics, 13,* 111–126.

Davis, C., & Brown, C. (1988). *How to use color.* Tustin, CA: Walter Foster.

Mohan, B. A. (1979). Relating language teaching and content teaching. *TESOL Quarterly, 13,* 171–182.

APPENDIX A: *Materials*

Each pair of students will need

*   newspaper to cover the work area

*   a container of water

*   an egg carton with red, blue, yellow, and white paint in four separate compartments (requires extra preparation time before class)

*   four plastic spoons

*   one worksheet

*   one paintbrush

*   one sheet of newsprint

*   one paper plate marked with lines dividing it into sixths, labeled clockwise as Sections 1–6 (requires extra preparation before class; see Appendix D)

*   paper towels

APPENDIX B: *Worksheet 1*

1. Record all observations on the table below.

2. Brainstorm a list of six objects that are not black, white, brown, gray, or a primary color.

3. Predict how to make the color—or a close approximation of the color—of the objects using a blend of two primary colors. For a hint on making your predicting easier, look at the color wheel with the three primary colors.

4. Experiment with the primary-color paints to produce the colors of the objects.

5. Fill in the last column with a name of the color that you have blended.

6. Predict and experiment to create the following colors: brown, black, gray, and white. You can use white and more than two primary colors.

| Name of object | Colors to blend | | Color of object |
	Prediction	Actual	
1. grass			
2.			
3.			
4.			
5.			
6.			
7.			brown
8.			black
9.			gray
10.			white

APPENDIX C: *Worksheet 2*

1. List five objects and their color. Then write the two primary colors blended to make that color.

Object and color	Primary colors blended
1.	
2.	
3.	
4.	
5.	

2. Give two examples for each of the following:
    *   primary colors
    *   secondary colors
    *   complementary colors (any two colors directly across from each other on the color wheel)

    Note: Any two complementary colors mixed together will make brown!

APPENDIX D: *Color Wheel*

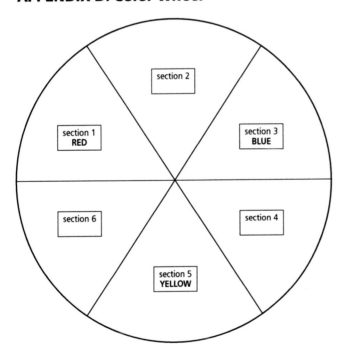

Organizing Ideas With Pictures

Ilse A. Rodriguez

Levels	*Intermediate*
Aims	*Organize ideas*
	Describe events in the past
Class Time	*2 hours*
Preparation Time	*1 hour*
Resources	*Envelopes*

Sequential pictures can help students speak coherently and organize ideas related to one topic. In this activity, the pictures are used to describe events in the past.

PROCEDURE

1. Select sets of sequential pictures showing different events, and arrange them in the wrong order. Put the sets in envelopes.

2. Give each student one envelope. Ask the students to organize the pictures into a logical order.

3. After a few minutes of observation, ask each student to describe the events shown in the pictures orally, as if they occurred yesterday.

FEEDBACK AND SCORING

Score the students' performances on this activity in the areas of organization of ideas, coherence, fluency, pronunciation, accuracy, and appropriateness, as shown in the scoring sheet (see Appendix B).

CAVEATS AND OPTIONS

1. Instead of small pictures, make big cards and have the whole class describe a single series of events.

2. Have the students discuss different ways to describe the same events.

3. Based on this oral description of the events, have the students write a short composition about what they have described.

4. The scoring sheet gives more weight to organization of ideas and appropriateness than to the other categories. Weight the categories equally by using 4-point scales for all of them.

APPENDIX A: *Model Sequential Picture Cards*

APPENDIX B: *Model Scoring Sheet*

Student's name _____

Criterion	Low				High
Organization	0	1	2	3	4
Coherence	0	1	2	3	4
Fluency	0	1	2	3	4
Pronunciation	0	1	2	3	4
Accuracy	0	1	2	3	4
Appropriateness	0	1	2	3	4

Total _____

Observation, Feedback, and Individual Goal Setting

Brian Paltridge

Levels	*Beginning +*
Aims	*Demonstrate strengths and weaknesses in oral interaction tasks*
	Set individual learning goals based on teacher's assessment
Class Time	*30–45 minutes*
Preparation Time	*15 minutes*
Resources	*Oral communication task*

Recent years have seen important changes in the way that students' L2 development is reported on and assessed. In particular, attention to the notions of communicative performance testing and "evaluation as an aid to learning" (Brindley, 1989, p. 5) in L2 classrooms has increased. The assessment tasks here aim to draw these concerns together. In this activity, the teacher observes and evaluates the students' oral performance and gives detailed feedback based on specific, performance-related criteria. The students draw on this evaluation and feedback to set individual language learning goals.

PROCEDURE

1. Choose an oral communication task—or a series of tasks—where the students work in pairs or in a group, whose topic is linked to the aims of the students' course of study, as well as the aspect of language use they are currently focusing on (e.g., see Nolasco & Arthur, 1987).

2. Make a copy of the observation schedule (see Appendix A) for each of the students in the class.

3. Set up the communication task(s) so that the whole lesson takes approximately 30–45 minutes to complete. If desired, use only one task for the lesson but ask the students to perform it a number of times with different partners or in a different group, depending on the nature of the task.

4. Observe the students' oral interactions pair by pair, or group by group, as appropriate.

FEEDBACK AND SCORING

1. Make notes about individual students' performance according to the categories on the observation schedule. Use the criteria in Appendix B as the basis for the comments noted.

2. Hold a general feedback session on the activity for the class as a whole, highlighting the positive aspects of the students' performance as well as areas of their performance that they could improve.

3. Write up individual assessments of each student's performance under the categories listed in Appendix A. Use the assessment criteria in Appendix B to refer to specific areas of the students' performance that would benefit from attention.

4. Give the students their assessments in a subsequent lesson. Then make appointments for the students to discuss their assessments individually one-on-one. When discussing the assessments with individual students, ask them to identify one area from the assessment they will work on for their next in-class observation and assessment. In this way, students establish learning goals.

CAVEATS AND OPTIONS

1. Repeat this assessment activity after a further period of instruction, using the previous assessment as the starting point for teacher observation and feedback.

2. Assign the students a grade for each of the areas of assessment as well as an overall score for their performance. Then use the grades as a reference point against which to measure future assessments and as a way of showing the students how they are progressing toward the learning goals they have set.

3. Give higher-level students copies of the criteria used for teacher assessment, and write feedback in light of the terminology they use. Be sure, however, to spend time explaining the meaning of some of the more technical terms used in the criteria sheet. The criteria are explained in detail in Paltridge (1992).

4. Give the students an opportunity to assess each other's performance in the same way they have been observed and assessed. Then have them give each other feedback and help each other establish individual learning goals based on these assessments.

REFERENCES AND FURTHER READING

Brindley, B. (1989). [Editorial]. *Prospect, 4,* 5–8.

Nolasco, R., & Arthur, L. (1987). *Conversation.* Oxford, England: Oxford University Press.

Paltridge, B. (1992). EAP placement testing: An integrated approach. *English for Specific Purposes, 11,* 243–268.

APPENDIX A: *Observation Schedule*

Student's name _____

Focus of assessment	Comment
Overall impression	
Accuracy	
Fluency	
Appropriateness	
Intelligibility	
Comprehension	
Strength(s) of spoken English	
Area(s) for improvement	

III

APPENDIX B: *Assessment Criteria for Oral Interaction*

Source: (Paltridge, 1992). Reprinted with permission from Elsevier Science Ltd.

Level	Overall impression	Accuracy	Fluency
0: Beginner	Nonuser. Cannot communicate in English at all.		
1: Elementary	Intermittent user. Communication occurs only sporadically.	Very limited grasp of lexical, grammatical, and relational patterns and functional language use.	Utterances consist of isolated words or short, memorized phrases. Frequent pauses may occur. Lack of range, subtlety, and flexibility.
2: Intermediate	Limited user. Neither productive skills nor receptive skills allow continuous communication.	Limited grasp of lexical, grammatical, and relational patterns. Initial grasp of functional language use.	Speech hesitant but self-correction occurs. Little ability to take the initiative in developing a conversation. Limited range, no subtlety or flexibility.
3: Upper intermediate	Moderate user. Can get by without serious breakdowns. However, misunderstandings and errors may still occur.	Moderate grasp of lexical, grammatical, and relational patterns, enabling the expression of a broader range of meanings and relationship between those meanings.	Can sustain conversation but reformulation sometimes necessary. Moderate range, subtlety, and flexibility.
4: Advanced	Competent user. Copes well in most situations. Will have occasional misunderstandings or errors.	Competent grasp of lexical and grammatical patterns and functional language use. Relationships between meanings generally well expressed.	Can generally engage in spontaneous conversation on most general-purpose topics. Competent range, subtlety, and flexibility.
5: Special purpose	Good user. Copes well in most situations. Can perform competently within own special-purpose areas.	Confident and generally accurate use of lexical and grammatical patterns and functional language use. Relationships between meanings well expressed.	Can engage in spontaneous conversation on general topics as well as matters relevant to own special-purpose interests. Good range, subtlety, and flexibility.

Appropriateness	Intelligibility	Comprehension
Use of language minimally appropriate to context, function, and intention.	Can convey only very simple meanings. Concentration and constant verification necessary on the part of the listener. Lacking strategies to compensate for low level of language ability.	Can understand only slow, careful speech. Frequently requires repetition.
Use of language appropriate to function, context, and intention within a limited range of situations.	Can convey basic meanings. Can be understood with effort but patient understanding necessary. Simple mastery of basic communication strategies.	Can understand speech related to familiar topics phrased simply. Repetition may still be required.
Use of language generally appropriate to function, context, and intention within a moderate range of situations.	Can be understood without undue difficulty when discussing familiar topics, but problems may arise with detailed explanations. Moderate command of a range of communication strategies.	Can generally understand and interpret meanings related to familiar subjects spoken by a native speaker at normal speed.
Use of language generally appropriate to function, context, and intention within a range of situations.	Communicates meanings competently in general communication contexts. Competent command of a range of communication strategies.	Can understand and extract information from native-speaker speech at normal speed. Some repetition may be required in special purpose areas.
Use of language mainly appropriate to function, context, and intention within a good range of situations.	Communicates meanings well in general and within own special-purpose areas. Good command of a range of communication strategies.	Can understand and extract information from most native-speaker speech. Will also have some competency within own special-purpose areas.

Consolidate Yourself

Chris Samsell

Levels	*Any*
Aims	*Review course objectives in an enjoyable way*
	Receive feedback and a score on performance
Class Time	*30–60 minutes*
Preparation Time	*15–30 minutes*
Resources	*Dice*
	Small objects to use as tokens

For instructors who teach within a curriculum that has an achievement test scheme, it is typically difficult to get students to show a gain on the final test. To do this, use the Consolidate Yourself game board periodically during the course as reinforcement as well as a review of course objectives toward the end of the course. Students enjoy the visual aspect of this game, and the instructor reaches his teaching objective: the students show a gain. Also, the game lends itself to free (real) conversation in an English classroom—something not easily done.

PROCEDURE

Making the Game Board

1. Choose items from the course objectives that the students need to review.

2. Make a game board (see Appendix A). Fill in the spaces with tasks that are based on the objectives you have chosen. Several times on the game board, repeat tasks based on one objective that is especially meaningful (e.g., comparing Japan with other countries). The sample game board (see Appendix B) contains this objective four times on the board so that the teacher can assess every student.

Playing the Game

1. Put the students in pairs or in groups of 3–4 students each. Groups of three can be monitored more easily and, if so desired, surreptitiously.

2. Distribute one game board, one die, and objects that serve as tokens (e.g., coins, erasers) to each pair or group. Do not read the game board to the students before they play. To prepare the students to play, tell them to

- supply details, not short answers

- start again when they finish the game (as the game lends itself to digressions)

- not play to win

3. Have the students roll the die and move their selected token across the game board.

FEEDBACK AND SCORING

1. Assess the students' responses with the assessment form (see Appendix C).

2. Either return the form to the students at the end of class, or record the assessment on the teacher's assessment (see Appendix D). Returning the form to the students immediately prevents forgetting to do it later and, more importantly, the students truly appreciate the immediate feedback.

CAVEATS AND OPTIONS

1. Vary the design of the game board each time a new one is made by using different colors, sizes, and so on. This prevents both students and teacher from becoming bored.

2. Either use computer-designed game boards, or make them by hand.

3. Don't assess the students during the first part of the game; let them warm up. When they answer the same question more than once, the students naturally tend to give better and better answers, showing that they are taking advantage of the learning environment.

4. This assessment activity, initially designed for adults and high school students in Japan, can be adapted to any level.

5. Instead of using one type of game board, give each group a different one.

6. After the students have gone through the game board once, rotate one student from each group into another group. This option gives the groups a chance to communicate and compare their English with more combinations of students and gives the students more chances to learn.

APPENDIX A: *Blank Game Board*

Consolidate Yourself

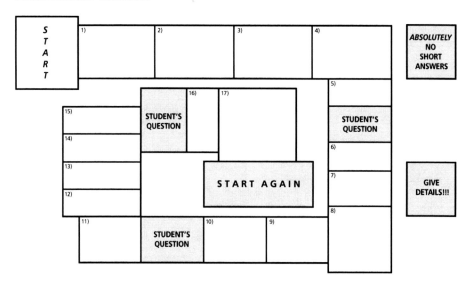

APPENDIX B: *Sample Game Board*

Consolidate Yourself: The Basics

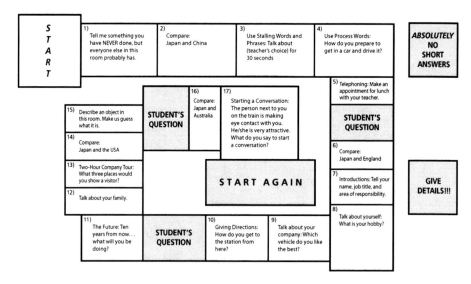

APPENDIX C: *Direct Assessment Form*

Student _____

Date	Rater	Objective assessed	Score					Average
			1	2	3	4	5	
			1	2	3	4	5	
			1	2	3	4	5	
			1	2	3	4	5	
			1	2	3	4	5	
			1	2	3	4	5	
			1	2	3	4	5	
			1	2	3	4	5	
			1	2	3	4	5	
			1	2	3	4	5	

Explanation of Scores

5 **Excellent response**; student adds to discussion, involves others, or both

4 **Good response**; student responds appropriately

3 **Fair response**; student makes obvious grammar and fluency errors

2 **Inappropriate response**; student tries to respond or clarify

1 Student does not respond or ask for clarification; uses L1

APPENDIX D: *Teacher's Assessment of Student's Form*

Date _____ Class _____

Teacher _____

Student	Objective assessed	Score					Average
		1	2	3	4	5	
		1	2	3	4	5	
		1	2	3	4	5	
		1	2	3	4	5	
		1	2	3	4	5	
		1	2	3	4	5	
		1	2	3	4	5	
		1	2	3	4	5	
		1	2	3	4	5	
		1	2	3	4	5	

Explanation of Scores

5 **Excellent**. Student answers appropriately, freely adds to response, and involves others in discourse

4 **Good**. Student answers appropriately; minor mistakes—if any—don't hamper comprehension

3 **Fair**. Student gives fair response and makes obvious grammar and fluency errors

2 **Poor**. Student tries to respond, but response is inappropriate

1 Student doesn't understand, ask for clarification, or respond in any way; uses L1 profusely

Whose Shoes Do You Use?

Mark D. Stafford

Levels	*Intermediate +*
Aims	*Understand and demonstrate functions and uses of pronouns*
Class Time	*60 minutes*
Preparation Time	*15–20 minutes*
Resources	*Realia (optional)*

PROCEDURE

Preparation

1. If desired, collect realia (e.g., household items: clocks, toothbrushes, dishes, food items, shoes, books) to bring to class.

2. Based on the realia, fill in the list of items (see Appendix A) so that all the items are listed next to the characters who own them.

Explanation

1. Tell the students that they will do an activity to help them learn the use of pronouns.

2. Go over the basic pronouns: *I, me, my, he, him, his, she, her, her, they, them, their, we, us, our, you, you, your.*

3. Practice some of the pronouns by having the students make sentences using the teacher, their classmates, or themselves as subjects.

Warm-up Activity

1. Ask the students to form groups of 3–5 people each and to list conversational situations in which they might use pronouns.

2. Regroup the class and discuss each group's findings.

3. Explain that the students will be doing a role-play about college housemates who are all moving away after graduating.

Assessment Activity

1. Form pairs of students.

2. Pass out the directions and list of items (see Appendix A).

3. Go over the role-play directions, and discuss new vocabulary (using the realia to stimulate discussion) and any questions that arise.

4. Assign each student a role description from Appendix B, and help individual students understand their parts.

5. Have the students perform their role plays. Observe and make notes on how they use pronouns.

FEEDBACK AND SCORING

1. After the role-play is complete, give the students feedback on their use of pronouns.

2. If desired, record the interaction while noting nonverbal communication, and fill out the assessment form (see Appendix C).

CAVEATS AND OPTIONS

1. Use the students' ideas to design a similar role-play.

2. If finding realia proves difficult, draw items on paper, or simply have the students use their imaginations.

3. This type of role-play activity is also good for practicing the use of modals and the language of negotiation.

REFERENCES AND FURTHER READING

Ellis, R. (1993). Interpretation tasks for grammar teaching. *TESOL Quarterly, 29*, 87–105.

Nunan, D. (1995). Closing the gap between learning and instruction. *TESOL Quarterly, 29*, 133–158.

Pica, T., Canoga, R., & Fellation, J. (1993). Choosing and using communication tasks for second language instruction and research. In G. Crookes & S. M. Gass (Eds.), *Tasks and language learning: Integrating theory and practice* (pp. 9–34). Clevedon, England: Multilingual Matters.

APPENDIX A: *Directions and List of Items*

DIRECTIONS: You are all roommates who have been living in the same house while going to college. It is now the end of the school year, so everybody will be graduating and moving away to start jobs in different cities. There are lots of things in the house that need to be packed, but it isn't clear which things belong to which roommate. Try to sort out everybody's belongings.

ITEM [Add names of items here.]	OWNER [Add names of owners here.]

APPENDIX B: *Role Descriptions*

AHMAD: You have been living in the house for 4 years. Because you have been living there so long, you have more things than everybody else. You are a leader of the house, so make sure everyone—including you—gets their things sorted out as peacefully as possible. Below is a table of things in the house and who owns them. This should help you sort out the household items.

Item	Yours	Somebody else's	Not sure whose

SHARON: You have lived in the house for 1 year. You brought a lot of things to the house when you moved in, so be sure to get them back. You're not too fond of Richard because he's really forgetful. Below is a table of things in the house and who owns them. This should help you sort out the household items.

Item	Yours	Somebody else's	Not sure whose

NOLAN: You've lived in the house for only 6 months, and you didn't bring much with you. Because you've lived in the house for such a short time, you don't have very many things and you remember exactly what is yours and what isn't. Below is a table of things in the house and who owns them. This should help you sort out the household items.

Item	Yours	Somebody else's	Not sure whose

YOKO: You have lived in the house for a year and a half with Richard, your boyfriend. Richard is forgetful, so he might not be so accurate about what he owns and what you own together. Be sure to get what is yours, and try to do it as smoothly as possible. Below is a table of things in the house and who owns them. This should help you sort out the household items.

Item	Yours	Somebody else's	Not sure whose

RICHARD: You and your girlfriend Yoko have lived in the house for a year and a half. You're not so sure about what is yours and what isn't, so try to get as many things as possible just to be sure. Sharon thinks you're forgetful. Below is a table of things in the house and who owns them. This should help you sort out the household items.

Item	Yours	Somebody else's	Not sure whose

APPENDIX C: *Assessment Form*

1. Does the student use pronouns that correspond to their antecedents?

2. Does the student use pronouns in appropriate places within sentences?

3. Does the student use pronouns as frequently as possible?

4. Does the student use pronouns appropriately within discourse?

5. Does the student use means of clarification, such as circumlocution and gesturing, when difficulties with pronouns arise?

6. Does the student get the items that belonged to him or her? If not, is it because of a lack of proficiency in using pronouns?

7. Does the student's use of pronouns contribute to settling the entire group's situation?

8. Does the student use pronouns while speaking to individuals as well as with the entire group?

Part IV

Alternative Ways of Accomplishing Classroom Chores

- **Preparing Students for Tests**

- **Creating Assessment Procedures**

- **Making Grading Easier**

- **Evaluating Curricula**

IV

Part IV: Alternative Ways of Accomplishing Classroom Chores

EDITOR'S NOTE

Traditionally, preparing students for tests, creating assessment procedures, grading, and evaluating curriculum have all been prerogatives of the teacher. Yet a number of the contributions to this book clearly offer alternative ways of accomplishing these classroom chores. In some cases, the contributors appear to be trying to save teachers work by using the students' energy to complete these requirements. In other cases, the contributors appear to have a genuine and healthy interest in involving students in the decision-making processes as part of their learning experience. In most cases, the teachers who contributed to this book seem to be recognizing the central role of assessment in curriculum development (for more on this issue, see Brown, 2005, pp. 252–261). Regardless of their motivations, the contributors are advocating that students be involved in (a) preparing themselves for tests, (b) making their own assessment procedures, (c) helping make grading easier, and (d) evaluating their own curriculum.

The four contributions involving the students in the processes of preparing themselves for tests have a variety of purposes: to help students appraise their multiple-choice test-taking skills ("Test-Wiseness Minitest"), to anticipate essay exam questions and create appropriate answers by putting themselves in the place of university professors (" 'Now You're the Professor!' Anticipating Essay Exam Questions"), to identify answers in their returned tests that warrant reconsideration by the teacher and encourage them to politely reason and negotiate with the teacher about those answers ("It's OK to Argue"), and to anticipate and answer various types of reading test questions ("Round Robin: Reading Test Prep").

The four contributions that show how students can develop their own assessment procedures focus on different goals: to assess students' reading comprehension and question-formation abilities based on questions they themselves formulate about a reading passage ("U Test U"), to provide a bridge between what teachers and students think should be learned ("Let Them Make Quizzes: Student-Created Reading Quizzes"), to introduce students to the assessment of their work using their own rubrics ("Developing a Student-Centered Scoring Rubric"), and using student involvement to create criteria and standards for assessing aspects of language that are seldom evaluated ("A Continuous Assessment Framework").

The three contributions that help make grading easier do so with several purposes in mind: to assess students' abilities to understand a reading and answer questions on it ("Raise Your Hand and Be Counted"), to assess students' abilities to integrate and sequence events ("Course of Events"), and to help students better understand, control, and predict their grades ("Getting the Point(s): An Adaptable Evaluation System").

Finally, the four contributions that utilize students in evaluating their own curriculum do so for different reasons: to assess students' degree of satisfaction with and involvement in various classroom activities ("Thermometer"), to assess students' understanding of classroom activities and involve students regularly in evaluating those activities ("Multiple Assessment Action Logging"), to get teachers to learn from students what works and what doesn't ("Wow! Marvelous Task"), and to get students to write a critique of the course ("Writing a Course Review").

REFERENCES AND FURTHER READING

Brown, J. D. (2005). *Testing in language programs: A comprehensive guide to English language assessment* (New edition). New York, NY: McGraw-Hill.

Brown, J. D. (2009). Using a spreadsheet program to record, organize, analyze, and understand your classroom assessments. In C. Coombe, P. Davidson, & D. Lloyd (Eds.), *The fundamentals of language assessment: A practical guide for teachers* (2nd ed.) (pp. 59–70). Dubai, UAE: TESOL Arabia Publications.

Carr, N. T. (2011). *Designing and analyzing language tests.* Oxford, England: Oxford University Press.

Cohen, A. D. (2006). The coming of age of researcher on test-taking strategies. *Language Assessment Quarterly, 3*(2), 307–331.

Test-Wiseness Minitest

Alastair Allan

Levels	*Intermediate +*
Aims	*Estimate skill at taking multiple-choice tests*
Class Time	*15–20 minutes*
Preparation Time	*5 minutes*
Resources	*Nothing additional*

Quite often, items on classroom tests—especially multiple-choice tests—contain unintended clues to the correct answers. Students who are test-wise are able to exploit these weaknesses and select the correct answers without necessarily possessing the knowledge or skills that the items are intended to measure. The Test-Wiseness Minitest gives a broad indication of test-wiseness. Low-scoring students are sensitized to their possible lack of this skill and can be suitably counseled and trained.

PROCEDURE

1. Tell the students that they are to work individually on a test. Remind them to use their skill, judgment, experience, and any tactics they can think of (apart from copying from each other!) to find the correct answers.

2. Hand out the minitest (see Appendix A).

3. Tell the students to select the best option (a, b, c, or d) for each question.

FEEDBACK AND SCORING

1. When the students have completed the test, read out the correct answers (see Appendix B) so they can mark their responses. The higher the students' total scores, the more test-wise they are. Anyone scoring higher than 3 (the level expected from blind guessing) has some amount of test-wiseness.

2. Have the students in pairs or threesomes try to identify the items making up the three subscales, each measuring one aspect of test-wiseness, in the test (see Appendix C).

CAVEATS AND OPTIONS

1. Remind the students not to take their scores too seriously. The test should produce valid scores, but it is very short, so the scores may not be reliable. They are merely suggestive.

2. Have the students note the strategies they use when responding to each item and compare them with their classmates' strategies.

REFERENCES AND FURTHER READING

Allan, A. (1992). Development and validation of a scale to measure test-wiseness in EFL/ESL reading test takers. *Language Testing, 9*, 101–122.

APPENDIX A: *Test-Wiseness Minitest*

1. Anna looked at the bowl of fruit then chose an
   a. banana.
   b. orange.
   c. mango.
   d. pear.

2. The herb called Eyebright was traditionally used
   a. to treat weak eyesight.
   b. for flower arrangements.
   c. in cooking vegetarian food.
   d. as a perfume.

3. A copper beech is a
   a. police dog.
   b. tree.
   c. mineral deposit.
   d. coin.

4. Steve has consulted many chiromancers, but only one
   a. are willing to give him advice.
   b. seems to understand him.
   c. charge him reasonable fees.
   d. offer to help him.

5. Mr. Park was dismissed from his job unfairly. This made his friends
   a. going on strike.
   b. to be sad.
   c. sympathizing.
   d. angry.

6. The leaves of the copper beech
    a. must be turned over every day.
    b. look similar to the leaves of most other trees.
    c. are the color of copper.
    d. should be used for protecting house walls from heavy rain.

7. My teacher, Mrs. Lee, said that my handwritten essay was a good example of cacography. This means
    a. my essay was too short.
    b. I had included some interesting ideas.
    c. I had written on the wrong topic.
    d. my handwriting was hard to read.

8. The Ashcan School was a
    a. old school that was closed down because it was so bad.
    b. ugly, unpleasant place used temporarily as a school.
    c. group of artists who painted scenes of city life in the early 20th century.
    d. organization that wanted to reform society by destroying poor-quality buildings.

9. Mrs. Lee
    a. was a ballet dancer.
    b. was a music lover.
    c. worked in a school.
    d. worked in a bank.

10. Small lakes found in mountainous areas are known as
    a. turns.
    b. tarns.
    c. terns.
    d. tiryns.

11. Jenny's crazy about books. She collects dozens of them. You could call her
    a. a woman.
    b. a person.
    c. Jenny.
    d. a bibliomaniac.

12. While climbing in the mountains, my brother Vic found a tarn and
    a. nearly fell into it.
    b. wore it all day to keep off the rain.
    c. kept it as a pet.
    d. sold it later for a large sum of money.

IV

13. My parents have gone out for a preprandial walk. This means
    a. a healthy walk.
    b. a long walk.
    c. a walk for pleasure.
    d. a walk before dinner.

14. I told my dog to keep quiet, but it barked
    a. loud and loud.
    b. even louder.
    c. ever loud.
    d. too loud.

15. Who among the following sometimes goes on hiking holidays?
    a. Anna.
    b. Mr. Park.
    c. Vic.
    d. Mrs. Lee.

APPENDIX B: *Answer Key*

1. (b) orange. ("*an* orange")

2. (a) to treat weak eyesight. ("*Eye*bright")

3. (b) tree. (See clue in Question 6(b), "most other *trees*.")

4. (b) seems to understand him. ("only *one* seems to understand him")

5. (d) angry. (The phrase "made his friends" must be followed by an adjective [angry].)

6. (c) are the color of copper. ("*copper* beech")

7. (d) my handwriting was hard to read. ("*hand*written" … "*hand*writing")

8. (c) group of artists who painted scenes of city life in the early 20th century. (Indefinite article *a* should be followed by a word beginning with a consonant.)

9. (c) worked in a school. (See clue in Question 7, "my *teacher*, Mrs. Lee.")

10. (b) tarns. (See clue in Question 12, "climbing in the mountains.")

11. (d) a bibliomaniac. ("*crazy* … biblio*maniac*")

12. (a) nearly fell into it. (See clue in Question 10(b), *tarns*.)

13. (d) a walk before dinner. ("*pre*prandial … before dinner")

14. (b) even louder. (This is the only grammatically correct option.)

15. (c) Vic. (See clue in Question 12.)

APPENDIX C: *Subscales*

The three item groups (subscales) in the test measure different aspects of test-wiseness, as follows:

	Measures ability to	Items
1.	Recognize a clue in the question stem	2, 6, 7, 11, 13
2.	Recognize that the grammar in the question stem or in one of the options points to the correct answer	1, 4, 5, 8, 14
3.	Recognize that a word or phrase in the stem or options in one question gives a clue to the answer in a different question	3, 9, 10, 12, 15

"Now You're the Professor!" Anticipating Essay Exam Questions

Debra Deane

Levels	**High intermediate +**
Aims	**Anticipate essay exam questions**
	Determine salient features of appropriate essay exam answers
	Gain insight into the creation of essay questions and the evaluation of answers
	Improve study habits for exams
Class Time	**2–3 hours**
Preparation Time	**30–60 minutes**
Resources	**Overhead projector, transparencies, and markers**

Students often have difficulty predicting what a professor will ask them on exams and knowing how to study effectively. Essay exams can be particularly problematic for ESL students. In this activity the students imagine they are professors and write essay exam questions while the teacher takes the role of the student and writes essay answers to the questions written by the students. The professors then evaluate the answers and give feedback to the students. In this way, ESL students not only learn strategies to prepare for and succeed on essay exams, but also come to understand better the material they are studying.

PROCEDURE

1. After the students have completed a content unit, ask them to imagine that they are professors, that they have just given their students the lectures and readings in the unit, and that they are now ready to test their students on their understanding of the material.

2. Ask the "professors" to form groups of 3–4 members and, using their lecture notes and academic readings, to write essay exam questions on the material they've taught their students.

3. After class, choose the 4–5 best questions from the groups and, in the instructor's new role as student, write answers to the essay questions. Make some answers appropriate and correct; in others, include erroneous information and write in a confused manner. Make photocopies of the answers for the class.

4. At the next class, give the answers to the professors. For homework, ask them to grade the answers and write positive and negative feedback, pointing out what is good in the answers and where there are errors or which parts seem confused.

5. Have the professors meet again in their original groups and discuss their grades and feedback. Ask the group members to come to a consensus and then to put their grades and written feedback for each answer on an overhead transparency.

6. Ask each group of professors to come to the front of the class and use their transparencies on the overhead projector to present their grades and written feedback to the rest of the class, justifying their decisions using the information from the content unit and specific details in the essay answers.

7. At the end of the presentations, elicit from the class the characteristics of good essay exam answers. Then examine these essay questions and the other questions generated by the groups earlier, and elicit characteristics of typical university essay exam questions. Also note which of the students' questions would probably not be asked in a university course and why.

FEEDBACK AND SCORING

As a culminating activity, have the students evaluate the following (see Appendix):

- their abilities to anticipate essay exam questions and recognize acceptable answers

- their understanding of the main ideas of the content unit

CAVEATS AND OPTIONS

1. Before doing this activity, discuss the terminology typically used in essay exam questions and the types of questions frequently asked.

2. If the class is quite advanced, have the students read, evaluate, and write feedback on the answers in class instead of assigning these activities for homework. This option allows lower-level or reticent students to think about their opinions and be prepared for the group work in class; it also gets

the students to think for themselves first without being influenced by the other group members' opinions.

3. Depending on their cultural backgrounds, the students may be hesitant or uncomfortable about evaluating and grading their teacher. The structure of the activity alleviates this problem: the students take the role of professors, work in groups to discuss their grading of the teacher, come to a consensus, and present it to the class. Humor can also defuse the situation; say things students have said to you, such as *Please don't make your test too hard! I haven't had a chance to study enough!* When the students understand the purpose of the activity, they usually enjoy testing their teacher.

REFERENCES AND FURTHER READING

Leki, I. (1989). *Academic writing: Exploring processes and strategies* (2nd ed.). New York, NY: St. Martin's Press. (See chapters 15 and 16 for tips on helping students prepare for and practice taking essay exams.)

McNamara, M. J. (1994). *Work in progress.* Boston, MA: Heinle & Heinle. (See chapter 6 for an explanation of types of essay questions and strategies to help students prepare for essay exams and cope with test-day anxiety.)

Weigle, S. C. (2002). *Assessing writing.* Cambridge, England: Cambridge University Press.

APPENDIX: *Self-Assessment Worksheet*

1. I rate my ability to anticipate essay exam questions as follows:

    ❏ Excellent   ❏ Very good   ❏ Satisfactory   ❏ Needs more practice

    Explanation: _____

    _____

2. I rate my ability to recognize good essay exam answers as follows:

    ❏ Excellent   ❏ Very good   ❏ Satisfactory   ❏ Needs more practice

    Explanation: _____

    _____

3. As a result of this activity, my understanding of the important information in this content unit has (choose one):

    ❏ Increased   ❏ Stayed the same

    Explanation: _____

    _____

It's OK to Argue

Kim Hughes Wilhelm

Levels	**Any**
Aims	**Be aware of ambiguous answers and poor questions on tests**
	Politely negotiate with the teacher over test answers
	Take responsibility for learning and assessment
Class Time	**60 minutes**
Preparation Time	**10 minutes**
Resources	**Completed test**

This assessment activity has three primary purposes: (a) to encourage students to identify answers that warrant reconsideration by the instructor, (b) to make students aware of ambiguous answers and poor questions, and (c) to encourage students to politely reason and negotiate with the teacher by explaining reasons for their answers and problems with the questions. In the activity, students also gain a host of skills: they assess their knowledge of content, use of strategies, and failure to follow directions on unit tests; develop their metacognitive awareness; and become motivated to improve their use of language and study strategies. Moreover, the activity encourages students to be responsible for their own learning and reinforces a collaborative approach to assessment.

IV

PROCEDURE

1. When introducing the course and again before giving the first major test,

    •   Tell the students that classroom policy is to give them 1 day in class to argue with the instructor about their test grade.

    •   Explain that this is a survival skill for academic work and that it is appropriate as long as students are polite and able to explain their thinking process.

    •   Assure them that the instructor will not consider them impolite or disrespectful if they question an item on a test because different people think in different ways and the instructor needs their help to identify confusing test questions.

2. As soon as possible after giving a test, bring the graded tests to class, and list the range of scores on the chalkboard from high to low. If desired, also include the following in the analysis of the students' performance on the test:

- the range of scores by section so that the students can compare their scores on each section with those of other students and assess their own abilities and needs. The range of scores also tells which skills and content are most difficult for the students (and require more work) and which the students have mastered.

- a question analysis (determining which questions were particularly good and which may have been ambiguous or poor questions)

- the number of students who missed a particular question and the breakdown of incorrect answers given

FEEDBACK AND SCORING

1. Hand out the evaluation sheet (see Appendix), and tell the students to fill it out as they go through the test.

2. Hand back the test—section by section if possible—and go over it one section at a time.

- If necessary, prompt the students to fill out the form for the first section. Discuss possible reasons for incorrect answers—for example, *just didn't know the answer* (hadn't studied well enough), *spent more time on the reading than on the film* (should have watched the film again), or *didn't follow directions*.

- List the range of scores for that section on the blackboard, and discuss any patterns you notice (e.g., say, *Most people did well on this section* or *I think we need more work on this*).

- Tell the students the questions that everyone got right, and concentrate on exploring questions that were frequently missed.

3. Explain to the students that in order to make sure their scores are accurate, they need to check the points per item and verify the point totals. Tell the students that this is the time to review their tests and discuss with you any answers they believe are in fact correct. Tell them you'll walk around the room to look at any answers they wish to discuss, and encourage them to speak up.

4. Walk around the room and discuss items that the students bring up. While reviewing alternative answers, require well thought out explanations of the students' thinking processes. For example, if a student is thinking correctly

with regard to an answer but can't provide a logical explanation, ask that student to prepare a better explanation in order to gain the points. With a very reluctant group, award a point just because a student was brave enough to argue.

5. Ask the students to revise their point totals, if necessary, on the evaluation sheet.

6. Also on the evaluation sheet, tell the students to summarize their performance, indicate whether they are satisfied with it, assess the test itself, identify skills they need to work on, tell how they would like you to help, and indicate what they will do to improve for the next test. (See the questions at the end of the sample in the Appendix.)

7. Have the students staple their evaluation sheet to the front of the test, putting the sections in order. Collect the tests, and tell the students that the tests will be in the office if they want to talk privately about them.

8. Follow up by confirming the final test scores, and arrange individual conferences if necessary. Revise the homework and lesson plans to respond to the students' expressed needs.

CAVEATS AND OPTIONS

1. This assessment activity is an excellent way to get the students to attend class the day after a test when attendance sometimes drops.

2. Some students from cultures with authoritarian classrooms may perceive this grading system as unfair. Spend time talking with the students about your rationale for allowing them to argue about their test grades. Reinforce the notion that doing so is an academic survival skill.

IV

APPENDIX: *Sample Test Self-Evaluation Sheet*

Name _____ EAP2, Test 2

DIRECTIONS: Look through your test and note the number correct in each section. Then describe what you missed or how you can improve next time. Add up the total points and the 3 points of extra credit possible to make sure your score is correct.

A. Focused Film Viewing: Fate of the Earth fill-in-the-blank

Points out of 12 possible   _____

Why missed? _____

_____

B. Topic Scramble: Save the Earth, Feed the World

Points out of 5 possible   _____

Why missed? _____

_____

C. Speed Read/Skim/Scan for details

Points out of 7 possible   _____

Why missed? _____

_____

D. Speed Read/Skim/Scan for main ideas

Points out of 9 possible   _____

Why missed? _____

_____

E. Sentence Analysis (relationship/referents)

Points out of 17 possible   _____

Why missed? _____

_____

F. Matching

Points out of 11 possible   _____

Why missed? _____

_____

G. Multiple Choice

Points out of 10 possible (2 each)   _____

Why missed?_____

_____

H. True–False

Points out of 10 possible   _____

Why missed?_____

_____

I. Essay Questions

Points out of 4/4 possible   ____ / ____

Required: _____

_____

Points out of 6 possible   _____

Option:_____

_____

+ 3 points if typed   _____

Total   _____

(Check one.)

_____ 85 or above? _____ 80 or above? _____ 75 or above? _____ 70 or above?

Are you satisfied with your performance on this test?   _____ Yes   _____ No

Were there any problems with the test itself (e.g., confusing questions, confusing or unclear directions)? Please explain.

What do you think you need to work on? Which skills do you need to practice?

How can the teacher help you?

Would you like an appointment with the teacher?

What will you do to improve your performance on the next test?

Round Robin: Reading Test Prep

Ashlea Allen Green

Level	*High beginner +*
Aims	*Practice anticipating and answering various kinds of test questions*
	Practice forming questions
	Demonstrate comprehension of a text
	Practice reading strategies
	Demonstrate acquisition of new vocabulary and collocations
	Engage in self- and peer assessment
	Encourage student ownership of the text and learning
Class Time	*30–90 minutes*
Preparation Time	*10 minutes*
Resources	*Index cards*
	Reading text
	Stopwatch
	Desks that can be moved

For many students, taking a reading comprehension test induces anxiety which can result in poor performance on the test. ELLs especially, who may have had culturally different assessment experiences, need to practice a number of skills before taking a typical ESL reading comprehension test. For example, they need to develop an understanding of various test question structures, strategies for answering test questions, and awareness of contextual, morphological and syntactic clues. Practice in a relaxed, peer-reviewed environment before the test will increase students' comfort levels and confidence in answering test questions during the test. In addition, this activity allows for the practice of vocabulary, collocations, and the grammatical formation of questions. Moreover, reading strategies such as scanning and skimming can be modeled.

PROCEDURE

Preparation

1. On 3x5 index cards, write the name of one test question format (e.g., *multiple choice, fill in the blank, true-false*.) The number of cards should equal the number of students so that each student will receive one card.

2. Select a reading text that the class has recently studied.

During the Activity

1. Ask students to move their desks so that they are sitting in a circle.

2. Ask students to take out a blank sheet of paper and have them write their names at the top of the paper.

3. Ask students to turn their attention to the selected text (i.e., book, article, or handout). Spend several minutes reviewing the text.

4. Give each student an index card. Ask the students what is written on their cards. Write some of the responses on the board.

5. Spend 10 minutes reviewing their responses and illustrating the different kinds of test-taking formats written on their index cards.

6. Tell students that they have 10 minutes to write one test question about the text using the format written on their index card.

7. In their questions they should use at least one vocabulary word (and preferably an appropriate collocation, if the class has studied them).

8. Circulate around the room to answer questions and to check that students are on the right track.

9. After 10 minutes, tell students to pass their paper to the student on the left.

10. Once the papers have been passed, tell students they have 3 minutes to answer the question on the paper in front of them. They should write their name next to their answer. Start your stopwatch to keep track of the time.

11. After 3 minutes, ask students to stop writing. Repeat steps 9–11 until each paper has circulated to all of the students.

12. Return the papers to their originator. Going around the circle, have each student read her question and all of the students' answers for it. Ask them to talk about any clues or strategies that aided in answering the question. Elicit questions or comments about this test question from the other students.

IV

FEEDBACK AND SCORING

Discuss the activity with the students. Ask questions such as

- What did you like/dislike about this process?

- Why did you ask the question that you asked?

- What strategies and clues did you use to answer questions?

- In your opinion, what test question format is easy/difficult?

- Without naming names, were there grammatical or spelling errors that you noticed in the questions and answers?

- On a scale from 1–5 (with 5 being the best), how did you do on the questions?

CAVEATS AND OPTIONS

1. The amount of time for this activity can be varied, depending on class size and the number of questions each student asks.

2. This activity can yield both informal and formal assessments by assigning points to the number of questions correctly answered. One could also assign points to grammar, spelling, and vocabulary usage.

3. After doing this assessment activity several times, teachers may choose to focus on specific kinds of test questions or other areas where students consistently need the most attention.

4. If students are required to keep a vocabulary journal, they may refer to their journals or dictionaries during the activity.

5. The round-robin setting is intended to create a less formal, more interactive atmosphere.

U Test U

Dafne Gonzalez

Levels	*Beginning to intermediate*
Aims	*Assess question formation, reading comprehension, and writing skills*
Class Time	*2 hours*
Preparation Time	*None*
Resources	*Content reading used in a study unit*

This activity checks what the students have really understood from a text and what they consider the most important information in it. It also serves as a sample of the students' reading comprehension and writing abilities in a portfolio. Teachers may use the information derived from this activity to reteach or promote practice in weak areas.

PROCEDURE

1. Locate a source text on the topic being studied.

2. Tell the students to read over the text as homework.

3. In class, give each student three sheets of paper (sheets A, B, and C).

4. Ask the students to

   • write their names on the top of each sheet

   • write four questions on Sheet A that can be answered from the reading and that represent the most important information contained in the text

   • write the answers to the questions on Sheet B

5. Have the students exchange their Sheet A for a classmate's. Ask each student to

   • write their name at the bottom of the classmate's Sheet A

   • rewrite any questions they consider to have mistakes

   • answer the questions on the partner's Sheet A

6. Tell the students who exchanged papers to work as a pair to check their questions and answers against Sheet B and write a revised version on Sheet C.

7. Collect Sheets C. Take notes on each student's reading comprehension and writing skills (including question formation) and on the content points brought up in the questions.

FEEDBACK AND SCORING

1. Use the information on Sheet C for a qualitative assessment.

2. Establish a scoring procedure for each answer (see Appendix).

3. Discuss all the questions and answers with the whole class, and reteach weak points.

CAVEATS AND OPTIONS

1. Before using this activity for assessment, have the students do it in groups in class to practice question formation and writing. In this case, the questions asked by one group are answered by another.

2. This activity has been used in an English for Science and Technology class, focusing the assessment strictly on reading comprehension and having the students write the questions and answers in Spanish, their L1.

3. In a content-based class, use the content of the questions asked by the students as part of later progress or achievement tests. In this way, the instructor can take into account what the students have learned and involve the students in the test-making process (Murphey, 1994/1995).

REFERENCES AND FURTHER READING

Murphey, T. (1994/1995). Tests: Learning through negotiated interaction. *TESOL Journal, 4*(2), 12–16.

APPENDIX: *Suggested Rating Scale*

Scoring Guidelines

1. Either have one rater read each answer on two separate occasions, or have two raters read each answer. The total points for each answer will be the average of the two scores.

2. Adjust the scores to fit the grading system.

3. Give more weight to language use and mechanics if the class focuses strongly on the form of the language. The example below reflects a concern with content.

4. Give 0–5 points for each correct answer based on the criteria indicated.

Content
3.0 points   Answer is correct, based on text
1.5 points   Answer contains only 50% of the required information
0.5 point   Answer contains almost none of the required information
0.0 points   Answer contains none of the required information

Language use
1.0 point   No errors in agreement, prepositions, pronouns, articles, verb tenses
0.5 point   Message conveyed, but some grammar mistakes
0.0 points   Grammar interferes with message getting across at all

Mechanics
1.0 point   Good use of writing conventions: capitals, punctuation, and spelling
0.5 point   Spelling or punctuation mistakes distract from message
0.0 points   Spelling or punctuation mistakes interfere with message getting across at all

Maximum points possible = 5 points/question × 4 questions = 20 points

IV

Let Them Make Quizzes: Student-Created Reading Quizzes

Greta J. Gorsuch

Levels	*Low intermediate +*
Aims	*Keep an ongoing assessment log*
	Discuss texts in a focused way
	Bridge the gap between what teachers and students think should be learned
Class Time	*15–45 minutes (write items)*
	15 minutes (administer and grade quiz)
	10 minutes (discuss)
Preparation Time	*10–30 minutes*
Resources	*Class textbook*
	Folders

After years of giving students weekly quizzes, there was evidence that the 2-week cycle required to make quizzes, give them, and grade them was taking too much time and that quizzes were really more for the instructor than for the students. Once the students found out their scores, they simply tucked the quizzes away somewhere. Not surprisingly, at the end of the term the students didn't have any idea of what progress they had made—something their cumulative quiz scores could have told them. Using input from Murphey (1994/1995) on student-created tests, a basic framework was devised, and structures were added to ensure that the students kept ongoing records of their own quiz scores, and a way was found to use the quizzes to discuss aspects of the texts that students were reading.

PROCEDURE

Preparation

1. Prepare a series of quiz items based on the chapter of the text that the students are reading. The items can be questions about the plot or about a

particular character in the text. Make sure the questions require a definite answer (i.e., they shouldn't be opinion questions).

2. After the students have read the chapter, divide them into groups of three. Ask the students to write down words or expressions from the text that they had trouble with or are interested in.

3. Elicit the words and expressions from the students, writing them on the blackboard. Get the students to explain what they think the words mean, then add any remaining information.

4. Tell the students to choose six words (or another appropriate number) for their next quiz. Write the words in the instructor notebook, and make sure the students understand that the material will be on the next quiz. Give the students at least a minute to ask questions.

5. Keep the students in their groups. Introduce the questions prepared in Step 1 by writing them on the blackboard and having the students read them silently. Allow ample time for questions.

6. Ask the students to write two questions about the text that are not vocabulary questions. Either tell them to use instructor questions as models, or have them write questions that seem different.

7. Circulate as the students talk and write. (Allow at least 15 minutes for this step.)

8. Elicit the questions from the students and write them on the blackboard. After at least six are on the blackboard, briefly and objectively explain any grammar or spelling changes needed. Praise the questions as creative artifacts of the students. For example, say *I really like the question, but change this word and put that word there, and the question will be more clear . . . . Do you see?*

9. Choose the clearest four questions. Tell the students that, in addition to the six vocabulary questions, those four will be on the quiz.

Quiz 1

1. Type up the questions and make sufficient copies for the students.

2. Administer the quiz.

3. When the quiz is over, either give the answers or have the students give theirs. Have the students grade their own papers.

4. Ask the students if they have other answers that they are not sure about, and write alternative answers that the students suggest on the blackboard. Get the students to refer back to the text itself to form their opinions about the answers. If there needs to be a judgment call, explain clearly the reasons for

accepting or rejecting the answer, based on the text. Let the students know what page and passage in the text that judgment is based on.

5. Hand out copies of the score sheet (see the Appendix), and have the students glue them into the inside front cover of their textbook or notebook. Then have the students record their percentage scores for Quiz 1. (If future quizzes contain 10 items, it will be easy for the students to record their percentage scores and keep track of their progress.)

Subsequent Quizzes

1. Begin the next cycle of student-created quizzes. If the cycle keeps going, the students shouldn't need nearly as much time to write their questions. From time to time, provide models of different types of questions, such as multiple choice or fill-in-the-blank.

2. Have the students keep their quizzes in a special folder and bring it to every class.

3. At frequent intervals, set tasks that will require the students to look back through previous quizzes. For instance,

   • ask the students to locate a question type they'd like to use on a new quiz

   • have the students read the quizzes to review the plot quickly or to review an aspect of a character the students are currently reading about

FEEDBACK AND SCORING

See **Quiz 1**, Steps 3–5, and **Subsequent Quizzes**, Step 3.

CAVEATS AND OPTIONS

1. Be sure to give the students plenty of time to respond to questions in classroom discussions. In Japan, students really get going after a minute of silence—it's worth the wait!

2. Be patient as the students learn how to write quiz questions. Their ability will increase quickly as time passes.

3. Consider allowing open-book quizzes (i.e., letting the students look at the books as they take quizzes).

REFERENCES AND FURTHER READING

Murphey, T. (1994/1995). Tests: Learning through negotiated interaction. *TESOL Journal, 4*(2), 12–16.

APPENDIX: *Quiz Score Sheet*

Score (%)

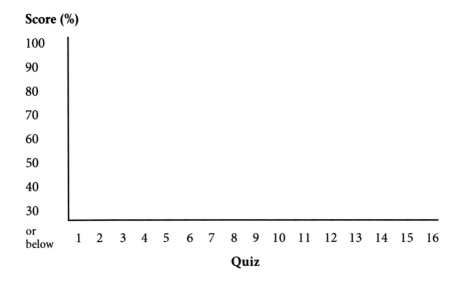

IV

Developing a Student-Centered Scoring Rubric

Michael A. Power

Levels	*Any*
Aims	*Understand assessment through rubrics*
Class Time	*15–30 minutes*
Preparation Time	*None*
Resources	*Overhead projector (optional)*
	Chart paper

Rubrics are elaborated scoring guides that clearly delineate the levels of students' performance at points on a scale, typically 1–4 or 1–5 (see Appendix). Scoring students' performance with a rubric has many advantages, including the ability to set clear performance targets, show growth qualitatively, and discuss students' work with them (as well as with other teachers and parents) based on a common understanding of expectations. One difficulty faced by second and foreign language teachers, however, is that often the language of the rubric is beyond the comprehension level of the students. Additionally, few students are familiar with rubrics, and it is difficult to explain their use and value (even in the students' native language). This activity models the construction of a rubric with the students, basing it not on an academic abstraction but on a concrete object familiar to them all.

PROCEDURE

Introduction/Warm-up

1. Ask the class *Who likes hamburgers? Where do you buy them? How much do you pay? Where can you get the best hamburgers?* and so forth. Continue until the students are all comfortable talking about the topic. (If hamburgers are not familiar to your students, use some other familiar food, either simple or deluxe.)

2. Tell the class *Today we're going to think about what a hamburger is, what a simple hamburger is, and what a great hamburger is.*

Building the Rubric

1. Write the numbers 1–5 on a piece of chart paper, leaving enough space to draw a picture and write a description after each number.

2. Ask the class *What is a hamburger? What does it have to have?* A likely student response is *Bread, meat, lettuce.* Then ask the class *If I have only bread, is that a hamburger?*

3. Draw one half of a hamburger bun on the blackboard. Ask *How many pieces of bread do I need?* Through questions like these, get the students to describe a simple hamburger: two pieces of bread and a piece of beef. Draw this on the blackboard, or have a student draw it next to the number 1 on the rubric. Next to the drawing, write the key words to describe this level of quality.

4. Again through questions and answers, develop what the students agree is a Level 2 hamburger: two pieces of bread, a piece of beef, lettuce, and ketchup, perhaps. Draw this on the blackboard along with the key words differentiating this level from the previous one.

5. Work through the other levels on the scale in this way. A Level 5 hamburger may be a double or triple with a special sauce, bacon, and cheese—the works!

6. Once the students have developed their rubric, have them work in small groups either to draw their own version of the hamburger rubric on chart paper or to think of their own example (e.g., a movie, a friend) and develop the descriptions for each quality level with words or pictures, depending on their language ability.

Developing the Concept

1. Make the connection between building the rubric for hamburgers and building as well as using scales to show students how well they are doing their work, whether in writing, speaking, or content mastery.

2. Hang the students' rubrics in the room, and refer to them whenever the students should be thinking about levels of quality in their work.

Developing the Rubric

1. Decide with the students what aspect of language learning to develop a rubric for (e.g., class speeches, compositions, essays).

2. Have the students work in groups to develop such a rubric on chart paper.

3. When the groups have finished, put the sheets of chart paper containing all their results up around the room.

4. Work as a class to develop a single agreed-upon rubric based on the efforts of all the groups.

FEEDBACK AND SCORING

See the **Procedure**.

CAVEATS AND OPTIONS

1. As much as possible, involve the students in the creation of the rubrics used for day-to-day assessment of their progress. Naturally, if a rubric for a high-stakes assessment, such as end-of-term grades or reports to parents is used, it is necessary to exercise a great deal of control over the criteria for performance at each level. Remember, however, that the more students are involved in creating the rubric, the more they will internalize the standards as well as become proficient at assessing themselves and demonstrating the desired skills and knowledge.

2. Have parents make hamburger rubrics on parents' night or at parent-teacher meetings, and explain to them the actual rubrics used for scoring in the class. This activity gives the parents insight into how their children are being assessed and makes it much easier to discuss rubric-based assessment data with them throughout the year.

3. With young or low-level language learners, use a 3-point scale instead of a 5-point scale at first. Increase the number of levels in a subsequent lesson.

REFERENCES AND FURTHER READING

Herman, J., Aschbacher, P., & Winters, L. (1992). *A practical guide to alternative assessment*. Alexandria, VA: Association for Supervision and Curriculum Development.

Popham, W. (1995). *Classroom assessment: What teachers need to know*. Needham Heights, MA: Allyn & Bacon.

Stiggins, R. (1994). *Student-centered classroom assessment*. Upper Saddle River, NJ: Prentice Hall.

APPENDIX: *Sample Holistic Rubric*

A simple holistic rubric for L2 learners showing their mastery of writing a story might look like this. Naturally the rubric will vary depending on the features of story writing on which you wish to focus. Note that some rubrics do not define all the levels. Performance at these levels is considered to contain some features of the higher level and some features of the lower.

LEVEL 5: Strong theme. The story is exceptionally clear and engaging. Few grammatical or spelling errors of any kind.

LEVEL 4: Clear theme. The story is elaborated with examples and explanations. Few grammatical or spelling errors; handwriting clear.

LEVEL 3: Clear theme but not elaborated. The basic story line tells only what happened or goes off on unrelated tangents. Few grammatical and spelling errors that interfere with comprehensibility; handwriting adequate.

LEVEL 2: Some evidence of theme, not clearly organized, minimal story line. Grammatical and spelling errors limit comprehensibility; handwriting hard to decipher.

LEVEL 1: No clear theme or organization. Many grammatical and spelling errors that interfere with comprehensibility; handwriting very hard to decipher.

IV

A Continuous Assessment Framework

David Progosh

Levels	*Any*
Aims	*Develop lifelong learning strategies through assessment of features rarely evaluated in the language classroom*
Class Time	*A few minutes per class*
Preparation Time	*60 minutes*
Resources	*Nothing additional*

Are the grades students receive an accurate record of their true abilities? If not, perhaps it is time to ask what is currently used to measure students' abilities and how it is used. The continuous assessment framework developed in this activity makes clear to both the students and the teacher the method of evaluating features that are rarely assessed in the language classroom (e.g., natural English use, effort, participation, volunteering). It keeps the teaching agenda open for scrutiny, reminding the teacher to be fair and ethical. It provides the students with lifelong learning strategies and encourages the teacher to have a clear set of objectives in the classroom.

PROCEDURE

Thinking About the Framework

Before class, think about devising a new assessment framework. Answering the questions below will clear up much of the mystery surrounding assessment:

- What factors are being examined when assessing students (e.g., participation, attendance, effort, homework, fluency/accuracy, pronunciation, meeting deadlines)?

- How much value is placed on the above attributes (e.g., 20% for effort)?

- What methods (e.g., tests, notes) will be used to measure those attributes?

- How will the assessments to students and other concerned parties be justified (i.e., what are the criteria or standards for a good participation grade)?

Involving the Students

1. At the earliest opportunity, broach the subject of assessment with your students. Explain that an assessment framework is being planned and that it would be helpful to have some information on how they were assessed in other classes.

2. Prepare an information-gap activity about past testing experiences by creating two different question sheets (see Appendix A).

3. Have the students get into pairs, ask their partner the questions on the sheet, and write down their partner's answers.

Designing the Assessment Framework

1. Ask the students what components (e.g., participation, homework, effort, volunteering) they think they should be assessed on. List them on the blackboard.

2. Ask the students how they should be evaluated on each component (e.g., tests, projects, journals). List their ideas on the blackboard.

3. Tell the students how the instructor feels they should be assessed. Put the instructor list on the blackboard. Explain that by working together, the instructor and the students can make an assessment framework that will be best for everyone.

4. To determine the criteria for assessment, have the students in groups think about what makes a good student. Have them come up with a list while doing the same. Elicit the students' views, and write both lists on the blackboard.

5. Have the students imagine they are the teacher. Write the numbers 5, 4, 3, 2, and 1 vertically on the blackboard. Ask the students to describe a perfect student, and write their ideas beside Number 5 on the blackboard. Do the same for Number 1, imagining the worst student.

6. Distribute one piece of paper to each group. Have the groups complete the criteria for the students represented by the Numbers 4, 3, and 2.

7. Collect the papers from each group. For the next class, collate the information, and make up a table of standards and criteria for the class (see Appendix B).

IV

FEEDBACK AND SCORING

1. To make the framework immediately relevant, use it with a class activity at once.

2. Decide before class to observe 3–4 students only, without their knowledge. Take notes while they are on task.

3. Periodically discuss the assessment framework, as things may have changed and an adjustment may be in order.

CAVEATS AND OPTIONS

1. The framework should help the students, not inhibit them, by telling them what they are to be praised on. Do not use it as an overt formal instrument, as it may hinder the students' performance.

2. If the instructor and the students disagree on a particular area of assessment, or if the instructor would like to include something they did not mention or exclude something they suggested, be sure to explain those reasons. The purpose of involving students in assessment is to develop an open, non-threatening approach to classroom assessment. Keep the agenda open and honest!

APPENDIX A: *What Do You Think About Tests?*

Student's name _____

Partner's name _____

With your partner, ask and answer the following questions about tests and grades. Write down what your partner says. Later, your teacher will collect your papers and share your ideas with the class. Note: There are no correct answers!

1. Last year, in what subjects did you get the highest grades? The lowest grades?

2. How do you feel about tests?

3. Do you think tests describe your true English abilities?

4. What kind of tests do you prefer (e.g., speaking/listening tests, reading/writing tests)? Why?

5. If you were an English teacher, how would you grade the students?

APPENDIX B: *Sample Framework*

Continuous Assessment: Effort

5   Consistent and thorough in all class and homework assignments. Genuinely interested and eager to do well.

4   Usually works well, fairly eager, completes most of the homework. Occasionally leads but is inconsistent.

3   Not too persistent but tries. Does average class work, but rarely does more than asked directly. Is interested but not eager.

2   Soon loses interest. Sometimes tries but does not concentrate for long. Completes homework minimally or forgets altogether. Needs prompts to engage in activities.

1   Lacks interest. Dislikes learning and speaking English. Fails to do homework; loses concentration or interrupts others.

Class Assessment

Here are some suggestions you gave me for assessment in English class.

Participation (40%)	Journal (10%; teacher judges quality)	Volunteering (20%)	Tests (20%; teacher judges quality)	Remembering books (10%)	Total (100%)
A = Always comes to class (40%)	A =	A =	A =	A =	A =
B = Usually comes to class (30%)	B =	B =	B =	B =	B =
C = Often comes to class (20%)	C =	C =	C =	C =	C =
D = Sometimes comes to class (10%)	D =	D =	D =	D =	D =
F = Never comes to class (0%)	F =	F =	F =	F =	F =

IV

Raise Your Hand and Be Counted

Juergen J. Bulach

Levels	*High beginning to low advanced*
Aims	*Demonstrate ability to understand and answer orally questions based on assigned reading*
Class Time	*60 minutes*
Preparation Time	*15 minutes*
Resources	*Copies of an article*
	Slips of paper

This enjoyable and competitive assessment activity involves reading, writing, listening, and speaking. It makes the grading of students' oral participation very easy and unbiased.

PROCEDURE

Session 1

1. Before class, choose and read an article appropriate to the class's level. Prepare and copy a list of 10–15 questions based on the information in the article.

2. In class, assign the reading of the article to the class. After the students have finished the reading, distribute the prepared handout of questions, and tell the students to write the answers on the sheet for homework.

Session 2

1. Tell the students to review the article for 5 minutes or so.

2. Give the students the following information:

    • After the instructor asks a question on the handout, the first student to raise a hand will be given the chance to answer.

    • The students cannot read their answers from their handout. The handout is to be used only as a guide.

- When they answer a question correctly, ask a question, or make a comment about the article, they will be given a slip of paper that is worth 1 point.

3. Ask the questions on the handout.

4. Award each student with a slip of paper for a correct answer or for asking a question. Have the students write their names on the slips of paper.

5. After all the questions have been asked, collect all the slips.

FEEDBACK AND SCORING

1. Assess the students' ability to answer questions by counting the points as represented by the slips of paper.

2. Emphasize participation to the students. Participation translates into points received for a correct answer, and points received translate into a better grade.

CAVEATS AND OPTIONS

1. To keep the students from guessing what the next question will be, do not ask the questions in the same order as they appear on the handout.

2. Use this assessment activity as a backdrop for a variety of reading materials, such as magazine articles, chapters from a novel, newspapers, and poetry.

IV

Course of Events

Paul Lyddon

Levels	**Beginning +**
Aims	**Demonstrate integration of information**
Class Time	**10 minutes**
Preparation Time	**30 minutes**
Resources	**Story, process, or phenomenon**

This variation on a guided writing task encourages even beginning-level students to develop their overall understanding of a story, process, or phenomenon by requiring them to examine the relationships between individual events. A novel scoring system is used to grade the activity.

PROCEDURE

1. Analyze the story, process, or phenomenon the class is about to study, and make a list of the 11 most significant events.

2. Type up the list with a blank to the left of each item.

3. Scramble the items by cutting them up and pasting them onto another piece of paper. (To reduce unconscious bias, arrange them from the shortest to the longest utterance.)

4. At the top of the paper, add a set of directions (e.g., *Put the following events in order from first to last by numbering them from 1 to 11*; see Appendix A).

5. Teach the story, process, or phenomenon.

6. Hand out the assessment activity, and have the students complete it.

FEEDBACK AND SCORING

1. Create a scoring key (see Appendix B) and a scoring method such as the following to determine how well the students have synthesized the information.

   • In the column marked *Key* in the vertical scoring aid, list the numbers of the events in the correct sequence. (Item 1, *The War of 1812 ends*, comes fifth in the sequence, so the number 5 appears at the top of this column in the vertical scoring aid in Appendix C.)

- In the column marked *S1*, list the responses of the first student (or group of students) in the order in which they appear on the exercise. (The first student put *The War of 1812 ends* seventh, so the number 7 appears at the top of this column in the vertical scoring aid in Appendix C.) Continue for subsequent students (or groups of students).

- Transfer the information from the vertical scoring aid to the horizontal scoring aid. Make sure the students' answers still correspond as they do in the vertical scoring aid. (In the horizontal scoring aid in Appendix C, the first student's number 7 still corresponds to number 5 in the *Key* row, as it does in the vertical scoring aid.) The purpose of this transfer is to reconstruct the student's time line and discover the pattern.

  My first student's pattern goes as follows:
  $2 < 3 < 4 < 6 < 7 > 1 < 8 < 10 > 9 > 5 < 11$

  The pattern of the key, of course, is
  $1 < 2 < 3 < 4 < 5 < 6 < 7 < 8 < 9 < 10 < 11$

- Count every < as 2 points of raw score, for a maximum of 20 points. (The order ascends seven times in the row marked *S1* in the horizontal scoring aid, for a raw score of 14.)

2. If desired, use the following conversion scale: 20 = A, 18 = B, 16 = C, 14 = D, below 14 = F. (The first student would receive a grade of D.)

CAVEATS AND OPTIONS

1. Because this instrument indicates which way a student's chronology flows and not the proximity of the responses to the actual positions of the events on the correct time line, the instructor may not want to use it when the exercise involves absolute, direct cause-and-effect relationships (e.g., the functioning of an internal combustion engine).

2. This exercise is well suited to a variety of applications, including language arts, science, and history. Its purpose is to promote synthesis of information, however; therefore do not give students a list of events merely to memorize (e.g., the steps of photosynthesis). If the subject is history, deemphasize dates and stress context.

3. This exercise was originally designed as an individual checkup or as part of a larger test. It can be used as a cooperative learning tool in a modified jigsaw approach, as well:

- Prepare in advance 11 index cards, each listing an event from the exercise.

- During the last 15 minutes of class, assign each student to a group and administer the exercise as a test, making sure to collect all materials and scratch paper at the end.

- During the first 15 minutes of the next day's class, assign each student to a different group, making sure that no two students who worked together the previous day work together again, and readminister the exercise.

- Once all the papers have been turned in, give immediate feedback using the following method:

  — Give 11 students each an index card. Ask them to put the cards in sequence by forming a line at the front of the room.

  — Have the whole class participate by negotiating the place of each event in the sequence.

  — Verify the order of the cards.

REFERENCES AND FURTHER READING

Good, T. L., & Brophy, J. E. (2007). *Looking in classrooms* (10th ed.). Boston, MA: Allyn & Bacon.

APPENDIX A: *Sample Assessment Handout*

Name _____

Course of Events (20 points)

DIRECTIONS: Put the following events in order from first to last by numbering them from 1 to 11.

_____ The War of 1812 ends.

_____ Mexico becomes a free country.

_____ Thomas Jefferson becomes president.

_____ The United States buys Louisiana from France.

_____ British soldiers burn Washington, DC.

_____ The United States wins the Battle of New Orleans.

_____ Cherokee Indians begin the Trail of Tears.

_____ James Monroe issues the Monroe Doctrine.

_____ American soldiers return from World War II.

_____ Lewis and Clark explore the Louisiana Territory.

_____ The American public elects its first Western president.

IV

APPENDIX B: *Scoring Aid Templates*

Vertical Scoring Aid for Course of Events

Student response										Key
S1	S2	S3	S4	S5	S6	S7	S8	S9	S10	

Horizontal Scoring Aid for Course of Events

	Key											Score
	1	2	3	4	5	6	7	8	9	10	11	20
S1												
S2												
S3												
S4												
S5												
S6												
S7												
S8												
S9												
S10												

APPENDIX C: *Scoring Aids for Sample Assessment Handout (Appendix A)*

Vertical Scoring Aid

Student response			Key
S1	S2	S3	
7	6	10	5
8	7	11	7
2	1	7	1
3	2	5	2
6	5	4	4
1	4	3	6
5	10	2	10
10	8	8	8
11	11	1	11
4	3	6	3
9	9	9	9

Horizontal Scoring Aid

	Key											Score
	1	2	3	4	5	6	7	8	9	10	11	20
S1	2	3	4	6	7	1	8	10	9	5	11	14
S2	1	2	3	5	6	4	7	8	9	10	11	18
S3	7	5	6	4	10	3	11	8	9	2	1	8

IV

Getting the Point(s): An Adaptable Evaluation System

Ron Grove

Levels	Any
Aims	Understand, control, and predict class grade
	Be evaluated appropriately and individually
	Be recognized for effort
Class Time	One or more class sessions
Preparation Time	Variable
Resources	Nothing additional

This assessment activity helps students understand, control, and predict their grade in a class or their progress through a program. The students are evaluated appropriately and individually, regardless of class or program size, and they are recognized for the effort spent, regardless of their level relative to other students. The point system provides a range of different but equivalent ways to earn points. This allows the students to choose those they find most congenial without increasing the teacher's record-keeping burden, as well as allows students in multilevel classes (from true beginning- through advanced-level students) to work at a level appropriate for them.

PROCEDURE

1. List and prioritize, or have the students list and prioritize, what they should do to succeed in a class or program.

2. Assign points to each item on the list such that students must meet absolute requirements in order to acquire sufficient points to pass. Let them know options of equal importance receive equal points, greater effort or better performance receives more points, and so on (see Appendix).

3. Explain the system to the students.

FEEDBACK AND SCORING

1. Monitor the students' accumulation of points.

2. For the final evaluation, simply add up the points accumulated.

CAVEATS AND OPTIONS

1. The amount of time needed for this assessment activity varies. If the students tailor their own system, allow one class period or more for setup plus 10–15 minutes periodically for fine-tuning. If using a prepared system, allow 10–15 minutes to explain initially plus time for later clarification as needed. Collect data for the awarding of points during or outside class.

2. The preparation time needed depends on the complexity of the class or the program. To devise a system for one Japanese university class can take about an hour, mostly spent on prioritizing factors and playing with numbers. The time required to add the number of points naturally depends on how often it is done and how many students there are.

3. The students should be able to keep track of their own points and know exactly how they are doing at any time, but remind them periodically of how many points they have.

4. Adapt the system for more complex or intensive learning contexts (e.g., full-time intensive ESL programs).

5. Periodically, award points for various activities in the form of merit badges or other tangible tokens of accomplishment. Devise a system whereby the acquisition of certain badges or a certain number of badges indicates progress through a program.

6. Award points for work in self-access centers or off-campus tasks. One possibility is to issue passports that are stamped or signed by persons with whom the students have interacted in English. Or, in a scavenger hunt approach, convert into points tangible evidence of tasks done in English.

7. Factor test scores into the evaluation by assigning points that clearly indicate the importance of those scores relative to other factors.

8. Adapt the information in the evaluation system for progress report forms. For example, the arrangement of attendance points in the Appendix resulted in much less tardiness. Use similar provisions to encourage or discourage other behavior.

REFERENCES AND FURTHER READING

Davis, R., & Armstrong, H. (1995). Using English beyond the classroom. *The Language Teacher, 19*, 52–53, 55.

Stoda, K. (1994). An aggressive "AET Money Contest": Ask me three questions, please! *The Language Teacher, 18*, 7–9.

APPENDIX: *Sample Grading System*

Below is the point system from a first-year English reading class at a Japanese university. Most students assume that they will pass if they are physically present in around half the classes, even if they do nothing else. The system was designed to discourage chronic tardiness and to convey the message that students must do something to earn points and that using a language is a better way to learn it than talking about it in another language. Points were assigned based on the following assumptions: 25 class sessions with about 10 spot-checks and about 10 quizzes, resulting in an ideal total of around 600 points. In the Japanese system, an A is considered to be above 79%; a B, 70–79%; a C, 60–69%; and a D (no credit), below 60%.

Evaluation

Grades at the end of the year will be based on the points earned by each student. The points needed for each grade follow:

A: ≥480   B: 420–479   C: 360–419   D: ≤359

Below are the ways to earn points.

Item		Points
Attendance (each class):	On time (seated and ready before the chime finishes)	10
	Late (up to 15 minutes)	5
	Very late (more than 15 minutes)	2
Working seriously in class (unannounced spot-checks):	No problem during the spot-check	2
	Working but not well	1
Surprise quizzes:	All answers correct	6
	Some answers correct, some not	3
Homework: SRA rate builders (per card, up to five/week)	Well done	1
	Poorly done	½
SRA power builders (per card, up to five/week)	Well done	2
	Poorly done	1
SRA skills development cards (per card, if needed)	Done	1
Reading reports (up to 1/week, including summer vacation)	Well done	10
	Poorly done	5
Language journals (per entry, up to five/week, including summer vacation)	Well done	1
	Poorly done	½

Thermometer

Claudia A. Becker

Levels	*Any*
Aims	*Demonstrate comfort level and involvement with classroom activities*
Class Time	*5 minutes*
Preparation Time	*None*
Resources	*Nothing additional*

T his activity represents a whole-class assessment technique that allows students to react immediately to a certain classroom activity. It can also be used to assess their reactions to a particular topic or issue discussed in class or covered in reading material. The "Thermometer" is a feedback device that indicates trends within the group of students, enables students to influence the continuum of the class, and serves as a tool for starting a dialog between the instructor and the students. For instance, a teacher who finds out via the Thermometer that most students do not feel comfortable with a certain activity or topic could explain that activity more carefully or provide more background information on the topic. Students like this activity because they value the fact that the instructor cares about what they think of a classroom activity or assignment.

PROCEDURE

1. After a classroom activity or reading assignment, draw three thermometers on the blackboard: one showing a temperature associated with a day at the beach, another reflecting the temperature on a mild rainy day, and the third reflecting the temperature on a chilly day.

2. Ask each student to reflect on the classroom activity or the reading assignment for a short while.

3. Ask the students to select the thermometer that best reflects their comfort level or degree of involvement with the classroom activity or reading assignment. Allow each student only one choice, and have the students indicate that choice by standing by whichever thermometer best matches their opinion.

FEEDBACK AND SCORING

1. The feedback on the teaching activities or reading topics goes to the teacher. Quickly count the students standing near each of the three thermometers, and jot down the count next to each thermometer.

2. Afterwards, ask the students why they felt a certain way by having them jot down next to "their" thermometer reasons for their ideas, thoughts on the assignment, and so on.

CAVEATS AND OPTIONS

1. Allow a maximum of 3 minutes on the first occasion to explain the concept of the Thermometer. Usually, the students quickly learn how to respond to this classroom assessment technique.

2. Leave the room while the students are responding to this classroom assessment technique so that their responses will be anonymous and more reliable.

IV

Multiple-Assessment Action Logging

Tim Murphey

Levels	*Any*
Aims	*Demonstrate understanding of classroom activities*
	Be involved in evaluating classroom activities
Class Time	*0–5 minutes*
Preparation Time	*30 minutes*
Resources	*Nothing additional*

In an action log, students evaluate classroom activities after each class by writing in a notebook that teachers read weekly. Teachers can then assess students' understanding of—as well as success with—the activities and make appropriate adjustments. The logs are not diaries, in that the students write only about things related to class; thus they are of high interest for teachers and encourage continual teacher development (Murphey, 1992, 1993).

PROCEDURE

1. Prepare a log handout according to class level (see Appendix A or B).

2. In class, ask the students to write in their notebooks outside class either freely about what happened in class or explicitly by choosing interesting topics in order to hear their reactions. For the latter option, list the activities or points on the same part of the blackboard each day to remind the students to comment on them.

3. Set a time for collecting the logs or having students drop the logs off (e.g., have different classes drop their logs off on different days of the week).

FEEDBACK AND SCORING

1. Read the logs, writing comments where appropriate.

2. Keep instructor responses short except when individuals show a special need, but make responses longer at the beginning of the term to let the

students know their help is appreciated. After using the logs for more than 150 students a week for 2 years, it usually takes only a minute per log to read and comment. Ninety percent of the comments are short phrases like *Thanks for the feedback, you're doing great!* with perhaps a smiling face and the instructor's initials.

3. Tag certain pages, and make photocopies of them to keep for use in future classes. Return the logs in the next class, or have the students pick them up at a designated time.

CAVEATS AND OPTIONS

1. Give beginning-level students certain formulas for reacting to classroom activities (e.g., *Today we did .... I liked .... I didn't like .... I want to do ... more*).

2. Have a beginning-level class give grades or number ratings to classroom activities (see Appendix B).

3. Give the students the last 5 minutes of class to write in the logs, and collect them in class.

REFERENCES AND FURTHER READING

Murphey, T. (1992). Letting the students in on teacher reflection processes. *The Teacher Trainer, 6*, 20–21.

Murphey, T. (1993, January). Why don't teachers learn what learners learn? Taking the guesswork out with action logging. *English Teaching Forum*, 6–10.

IV

APPENDIX A: *Action Log Requirements for Higher-Level Students*

As soon as possible after every class (so you remember well what happens), write a short description of the class in a notebook. (1) Say briefly what we DID and (2) COMMENT about what you learned and what you liked. List the different activities and segments. You may want to take short notes in class to remind yourself. Comment on those activities you especially liked and could learn from, as well as those you didn't like and think could be improved. I need your feedback so that I can teach you better. I read your Action Logs. I like your suggestions and will try to use them if possible.

If there is anything else (e.g., outside problems) that you think I should know (and that influences your learning), please write that in your log as well.

An example of an entry:

Written April 8, 21:00

1. DID: Today we listened to a story; did shadowing, retelling, and speed reading; and sang a song.

2. COMMENT: Shadowing seems especially interesting. I'm going to try it in my other classes. I didn't understand some of the points in speed reading: What is chunking? Sometimes you spoke too fast. Please speak slower. My partners were Yuki and Hiroko and I enjoyed getting to know them. We got a lot of homework, but it looks like fun. I'm looking forward to the rest of the classes. Oh, and I like singing.

Note: Always put the date of the class and the time you write, and always use people's names when you refer to partners.

APPENDIX B: *Action Log Requirements for Lower-Level Students*

After every class, write in a notebook a grade for each activity that we did in class. I will list the activities in the upper left-hand corner of the blackboard in each class. You are also free to comment on the class if you want to. I read your Action Logs. I like your suggestions and will try to use them if possible.

An example of an entry:

Written April 9, 20:00

DID	Grade on interest	Grade on usefulness
story	A	A
shadowing	B	A
retelling	B	A
speed reading	B	C?
song	A+	B

Note: Always put the date of the class and the time you write.

Wow! Marvelous Task

Tim Murphey

Levels	Any
Aims	*Try out suggested behaviors in class*
	Tell teachers which tasks work
	Identify barriers to following teachers' suggestions
	Change limiting beliefs
Class Time	*5–10 minutes*
Preparation Time	*Variable*
Resources	*Students' environment*

In this activity the teacher learns from students what tasks work and what the barriers are to following the teacher's suggestions. The task test is used to assess classroom activities and plausible or possible student behavior with a view toward constructing a richer acquisition environment. The activity reflects a *trying-is-succeeding* philosophy: if the students do the task and report what happens, they earn a high grade (and the teacher finds out whether the tasks work as they are intended to).

PROCEDURE

1. List learning concepts from class and behaviors the students should try out.

2. Make a list of tasks around these concepts (see Appendix). Copy the list.

3. In class, pass out the task list and explain the tasks if necessary. Give the students a deadline (e.g., 1–2 weeks) for completing the tasks and writing a short paragraph about each.

FEEDBACK AND SCORING

1. Tell the students that their grade depends only on whether they do the tasks and write about them, not on whether they are particularly successful at the tasks.

2. If the students do the task and report what happens, give them a high grade.

CAVEATS AND OPTIONS

1. After doing such tests several times, adapt the tasks to make them more per-formative. For example, when some students were approaching foreigners in groups of three to ask the time, in later assessments, the students were told to do this individually.

2. Tell the students about past students' successes at doing the tests, previous students' courage to try new things, and the rewards of trying new things.

3. In an ESL environment, have the students perform other real-world tasks in English (e.g., ask for directions and information from local people, call numbers for recorded information).

REFERENCES AND FURTHER READING

Murphey, T. (2006). *Language hungry! An introduction to language learning fun and self-esteem.* Innsbruck, Austria: Helbling Languages.

APPENDIX: *Sample Task List*

The following task test was given in a large-city EFL setting. Tasks correspond to individual learning strategies (1–9), interactive learning outside class (10–12), and collaborative learning (13–17) that the teacher gave lessons on or suggested.

DIRECTIONS: "Wow! Marvelous!" Test due _____. Do the following tasks within the next 2 weeks and write a short report (a short paragraph) about each one. Write in dark ink. You are not allowed to show your answers to anyone, but you can talk to them and tell them your answers (in English only).

Scoring: All tasks done and commented upon = A+; one grade lower for each task not done or not completely done; one grade lower for every day late.

1. Talk to yourself in English every morning when you wake up. Tell yourself what you are going to do that day (e.g., *First I'm going to eat, then brush my teeth, then . . . go to school, eat lunch with friends*).

2. Listen to bilingual radio when you get up in the morning (at least five mornings for the next 2 weeks), and write down at least three expressions you hear that you might use (e.g., *Wow, what a marvelous day!*).

3. Notice and write down at least five words or phrases in English from advertising that you see around you every day on your way to and from school. The words

IV

and phrases should be interesting things that you could use (e.g., "Just do it!" in the Nike advertisement with Michael Jordan).

4. Sing a song in English to yourself every morning while you are coming to school for at least a week. Did you memorize it easily? Write about it.

5. Wear your watch upside down for 2 weeks. Ask two different classmates each day for 10 days (20 different people) *What time is it?* (a) If they answer *Now is the best time to be happy!* say, *Yes, and smiling makes you beautiful.* (b) If they tell you the time, say, *Thanks, and what a great time it is to be happy, too!*

6. Silently shadow or echo another professor in one of your classes, then reformulate what the professor said to someone right after class (as soon as possible). Could you remember more? What was the experience like?

7. Shadow or echo an easy radio or TV program for 15 minutes (e.g., *Sesame Street,* an English lesson). Was it easy or difficult?

8. SPURR (Specifically Personal Use Repeat and Recycle) three words or expressions from your language lab class that you want to learn. Write the SPURR items here and say how you practiced them meaningfully.

9. (Note: do this alone, not with friends.) Ask at least three different foreigners, *Excuse me, what time is it please?* What did they say? How did you feel?

10. Greet (say *hello* or *good morning*) to your Japanese English teachers in English at least three times in the next 2 weeks (and longer if you like).

11. Teach a friend or member of your family the 10 gesture-idioms. Write about it. Retell two of Murphey's stories to friends or family, using as much English as possible so that they understand.

12. Think of a mistake you made. Tell three different classmates about it in English. Make it funny when you tell it. How did it feel?

13. Find a special partner in your regular oral communication class, and agree to speak mostly English with that partner for 2 weeks, in and out of class. Support each other. Remind each other. Write your partner's name and describe what happened, when you started, and when you finished. When you speak, it's OK to use some Japanese when you don't know the English. Maybe your partner can translate it for you. Shadow your partner!

14. Find another friend (different from the one in No. 13) who is willing to talk to you in English, and telephone each other four nights straight (in a row). Tell each other what you did that day. Prepare what you want to say during the day. How did it work? Was it useful? Would you like to continue?

15. In English, write one note of encouragement and friendship a day for 5 days to your friends in your English classes. Ask a question or two also. Give the notes to them outside class (e.g., *Yuki, I really like the way you speak English. Your pronunciation is very clear. Thank you for talking to me so much in English. I can learn a lot from you. Your Friend, Yuko. P.S.: Can I borrow your notes for the day I was absent? Don't you think [name] is handsome?*). When you get a note, respond to the question, and ask another if you'd like.

16. Ask your friends if they know the word *tickle* in English. If not, show them what it means by tickling them. (Blame it on your homework if they get angry.)

17. Give an unexpected compliment a day to someone in English (e.g., *I like your hairstyle!*).

18. Loan the person you sit with in class an audio recording of one of your favorite songs in English with a lyric sheet and a note telling why you chose that song. Listen to the song (shadow it), and read the lyrics and note. Write your partner about the song, and return the recording in the next class.

19. Find at least two friends in this class, and talk about your answers to each of these tasks only in English. Write the friends' names and what you learned.

Daily In-English Reminder: Talk to myself when I wake up, listen to bilingual radio, notice English advertising going to school, sing an English song in my head, give a compliment to someone, speak English mostly to my 2-week partner, give a note to a friend, ask a few classmates *What time is it?,* say *hello* to my English teachers, shadow my teachers, ask friends if they know the word *tickle* (tickle them!), find an at-home telephone partner, write and answer notes.

Occasional: SPURR words, loan a favorite song to a classmate, teach 10 gesture-idioms, ask three foreigners the time, tell three friends a mistake I made, shadow TV English and songs, retell stories, talk about tasks with two friends.

IV

Writing a Course Review

Nathan Ducker

Levels	**Intermediate +**
Aims	**Doubles as writing assessment and autonomous reflective review of the course**
Class Time	**1 class**
Preparation Time	**60 minutes**
Resources	**Nothing additional**

PROCEDURE

1. In the evaluation phase of the course, set aside a lesson for a writing evaluation. Preferably before the class, distribute the questionnaire and have students fill it in (see Appendix).

2. Depending on the length of the questionnaire and class time available, have students either write a paragraph for each of the questionnaire sections, or for the ones they are most interested in.

3. For each section of the questionnaire, students must select 2–3 points to write about. (Complementary points will make a paragraph much easier to write.)

4. Instruct students to write a topic sentence based on their evaluations from section 1 of the questionnaire, such as *I have satisfactorily developed teamwork skills in this course.*

5. Instruct students to use several different questionnaire responses in section 1 to create the supporting sentences of paragraph 1.

6. Have students use their own evidence such as graded work, assignments, and memories to add details to the evidence of paragraph 1.

7. Monitor students as they repeat Steps 3, 4, 5, 6 for further sections of the questionnaire.

8. For more advanced classes, have students add an introduction and a conclusion.

FEEDBACK AND SCORING

This entire activity is a form of feedback for both students and teacher.

CAVEATS AND OPTIONS

1. During the course, the teacher and students will have encountered various learning phenomena. They may come either in the form of activities or various skills. The teacher should prepare sets of questionnaires that elicit students' opinions on each aspect of the course.

2. Students should be familiar with writing a structured paragraph or essay.

3. If students are handwriting, a pre-prepared template including boxes for each paragraph will make it much easier for students to edit and plan the essay.

REFERENCES AND FURTHER READING

For survey making, see www.surveymonkey.com

Barfield, A., & Nix, M. (Eds.). (2003). *Learner and teacher autonomy in Japan 1: Autonomy you ask!* Tokyo, Japan: Japan Association for Language Teaching Learner Development Special Interest Group.

Skier, E. M., & Kohyama, M. (Eds.). (2006). *Learner and teacher autonomy in Japan 2: More autonomy you ask!* Tokyo, Japan: Japan Association for Language Teaching Learner Development Special Interest Group.

IV

APPENDIX: *Example Survey Used in a Recent Projects Course*

Please answer the following questionnaire concerning your feelings about this course.

Part 1: Topic

	I strongly disagree	I disagree	I partially disagree, I partially agree	I agree	I strongly agree
I would like to study more about the topic we chose					
I learned a lot about the topic we chose					
If I could go back in time, I would choose the same topic again					
If I could go back in time, I would like to have a wider choice of topics					
I think this topic could be useful for me in the future					

Part 2: Language Skills Development

	I strongly disagree	I disagree	I partially disagree, I partially agree	I agree	I strongly agree
I practiced and therefore improved my reading / writing / listening / speaking skills					
The teacher should have instructed us more on reading / writing / listening / speaking skills					
I learned lots of new vocabulary					
I learned how to use existing vocabulary knowledge better					
I learned lots of new grammar					

IV

Part 3: Critical Thinking and Study Skills

	I strongly disagree	I disagree	I partially disagree, I partially agree	I agree	I strongly agree
I learned to plan ahead for a longer assignment, such as a project or thesis					
I learned to plan a simple assignment, such as an essay or survey					
I learned to think ahead and predict problems when facing a challenge					
I learned to think in different ways					
I felt I could make decisions more easily					

Alternative Ways of Assessing Written Skills

- **Reading**

- **Reading and Vocabulary**

- **Vocabulary**

- **Writing and Grammar**

V

Part V: Alternative Ways of Assessing Written Skills

EDITOR'S NOTE

Traditionally, language tests were designed to test the four language skills as separately as possible. For instance, an overall English language proficiency test battery might be made up of five separate skills tests: four multiple-choice tests (grammar, listening comprehension, reading comprehension, and vocabulary) and a composition test.

A quick look at the skills from the point of view of channels and modes will indicate that it is not always possible, or indeed desirable, to separate the skills when doing assessment, especially classroom assessment. Each skill can be described in terms of its channel and its mode. *Channel* refers to the means used to communicate. The two possible channels are the written and the oral. In other words, the message is conveyed by either light waves or sound waves. The two skills involved in the written channel are reading and writing. The two skills involved in the oral channel are listening and speaking.

Mode refers to the direction of communication involved. The two possible modes are the *receptive* and the *productive*. In other words, the message is either received (receptive) or sent (productive). The two skills involved in the receptive mode are reading and listening. The two skills involved in the productive mode are writing and speaking. The following diagram (adapted from Brown, 1996, p. 28) shows how the modes and channels are related. Notice that reading is the receptive written skill, writing is the productive written skill, listening is the receptive oral skill, and speaking is the productive oral skill.

		Channels	
		Written	Oral
Modes	Receptive	Reading	Listening
	Productive	Writing	Speaking

Modes and channels help us separate the characteristics of the four skills in our minds, and such a separation is sometimes useful. Indeed, I have used the written channel to describe the assessment activities found in this part of the book, and the oral channel to describe the activities in Part VI.

....

The moment someone starts thinking about real language production or about language assessment, however, it becomes almost impossible to keep the skills separate. Consider what testers do when they assess reading comprehension ability. Typically, they ask the students to read a passage and answer multiple-choice questions. The students read the passage. They read the questions. Then they select the correct answer by circling it or filling in a little dot on an answer sheet. All of that at least somewhat imitates what people experience in real-life reading, and, at least, no other language skills are involved.

What about listening comprehension, however? Traditionally, testers have presented aural passages to the students via an audio recording and asked the students to read the responses and select the correct answer. In other words, the task mixes listening as well as reading skills and does so in a way that is not very similar to any real-life task. How often does anyone listen to something in real life, then select a written answer? I suppose it happens sometimes, but not often.

Similar problems arise in trying to test writing and speaking skills. How can an instructor give students a writing prompt without requiring them to read or listen? The answer is that it's not possible. And how does an instructor get students to speak without giving them some instructions that require them to listen or read in some way (as in an interview)? Again, the answer is that it's not feasible. And how authentic are writing and speaking tests devised with written prompts or with interview procedures, anyway?

Of course, using L1 prompts or pictures can circumvent some of these problems, but those strategies aren't exactly like real-life language activities either, all of which suggests that the quest to test pure language skills may have always been a bit quixotic, if not completely impossible.

Given recent trends in language teaching toward more authentic communication in the learning process, it is no surprise that the majority of contributions in this part and in Part VI—indeed, throughout the book—propose assessment activities that combine two or more skills. Apparently, teachers have recognized the futility of separating the skill areas in the teaching processes as well as in the related classroom assessment processes.

This part of the book, which focuses on written-channel skills, includes those contributions that deal primarily with reading, writing, vocabulary, and grammar.

The five contributions that focus primarily on reading do so with different purposes: to encourage active reading of longer and more substantial resource material ("Taking the Speed Out of Reading Tests"); to keep track of students' progress in reading while motivating them ("Keeping Track With Free Readin' "); to assess reading comprehension and critical thinking abilities ("The Reading Beat: Investigative Questioning and Reading Comprehension"); to help students read material above their level intensively for an extended period of time ("A

Window on the Reading Process"); and to practice reading by figuring out a text's organization ("Sort It Out").

The four contributions that primarily combine reading and vocabulary do so with the following purposes: to assess students' comprehension of written descriptions ("Have You Seen My Brother?"); to assess students' newspaper-reading skills ("Extra! Extra! Read All About It!"); to assess students' vocabulary development and reading comprehension ("On the Spot!"); and to read with a specific purpose while inferring words from definitions and context ("Definition-Resource Cloze").

The six contributions that deal primarily with vocabulary are all included here, even though some of them use the oral channel, because vocabulary is their focus. They are designed for the following purposes: to help learners be aware of their knowledge of vocabulary by examining everyday objects in stores ("Going to the Supermarket"); to help students demonstrate process organization and activate vocabulary related to food and cooking ("Party or Test: Who Cares? Let's Eat!"); to assess students' knowledge of numbers ("The Price Is Right"); to assess students' knowledge of color vocabulary ("Color-Coordinated Quiz"); to build vocabulary in real-time, on-line computer discussions ("Vocabulary Information-Gap Electronic Discussion"); and to reinforce the relationship between a word and its various meanings ("A Vocabulary Quiz Given by Students to Themselves").

The five contributions that concentrate on writing and grammar have these purposes: to help students understand the qualities of an acceptable library research paper and help teachers evaluate such papers ("Check It Out: A Library Research Checklist"); to assess students' production of the three spoken versions of the past tense ending -ed ("Tense Excitement Throwing a Die"); to help students understand and practice the comparative form ("Who Is He?"); to provide direct, continuous feedback on source-based writing ("Assessing Writing From Sources"); and to provide feedback that increases naturalness through reformulation ("Using Reformulation to Assess Paragraph Rhetorical Structure").

V

REFERENCES AND FURTHER READING

Alderson, C. (2000). *Assessing reading.* Cambridge, England: Cambridge University Press.

Brown, J. D. (1996). *Testing in language programs.* Upper Saddle River, NJ: Prentice Hall Regents.

Brown, J. D. (2005). *Testing in language programs: A comprehensive guide to English language assessment* (Rev. ed.). New York, NY: McGraw-Hill.

Purpura, J. E. (2004). *Assessing grammar.* Cambridge, England: Cambridge University Press.

Read, J. (2000). *Assessing vocabulary.* Cambridge, England: Cambridge University Press.

Weigle, S. C. (2002). *Assessing writing.* Cambridge, England: Cambridge University Press.

Taking the Speed Out of Reading Tests

Rex Berridge and Jenny Muzamhindo

Levels	*Intermediate +*
Aims	*Gain credit for active reading tasks*
	Use longer, more substantial resource material
Class Time	*Variable*
Preparation Time	*Minimal*
Resources	*Texts and reading task*

This assessment activity creates a situation in which students receive credit in a course for performing active reading tasks in which they read and do something with the reading. Such activities encourage students to take on lengthier and more substantial reading materials than they may have tackled previously.

PROCEDURE

1. Before class,

   - choose resource texts that are stimulating and challenging to students and that allow for active reading tasks.

   - prepare an active reading activity for the assessment (see Appendix). Skills to assess might include the standard range of analysis or application skills that require students to construct from the text or to reconstruct modified text. Tasks might include completing or constructing texts or diagrams, matching, generating questions or answers, creating or filling in tables, and marking the text in specified ways. Avoid tasks such as summarizing, for which the students can prepare a written draft.

2. A reasonable amount of time in advance, for example the evening before the assessment,

   - distribute the text to the students so that they can read through it for homework and remove any obstacles caused by time constraints.

- make it clear that the students will be required to do something with the text but do not indicate what that will be.

- tell the students to bring the text to the assessment activity.

3. On the assessment day, give the students the active reading task. Have spare copies of the text available. Do not allow time for the process of getting to know the text, but do allow time to use the material.

FEEDBACK AND SCORING

Score tasks like those in the Appendix by counting the number of correct responses.

CAVEATS AND OPTIONS

Colleagues may oppose the idea of allowing the students to see the text in advance, particularly in more formal examinations in which they feel that it amounts to cheating or giving an unfair advantage. Make it clear that the assessment is not being compromised or revealed in advance, and take great care to ensure that this is so.

REFERENCES AND FURTHER READING

Hughes, A. (1989). *Testing for language teachers*. Cambridge, England: Cambridge University Press.

Lunzer, E., & Gardner, K. (1984). *Learning from the written word*. Edinburgh, Scotland: Oliver & Boyd.

Nunan, D. (1989). *Designing tasks for the communicative classroom*. Cambridge, England: Cambridge University Press.

APPENDIX: *Sample Active Reading Tasks*

Trainee teachers were asked to read a magazine article on land degradation. To demonstrate their ability to use text and to plan for using texts in the classroom, they were then asked to carry out tasks such as the following:

1. Complete the table showing the causes of deforestation.

	Wildlife	Commercial felling	Population expansion	Agriculture
Causes				
Solutions				

2. One group of students: Underline the main points in the passage. Use these to prepare a set of 10 questions to ask other students as an assessment of their understanding of this passage.

3. Describe the process of soil erosion by filling in the flowchart.

4. Draw pictures to illustrate six factors that contribute to land degradation.

Keeping Track With Free Readin'

Nicholas O. Jungheim

Levels	Any
Aims	Receive formative evaluation of reading comprehension
	Become motivated to read
Class Time	20–25 minutes
Preparation Time	15–30 minutes
Resources	Short magazine or newspaper articles

For EFL students who are accustomed to traditional grammar and translation instruction, it can be a major task to motivate large classes to take charge of their own reading. Plotting their improvement during a short school term may also be difficult. This assessment activity gives students a chance to read and respond to a text of their choice and also gives the teacher a formative evaluation tool with which to regularly spot-check their progress.

PROCEDURE

1. Before class, choose 6–7 short magazine or newspaper articles (including pictures, if possible) appropriate to the students' level. Include articles on a variety of topics, such as sports, politics, economics, human interest, and entertainment. Arrange the articles on a single sheet of paper.

2. In class, explain the purpose of the task. For example, say *The purpose of this task is to give you a chance to read interesting articles in class and to help me check how well you understand what you read.*

3. Give each student a copy of the sheet of paper containing the articles.

4. Instruct them to scan the headlines and pictures, choose one article, and read it as quickly as possible, avoiding the use of dictionaries if they can, then write down what they feel about the article and indicate whether they learned anything new.

5. Allow the students a short amount of time to read and respond. About 20–25 minutes works well for articles up to 250 words. Make sure the students devote most of the time to responding to the article.

FEEDBACK AND SCORING

1. Collect the students' responses and rate them. Do not be tempted to correct writing errors. Use a simple three-level rating scale, such as the following, or a similar scale:

    ✔– Brief response with no direct reference to the contents of the article

    ✔ Brief response but some direct reference to the contents of the article

    ✔+ Lengthy response including direct reference to the article, feelings about the topic, and the relationship of new knowledge to previous knowledge

2. Read some of the responses aloud during the next class. Edit the writing before reading so that the class hears an error-free form of the original. Be sure to read 1–2 of the shorter responses to encourage the class to do a good job.

CAVEATS AND OPTIONS

1. Repeat this activity at regular intervals throughout the term. Adjust the difficulty of the reading according to the ratings.

2. Avoid stressing the evaluation side of the activity to the students. This activity is supposed to be a low-pressure, motivating experience.

3. Either keep the written responses, or have the students save them in folders. Use them in a portfolio assessment scheme.

4. If desired, use numbered ratings that can be averaged or totaled, but doing so is not recommended because it defeats the basic aim of the task as a formative evaluation.

5. Alternate this activity with written responses to articles that the students choose from newspapers and magazines found in the library. Provide feedback and scoring in the same way as for the in-class activity

6. Report to the class how many students read each article as a survey of their interests and to encourage the students to read texts on a variety of topics.

The Reading Beat: Investigative Questioning and Reading Comprehension

John M. Norris

Levels	*Advanced*
Aims	*Develop effective questioning strategies*
	Demonstrate comprehension of a text and critical thinking ability
Class Time	*50 minutes*
Preparation Time	*30–60 minutes*
Resources	*Narrative reading passage*

This assessment activity is a way to simultaneously enhance students' involvement with a text and provide a rough estimate of their comprehension of that text. If advanced-level ESL reading students respond enthusiastically to investigative reporting read during class, they may enjoy and benefit from trying their hands at the process themselves. By suspending the classroom reality, the activity allows students to picture themselves as investigative reporters following up a lead. The interview prompts written by the students give the instructor an idea of their ability to ask in-depth questions and to approach a text with a critical eye. The students have an opportunity to ask more questions than they would in a full-class discussion, and they can ask questions that they might not otherwise have asked (e.g., due to inhibitions). Assuming the roles of the characters in the story causes them to analyze the text from a different perspective and show the instructor how well they understand the relationships between particular characters and the overall text. The students enjoy this activity, and its repetition over the course of a semester can leave the instructor with strong impressions of their capacity to successfully finish a reading assignment.

PROCEDURE

1. Identify a reading of appropriate length for the students. The most effective reading for this activity will include a narrative story line. Assign the reading for homework.

2. Write a brief article assignment from the editor of a magazine or newspaper, explaining that the students will have to create an interview schedule that probes for the truth behind the reading.

3. Have students bring the completed reading assignment to class. Explain to them that they are now investigative reporters who must dig up the truth by interviewing a particular character from the story.

4. Give students the editor's article assignment. Have them choose a character that they would like to interview. Encourage students to develop questions that probe a character's motivation, an interpretation of the character's actions, and a rationale for actions and events in the story. Stress that the questions should not be of the *yes–no* variety. If desired, provide model questions (e.g., *What did you mean by . . . ?* or *What did you hope to accomplish in . . . ?*).

5. Tell students that there is a deadline for their story. Give them 15 minutes to come up with 10–12 questions before the interview.

6. After 15 minutes, assign partners to the students. Have one partner assume the role of the character that the other partner wants to interview. Tell the students to take notes on the answers to their questions during real-time conversation, just as an actual reporter would have to do.

7. Give each student 15 minutes to conduct the interview. After the first interview, have students switch roles, and give the second student 15 minutes to conduct an interview.

8. Collect the interview schedules and notes.

FEEDBACK AND SCORING

Follow up the activity with a writing session:

1. Look over the notes from the interviews, and return them to the students as approved stories that will run in the next edition.

2. Have students write up their interviews in a newspaper or magazine format (with a byline and boldfaced interviewee and interviewer dialog).

3. Publish the stories in a collection, and give a copy to each student.

CAVEATS AND OPTIONS

At first, students may rely heavily on questions such as, *What did you mean when you said . . . ?,* which does not provide much information on their critical relationship with the text. Before the next session, discuss methods of question formation that (a) give a context to the question being asked and (b) attempt to relate events in the text to other text-internal or text-external events (e.g., *Given this situation, how is it that you said X, but did Y?*). Such questions are much more revealing of the students' comprehension and questioning ability.

A Window on the Reading Process

Patrick A. Rosenkjar

Levels	*Any*
Aims	*Read intensively and for global meaning*
	Comprehend difficult reading passages
	Demonstrate understanding without traditional comprehension questions
Class Time	*20+ minutes per session*
Preparation Time	*Variable*
Resources	*Complete text of several pages*

This activity helps students read intensively for an extended period of time. It is especially useful in situations that require students to understand language that is above their level. The second purpose is to assess which students can cope with the reading demands of the activity and which students need additional work on reading skills. This method assists students enrolled in adjunct courses in any content discipline and encourages them to do the large volume of complex reading that is assigned.

PROCEDURE

1. Select a reading passage consisting of at least several dozen paragraphs. The passage should be slightly above the level that the students can comfortably handle.

2. Number each paragraph of the reading.

3. Select one-third to one-half of the paragraphs for paraphrasing. Rewrite the selected paragraphs, being careful to retain the propositional content and focus of the original. Be sure that the rewritten paragraphs are syntactically and lexically different from the originals, however.

4. Type up the rewritten paragraphs in random order. Place a blank for an answer before each paragraph.

V

5. Give each student a copy of the original reading passage (with paragraphs numbered) and a copy of the paraphrased paragraphs.

6. Have the students read the original passage and the rewritten paragraphs, determine which original paragraphs match the rewritten paragraphs in meaning, and write the original paragraph number in the blank space in front of the rewritten paragraph.

7. Assign the unfinished portion of the matching as homework.

FEEDBACK AND SCORING

1. Give the students feedback on their answers while they work (e.g., O = right; X = wrong).

2. Note how many correct matches the students make in the time allowed in order to identify students who are having problems with reading (as well as those who are reading fluently).

CAVEATS AND OPTIONS

1. Be sure that the rewritten paragraphs cannot be matched with the originals simply by scanning for lexical similarities. Part of the purpose is to induce the students to process text at a deeper level of meaning.

2. This activity is limited only by the amount of time available for preparation and by the instructor's skill at paraphrasing. The time the students spend on the activity can vary, too, but allow a minimum of 20 minutes per session so that they can experience sustained intensive reading.

3. Precede the activity by a schema-setting introduction, or use the activity itself as the introduction to further activities.

REFERENCES AND FURTHER READING

Craik, F. I. M., & Lockhart, R. S. (1972). Levels of processing: A framework for memory record. *Journal of Verbal Learning and Verbal Behavior, 11*, 67–84.

Widdowson, H. G. (1992). *Practical stylistics* (pp. 108–144). Oxford, England: Oxford University Press.

Sort It Out

Zully G. Tondolo

Levels	*Intermediate*
Aims	*Practice intensive reading*
	Learn how texts are organized
Class Time	*30 minutes*
Preparation Time	*60 minutes*
Resources	*Nothing additional*

Reading is fundamental in the process of language learning because it fosters cultural growth, gets students in contact with English-speaking cultures, encourages vocabulary building in meaningful contexts, and promotes thinking in order to draw conclusions.

PROCEDURE

1. Choose 2–3 short passages from the course text or any other source. Mix up the sentences in each text. With these, develop a passages handout and answer key (see Appendices A and B). Make a copy of the handout for each student.

2. Give students the passages handout and explain the directions. Allow them 10 minutes to read the texts.

3. When time is up, ask students *yes-no* or short-answer questions about each of the texts. Have them number and write their answers below the sentences for each text.

FEEDBACK AND SCORING

1. Use the answer key to score the handouts.

2. If desired, give 6 points for sorting each text out and 2 points for each of the short-answer responses.

CAVEATS AND OPTIONS

1. Instead of mixing up the sentences in the texts, put 3–4 nonsense sentences into a text and ask students to find them.

2. Use only one text. Create different versions by varying the details within it, and ask students to spot the mistakes.

3. Mix the sentences from all the texts together, and have students separate them into passages before ordering the sentences within each passage.

4. To make the activity easier, type out each sentence on a different line, stick the sentences onto a card, and cut the card into sentence strips. Then have students move the sentences around as they sort them out.

REFERENCES AND FURTHER READING

Phillips, S. (1994). *Young learners.* Oxford, England: Oxford University Press.

APPENDIX A: *Sample Passages Handout*

DIRECTIONS: Number the sentences in logical order from 1–6.

A.   Devi and the Tree

____   Sometimes she also liked to climb the trees and sit there in her secret place.

____   One of the trees was Devi's special reading tree.

____   Five hundred years ago, a young girl called Devi lived in a town in the mountains in India.

____   Her family's house had a big garden.

____   In later life, Devi liked to sit under the beautiful trees in the garden and read a book.

____   Sometimes Devi and her friends had picnics or played games together there.

B.   The Thieves

____   "Good idea!" said Taffy. "We are going to be rich."

____   "Let's go to the house tomorrow night. Let's steal the diamonds!"

____   "There are some diamonds in one of the rooms of the big house on the hill," Jack said.

____   Jack was a thief, too.

____   One day Jack saw some pictures in the newspaper.

____   Taffy was a thief.

APPENDIX B: *Sample Answer Key*

A.   Devi and the Tree

1.   Five hundred years ago, a young girl called Devi lived in a town in the mountains in India.

2.   Her family's house had a big garden.

3.   Sometimes Devi and her friends had picnics or played games together there.

4.   Sometimes she also liked to climb the trees and sit there in her secret place.

5.   In later life, Devi liked to sit under the beautiful trees in the garden and read a book.

6.   One of the trees was Devi's special reading tree.

B.   The Thieves

1.   Taffy was a thief.

2.   Jack was a thief, too.

3.   One day Jack saw some pictures in the newspaper.

4.   "There are some diamonds in one of the rooms of the big house on the hill," Jack said.

5.   "Let's go to the house tomorrow night. Let's steal the diamonds!"

6.   "Good idea!" said Taffy. "We are going to be rich."

Questions

1.   Where did Devi live?

2.   Where did she read the book?

3.   Who were Taffy and Jack?

4.   What did they find?

5.   Where is the big house?

Scoring: 6 points for putting the text into the correct sequential order and 2 points for each correct short answer.

Have You Seen My Brother?

Beatriz de Aguerrevere

Levels	*Any*
Aims	*Demonstrate comprehension of written descriptions*
Class Time	*10–15 minutes*
Preparation Time	*5–10 minutes*
Resources	*Sets of eight color pencils*
	Audio recording device (optional)

This activity assesses students' comprehension of written descriptions of people. In a situation similar to real life, students draw and color the person described.

PROCEDURE

1. Seat students in a row, allowing ample space between individual students.

2. Give each student a set of eight color pencils: black, white, blue, red, green, orange, brown, and yellow.

3. Give oral instructions for the activity (see Appendix), and answer the students' questions about the procedure.

4. Give each student a handout containing the written instructions and dialog (see Appendix). Allow students 3–5 minutes to read the instructions, and answer any remaining questions.

5. Give students 15 minutes to finish the task. Monitor them as they work.

6. Collect students' work when the time is up.

V

FEEDBACK AND SCORING

1. Give 1 point for each correct item. In the example in the Appendix, scoring would be as follows:

    Genre = 1 point

    Descriptive adjectives: 1 point for *short* and 1 point for *heavy* = 2 points

    Hair: 1 point for color, 1 point for length = 2 points

    Clothing: 1 point for each correct item of clothing = 4 points

    Color: 1 point for correct color of each item of clothing = 4 points

    Maximum possible = 13 points

2. Transform the scores into your grading system (e.g., a percentage).

CAVEATS AND OPTIONS

1. Be sure the students have already been introduced to and have thoroughly practiced the vocabulary and expressions needed for describing people (e.g., simple, short descriptive adjectives; body parts; clothing and colors; the present tense of *to be* and *to have* and the present continuous of *to wear* in their affirmative, negative, and interrogative forms), both in the oral and written forms and in the receptive and productive modes.

2. Prepare several similar dialogs, changing the person's gender, characteristics, and clothes.

3. Ask the students to bring their own color pencils (and have a few sets as backup) as a way of minimizing cost and effort.

4. To use the activity to assess oral comprehension, give the students a handout with the instructions and a space for drawing. Either read the dialog aloud, or audio record it (with two native speakers if you prefer) and play it back to the students. In either case, make the dialog realistic, or play it back three times. Use the same scoring procedure.

APPENDIX: *Sample Handout*

Name _____ Grade_____ Date _____

DIRECTIONS: Read the following dialog. Draw a picture of the person described in the dialog, and color your drawing according to the information given.

Setting: A dentist's office. A is a young girl, around 18 years old. B is the dentist's secretary.

A: Good afternoon.

B: Good afternoon. May I help you?

A: Sure. Did Arthur leave already?

B: Arthur?

A: My brother. He had an appointment at three. I came to pick him up.

B: Is he tall and thin?

A: No, he's short and heavy.

B: Does he have long brown hair?

A: Yes, he does.

B: Is he wearing blue jeans and a yellow T-shirt?

A: Yeah, he's also wearing a green jacket and black shoes.

B: Oh, I think he just went to the restroom.

A: What a relief! Can I wait for him here?

B: Certainly.

V

Extra! Extra! Read All About It!

Herman Bartelen

Levels	*Intermediate +*
Aims	*Understand the layout of a newspaper*
	Develop skimming, scanning, and vocabulary skills
	See the value of newspapers for developing English and getting information and opinions
Class Time	*90 minutes*
Preparation Time	*60 minutes*
Resources	*Daily newspaper, preferably short*

This activity allows teachers to assess students' reading skills in class with the morning newspaper. Thus it deals with current information that is likely to be relatively interesting to the students.

PROCEDURE

1. Buy copies of a daily newspaper for the entire class.

2. Write questions about the newspaper on a sheet of paper or on the blackboard in class. (See Appendix.)

3. Hand out the newspapers and questions in class, and have the students answer the questions.

4. Have the students write their names on their answer sheets and newspapers, and collect them.

FEEDBACK AND SCORING

1. Correct the answer sheets.

2. Bring them to class, and go over the answers.

CAVEATS AND OPTIONS

1. Use the newspaper as the basis of a 1-month course of study.

2. Focus each class on a different aspect of the newspaper. Select the features of the newspaper (e.g., headlines, articles, captions, standings, graphs) or use sections of the newspaper (e.g., front page, business, sports, entertainment, national, local, international, science, nature, and children's sections).

3. Once the class has looked at the various sections, bring a newspaper into the last class and assess the students with questions based on that day's entire newspaper.

APPENDIX: *Sample Questions for Newspaper Assessment*

General

1. How much does the newspaper cost?

2. What is the weather for today?

3. How many sections are there in the newspaper?

4. On what pages are the sports articles?

5. What is the exchange rate for the dollar and the yen today?

6. What movie [album, play, actor, musician] is featured in the entertainment section?

7. What is the theme for today's editorial?

Skimming and Scanning

Look at the advertisements and answer the following questions:

1. How much does the [item] cost?

2. How many cans of [item] can I get for $2.00?

3. Where is the store located?

4. How much does it cost to travel to [place]?

5. What's the telephone number of the agency that offers trips to [place]?

Vocabulary

1. Look at the headline [...] on page [number]. [Note: Give the page numbers sometimes to help the students find the article. For some of the scanning and skimming questions, do not give the page numbers.] The word [...] probably means

    a. [Add real meaning and distractors.]

    b.

    c.

    d.

2. [synonym study] Read the article entitled [...]. Look for words that mean the same as the following words.

Advice Column

1. Read the advice column. Explain why you agree or disagree with the advice.

2. Read the first letter in the advice column. Write a letter of advice to the author.

Entertainment Section

1. How many movies [concerts, plays] are reviewed?

2. Write the names of the movies [concerts, plays] that are reviewed today. Scan the reviews and check whether each is ___ positive, ___ negative, or ___ mixed.

3. When does [name of event] start? When does it end? Where can I get tickets?

Sports Page

1. Look at the sports standings and answer the following questions: Who's in first place in [...]? What player has the most [...]? Who has the most wins in the [...]? Who won the baseball game in [...] last night? What was the score of the basketball game in [...] last night?

2. I'm interested in football. Write the headlines of the article(s) in the sports sections I will be likely to read.

Specific Articles

Read the article entitled [...] and answer the following questions:

1. Who is the article about?

2. What happened?

3. Where does the story take place?

4. When does the story take place?

Letters Section

Read the letters to the editor section.

1. Which letter talks about [...]?

2. In which letter is the writer most angry? least angry? commenting on a previous letter? commenting on a previous article? complaining?

3. Write a letter to the editor based on a topic about which you feel strongly.

4. Write a letter to the newspaper based on one of the letters.

Editorial

1. What is the editorial theme for today?

2. Read the editorial and write whether you agree or disagree with the writer.

Imagination

1. Write a different headline for any article in the newspaper. Also write the original title and page of the article.

2. Look at the picture on page [...]. Write your own caption for the picture.

3. Look at the picture on page [...]. Write a completely different story for the picture.

Comics

1. Read the [...] cartoon. Why is [...] sad?

2. Read the [...] cartoon. What is the relationship between the two people?

V

On the Spot!

Carol MacLennan

Levels	Beginning +
Aims	Demonstrate vocabulary development and reading comprehension
Class Time	Variable
Preparation Time	Variable
Resources	Objects and pictures

For every new word children are required to learn, they have to master a rather large number of interrelated elements of information. Teachers need to be able to make formative assessments of students' ongoing learning on the spot. This activity gives teachers immediate information about each student's vocabulary development and reading comprehension at any moment without using a paper-and-pencil test.

PROCEDURE

1. To check the ability to match a target object with the appropriate sound symbols,

    - Show the class the target object (e.g., a pencil).

    - Ask a student, *What is this?* If the student can provide the correct answer, the student clearly can match the object with the correct sound symbols.

2. To check the ability to match a picture of the target object with the appropriate sound symbols,

    - Show the class a picture of the target object (e.g., a horse).

    - Ask a student, *What is this?* If the student can provide the correct answer, the student clearly can match a picture prompt with the correct sound symbols.

3. To check the ability to match the target print symbols with the appropriate sound symbols,

- Write the target object's print symbols (e.g., the word *book*) on the board and point to them.

- Ask a student, *What is this word?*

4. To check the ability to match the target object with the appropriate print symbols,

    - Write sets of print symbols (e.g., *engine, elephant, eraser, erase, error, ear, answer, anger*) on the board. Show the class the target object (e.g., an eraser).

    - Point to the board and ask a student, for example, *Which word is* eraser? Have a student select a word by pointing to it.

FEEDBACK AND SCORING

1. Count and record the number of correct responses.

2. Keep track of which responses were correct in order to give students diagnostic feedback. In this way, this assessment activity has positive backwash effects because it encourages students to focus on aspects of the target language in which they are weak.

CAVEATS AND OPTIONS

1. Assess the vocabulary development and concept learning of students at other levels of proficiency by changing the content and readjusting the focus appropriately. With more advanced-level classes, assume that the students are already familiar with the concepts involved in the teaching of the target language. If content at the appropriate level of difficulty is selected, however, the above procedures can provide a useful means of assessing the current language proficiency of individual group members.

2. Assessing whether students can match sounds with print is obviously not the same as asking them to match print with sounds. The instructor needs to know if students have mastered both these skills as well as many other skills involved in learning a concept. The skills assessed in the Procedure are the key elements that the instructor will want to assess.

3. If desired, assess the students' ability to match an object with a picture and a picture with an object, either at an earlier stage in the reading process or when pictures are stylized in some way.

4. Show the students different examples or categories of the target object. To learn how well students' concept of *dog*, for example, is established, offer

pictures of several different kinds of dogs, and ask the students to provide the print and sound symbols that match the pictures. Or, offer pictures of various breeds of dogs interspersed with examples of cats, horses, or other four-footed animals to determine if the students have learned category inclusion and exclusion.

5. The table below contains a matrix of the various combinations of matching procedures for assessing students.

	Object	Picture	Sound	Print	Concept
Object	—	✔	✔	✔	✔
Picture	✔	—	✔	✔	✔
Sound	✔	✔	—	✔	✔
Print	✔	✔	✔	—	✔
Concept	✔	✔	✔	✔	—

Definition-Resource Cloze

Edith Malagarriga

Levels	*Advanced; postgraduate EFL teachers-in-training*
Aims	*Read with a specific purpose*
	Infer words from definitions
	Use context to determine suffixes and inflections of words
	Understand the purpose of a text
Class Time	*60 minutes*
Preparation Time	*3 hours*
Resources	*Nothing additional*

This activity assesses the students' ability to ascertain missing words using the context itself and the definition provided for each word. Students also use their background knowledge on the topic as a resource.

PROCEDURE

1. Pass out the Definition-Resource Cloze Test (see Appendix A) to each of the students.

2. Have the students read the passage quickly to get the general meaning.

3. Ask the students to fill in the missing words by looking at the definitions provided for each of the blanks, and to decide on the specific morphology of the word according to the context.

4. Ask the students to create a title for the text.

FEEDBACK AND SCORING

Using an answer key like the one shown in Appendix B, score the test as follows: 22 total points—1 point for each of the blanks and 2 points for the title.

CAVEATS AND OPTIONS

For very advanced-level students, leave blanks in the definitions, resulting in another cloze test.

REFERENCES AND FURTHER READING

Hulse, S. H., Deese, J., & Egeth, H. (1975). *The psychology of learning.* New York, NY: McGraw-Hill.

APPENDIX A: *Definition-Resource Cloze Test*

This assessment activity is designed for students learning English in the field of psychology. Thus the criterion for leaving a word out was that it be a noun related to the field.

Name: _____

1. Read the passage quickly to get the general meaning.

2. Fill in the missing words using the definition given for each of the blanks as a resource.

3. Check your answers.

4. Give a title to the text.

Note: This is a 22-point test: 1 point for each blank, and 2 points for the title.

Title: _____

Extinction produces the most dramatic (1) of patterns of reinforcement upon behavior. All (2) affect resistance to extinction somewhat differently, but it is an important general (3) that a pattern that involves some (4) in the nature of reinforcement (5) from response to response will produce greater (6) to extinction than a condition where all (7) are reinforced immediately, 100 percent of the time, in just the same way.

Results obtained by many, many (8) show that a pattern of partial reinforcement greatly increases resistance to extinction. Skinner (1938) and Humphreys (1939) demonstrated this in some of the earliest (9) on the problem, and since that time, literally hundreds of experiments have repeated these results with a wide variety of (10), apparatuses, and experimental (11) (Jenkins & Stanley, 1950; Lewis, 1960; and Robbins, 1971, provide extensive reviews of the literature concerned with this (12). Resistance to extinction following (13) with a pattern of variable amounts of (14) increases as the range, or variability, of the amounts increases. Greatest resistance to extinction was obtained following (15) with 10 units on half the (16) and 0 units on the other half (partial reinforcement), and resistance to extinction was least if all trials had been reinforced with the mean (17) of 5 units (continuous reinforcement). The important point, however, is that intermediate resistance to (18) was obtained when the (19) in amounts given from trial to trial lay between the (20) of continuous and partial reinforcement.

1. _____
2. _____
3. _____
4. _____
5. _____
6. _____
7. _____
8. _____
9. _____

10. _____
11. _____
12. _____
13. _____
14. _____
15. _____
16. _____
17. _____
18. _____
19. _____
20. _____

Definition Resource

(1) anything brought about by a cause or agent

(2) a reliable sample of traits, acts, tendencies, or other observable characteristics of a person

(3) an established practice that serves as a guide

(4) the complete or partial alteration of an item in form, quality, or relationship

(5) attendant circumstances

(6) the tendency to respond in an opposite direction from that of an applied force

(7) any implicit or overt change in an effector organ, substance, or item consequent to stimulation

(8) someone who searches into; inquires into systematically

(9) any action or process undertaken to discover something not yet known or to demonstrate or test something known

(10) someone or something undergoing a treatment, experiment, or other procedure

(11) a particular course or method of action

(12) a fact, occurrence, or circumstance that is open to observation

(13) modification so that an act or response previously associated with one stimulus becomes associated with another

(14) strengthening of a conditioned response by reintroducing the original uncondi-tioned stimulus

(15) a process of helping others acquire skills and knowledge

(16) an act of testing something to see if it works

(17) a collection or mass considered as a unit in terms of its size, number, and so forth

(18) the process by which the repeated response to a conditioning stimulus reduces the response to a minimum

(19) the limits within which variable amounts or qualities are included

(20) either of two things that are as different or as far as possible from each other

APPENDIX B: *Answer Key*

Title: Patterns of Reinforcement and Extinction

(1) effect

(2) patterns

(3) rule

(4) change

(5) conditions

(6) resistance

(7) responses

(8) investigators

(9) experiments

(10) subjects

(11) procedures

(12) phenomenon

(13) conditioning

(14) reinforcement

(15) training

(16) trials

(17) amount

(18) extinction

(19) range

(20) extremes

Going to the Supermarket

Maria Irene Albers de Urriola

Levels	*Any*
Aims	*Be aware of one's own knowledge of English vocabulary*
Class Time	*Variable*
Preparation Time	*None*
Resources	*Nothing additional*

Many learners think they don't know any English vocabulary because they aren't aware of the copious numbers of words found on packages, bottles, bags, and canned goods in supermarkets, in different departments in stores, even in EFL situations. This activity helps students understand these resources and helps the teacher better understand the problems some students have in understanding simple instructions or producing certain sounds, for example.

PROCEDURE

1. Tell the students to go to a supermarket, look for five items in each department with brands or components (e.g., nutritional information, chemical elements) in English, and write down the information about the products.

2. Have the students bring their lists to class and read them to their classmates.

3. Make a chart like the following on the blackboard, and have the students organize the items into groups to assess their knowledge of the different groups of words.

Food	Cleaning products	Beauty aids	Gardening products
Cornflakes	Bold 3 mildew remover	shampoo	

FEEDBACK AND SCORING

1. Use the lists to assess the students' performance in a role-play in which one student is the customer and a second one, the clerk.

2. Prepare a checklist of factors that you want to give feedback on, or use the checklist in the Appendix to give the students feedback.

3. Consider having the students evaluate each other using some variant of the checklist.

CAVEATS AND OPTIONS

1. Ask the students to look for English words on appliances, manuals for appliances, or other items they have at home.

2. Instead of having the students read their lists to the whole class, have the students gather in groups of 3–4 to check their own lists, produce a new list, and read it to the class.

APPENDIX: *Language Skills Checklist*

Listening

_____ 1. Understands simple directions

_____ 2. Understands simple *yes-no* questions

_____ 3. Understands simple *wh-* questions

_____ 4. Understands vocabulary related to the activity

_____ 5. Understands contractions and common shortened forms

_____ 6. Understands language of peers

Speaking

_____ 1. Pronounces vowel sounds correctly

_____ 2. Pronounces consonant sounds well

_____ 3. Pronounces blends correctly

_____ 4. Uses word stress correctly

_____ 5. Produces simple *yes-no* questions

_____ 6. Produces simple *wh-* questions

_____ 7. Produces vocabulary related to the activity

_____ 8. Uses peer-group language properly

Party or Test: Who Cares? Let's Eat!

Jim Bame

Levels	*Intermediate +*
Aims	*Demonstrate ability to organize a process*
	Activate vocabulary
	Talk about food in an informed way within a nonthreatening atmosphere
Class Time	*3 hours*
Preparation Time	*60 minutes*
Resources	*Dictionaries*

Students usually talk about both the food of their native country and food from the U.S. in very general terms (e.g., *it's good . . . it's OK . . .*). This activity introduces the vocabulary of preparing foods and describing their various tastes. As an assessment, students prepare a dish from their own country for a lunch or dinner party, describe how to prepare their dish, and describe the flavors of the many dishes they taste.

PROCEDURE

Day 1

1. Ask the students to divide into groups of two or three, preferably with each of the students coming from a different language background.

2. Have the students use dictionaries (electronic or paper) to negotiate the meanings of the Terms Used for Food Preparation in the handout (see Appendix A). Add any other necessary vocabulary. Go from group to group and facilitate.

3. Tell the students to discuss the words on the handout and describe a food from their country that each word applies to.

Day 2

1. Have the students decide on a dish to prepare for a class lunch or dinner.

2. Ask the students to divide into groups of two or three. Tell them to practice vocabulary germane to their dish and practice telling how to prepare the dish. Circulate from group to group, and facilitate questioning about the tastes of the various dishes.

3. Ask the students to bring the dish to the next class meeting.

Day 3

1. Have the students taste the foods that their classmates have prepared.

2. Have the students describe the preparation and taste of their dish and the taste of two or three other students' dishes.

FEEDBACK AND SCORING

Use the scoring grid shown in Appendix B to assign and compute scores.

CAVEATS AND OPTIONS

1. Use the party format to practice or assess the ability to introduce others, engage in small talk, talk about past experiences, practice formal or informal language, and use this method for other conversational strategies.

2. This assessment activity works best at the end of a term or in the middle of a semester as a way of breaking the monotony.

3. Instead of preparing the food themselves, the students can opt to bring food prepared by a restaurant, but they should be able to describe how the food is prepared.

4. Hold several parties. Have part of the class prepare food for the first party, and rotate that duty for the next one.

APPENDIX A: *Terms Used in Food Preparation*

Adjectives Used to Describe Food

sweet	sour	delicious
gross	disgusting	nasty
tasty	thick	hot
spicy	bitter	salty

Phrases and Sentences Used to Describe Food

It tastes:

good	unusual	different	excellent	like [...]

Verbs Used in Preparing Food

Cutting	*Cooking*
slice	steam
dice	boil
quarter	simmer
	fry
	bake

Ingredients

Spices	*Main ingredients*
curry powder	cabbage, leeks, carrots, onions
soy sauce	tofu, rice, noodles
ginger	meat (e.g., beef, shrimp, chicken, pork)
salt	peanuts
pepper	tomatoes
red pepper (cayenne)	
garlic	
oregano	

Measurements

a pinch	a teaspoon
a tablespoon	a cupful
a package	a head [of cabbage]

Process Description

First	Then		After that
After cutting [cooking, mixing, ...]	Finally		

APPENDIX B: *Scoring Grid*

Maximum points possible = 40

Category	Score (0 = low; 4 = high)				
Use of appropriate phrases	0	1	2	3	4
Comprehensibility	0	1	2	3	4
Grammar (doesn't interfere with the meaning)	0	1	2	3	4
Natural speech (isn't scripted)	0	1	2	3	4
Pronunciation (doesn't interfere with meaning)	0	1	2	3	4
Sufficient description	0	1	2	3	4
Description of own food's taste	0	1	2	3	4
Description of method of preparation	0	1	2	3	4
Description of ingredients	0	1	2	3	4
Description of two dishes' tastes	0	1	2	3	4

V

The Price Is Right

Dennis R. Bricault

Levels	*Beginning to low intermediate*
Aims	*Demonstrate knowledge of numbers*
Class Time	*5–10 minutes*
Preparation Time	*45–75 minutes*
Resources	*Sunday newspaper advertising inserts*
	Large sheets of paper
	Glue

This activity livens up assessment activities by including a price component. The students give the teacher the prices of household items as they practice small and large numbers in context.

PROCEDURE

1. From the multicolored Sunday newspaper advertising inserts (e.g., from big electronics and department stores), cut out 10–20 pictures of different sale items (e.g., televisions, computers, cameras, articles of clothing) along with their prices. Choose items in various price ranges ($1–$20, $21–$99, $100–$999, and $1,000+).

2. Glue 4–5 items in different price ranges on each of several large sheets of paper.

3. Either give the students, or have them select, one sheet of pictures.

4. Ask the students to say aloud the price of each item on the sheet.

FEEDBACK AND SCORING

Grade the responses based on accuracy, pronunciation, or both.

CAVEATS AND OPTIONS

1. This activity is best done one-on-one while a test is being administered. Have one student meet with the instructor at her desk while the others are writing.

2. Include vocabulary (*The video cassette player costs $275*), adjective order (*I paid $25 for the dark blue blouse*), or functions (*I'd like to buy the TV for $499*) as part of the test. With more advanced-level classes, include fractions and percentages.

Color-Coordinated Quiz

Dennis R. Bricault

Levels	Beginning to low intermediate
Aims	Demonstrate knowledge of color vocabulary
Class Time	5–10 minutes
Preparation Time	30–60 minutes
Resources	Full-color Sunday newspaper advertising inserts or catalogues
	Large sheets of paper
	Glue

This activity adds a dimension to a unit test by including a color component that helps students demonstrate their knowledge of vocabulary and word order. This component is based on readily available material taken from the newspaper or catalogues.

PROCEDURE

1. From multicolored department store advertising inserts in the Sunday newspaper or from catalogues, cut out 10 pictures of different items (e.g., articles of clothing). Choose items in a wide selection of colors that the students have studied.

2. Glue the items onto a large sheet of paper. Number the items from 1–10.

3. Give one student the sheet, and ask the student to write a description of each item (e.g., *A woman is wearing blue jeans and a red t-shirt*) on a separate sheet of paper. Tell the student to pass the sheet of pictures on to the next person in class after finishing the descriptions.

4. Continue until everybody has had a chance to respond, and collect the students' descriptions.

FEEDBACK AND SCORING

Grade each response on accuracy of vocabulary, spelling, word order, content, or all of these features.

CAVEATS AND OPTIONS

1. Try not to choose articles of clothing with unusual colors or hard-to-describe designs (e.g., a paisley tie).

2. Do the activity orally.

3. For large classes, prepare several sheets, or use fewer items on each sheet.

4. Add language functions (*I'd like to buy a pair of black shoes*) or longer sentences (*He's wearing a blue and red tie*) to the required response.

5. Put each sheet in a plastic cover to protect it as the students pass it around the class.

V

Vocabulary Information-Gap Electronic Discussion

Rebecca Fisher

Levels	*Intermediate*
Aims	*Build and contextualize vocabulary*
	Develop grammar
	Participate in real-time, online discussion
Class Time	*Two class meetings (or regularly during the term)*
Preparation Time	*1–2 hours*
Resources	*Computer lab*
	Local area network (optional)
	Internet access (optional)

This assessment activity helps students contextualize vocabulary through an authentic exchange of new information and participate in a real-time, online discussion without the distractions of interruption, racism, genderism, social status, or accent (Warschauer, 1995, p. 44).

PROCEDURE

1. To set up the activity, do one of the following:

   - If your school has access to a computer lab but is not hooked up to a local area network (LAN) (or if you would rather split the class in half and have the students chat within the class), go to Step 4.

   - If your school district has a LAN but does not have access to the Internet, contact another teacher within the school district who has students at the same L2 proficiency level.

   - If your school has access to the Internet, contact another teacher with students at the same L2 proficiency level by e-mailing Tom Robb, a Student List Manager (trobb@cc.kyoto-su.ac.jp) or by posting a notice on *TESLCA-L* (the computer-assisted language learning branch of *TESL-L*, an e-mail discussion list).

2. With the other ESL teacher, create a long list of vocabulary from an agreed-upon lexicon or topic (e.g., animals, including words describing how and where they live). Divide the vocabulary list into two parts, one for each class.

3. Construct a worksheet with the vocabulary words that the other class (or group) will be explaining to your students. Be sure to provide ample room to take notes directly on the sheet.

4. With the other teacher, match the students up with electronic discussion pals (or pal groups), keeping in mind that 2–3 students can use a single computer.

5. Decide on a date and time for the discussions. Reserve the computer lab for that time.

6. The day before the electronic discussion is to take place, distribute the vocabulary that the students will explain to students in the other class, along with related information on the topic.

7. Teach the vocabulary to the students in whatever way preferred, giving them time to look up vocabulary words and ask questions, if desired. Alternatively, assign the students homework about the vocabulary as preparation for the electronic discussion the next day.

8. Explain how to do the activity and how to use the computer for an electronic discussion.

9. Have the students conduct an electronic discussion with their partners in the other class. Encourage the students to use their notes to relay information to their electronic pals and to ask clarification questions about the new vocabulary that they are learning from the other students. Provide help when needed.

10. Ask the students to complete their worksheets.

11. When the task is completed, have the students print out a hard copy of their discussion.

FEEDBACK AND SCORING

1. Gather and analyze the students' worksheets and hard copies.

2. Determine if the focus of the activity was to learn vocabulary, chat communicatively, implement discrete grammar points, or a combination thereof.

3. Construct a grading scale that reflects the activity's focus (e.g., recognition of target vocabulary 40%; correct use of verb tenses 20%; clear instructions given to the other student 40%).

4. Count the number of vocabulary words that the student filled out in the worksheet, and give points accordingly.

5. On the hard copy of the discussion, highlight all of the points that will be graded. Divide the number of correct attempts by the total number of attempts.

6. Highlight and count the number of unresolved miscommunications between the students that result from poor explanations of vocabulary. Or, count the number of successful attempts at informing the other student about a vocabulary word.

7. Adjust each set of scores to its percentage value in the final grade. For example, if a student writes down 18 vocabulary words and leaves 2 blank, and vocabulary accounts for 40% of the grade, the student would score 36%. Add the percentages together for a final grade.

CAVEATS AND OPTIONS

1. Be sure to allocate enough time to prepare this assessment activity. You will need at least 30 minutes to connect to and discuss the activity with the other teacher, 30 minutes in the computer lab, and 60 minutes to get the students ready for the activity.

2. To circumvent off-topic responses by electronic pals, advise your students that they may chat about tangential topics only after they have exchanged all of the information.

3. Advise students never to give any personal information, such as their home telephone number or address, over the Internet.

4. Encourage an e-mail exchange if the partners want to stay in touch.

5. If you are unable to arrange a meeting time with another class (because of time zone differences), set up an e-mail discussion. E-mail changes the nature of real-time discussion, but opens the door to process writing tasks.

6. Create an information-gap task that focuses on explicit grammar points (e.g., the past tense, English subject-verb agreement strings, adjective or adverb placement, relative clauses) or on process writing through an overall analysis of semester-long electronic discussions.

7. Instead of highlighting the points to be assessed by the teacher, have the students do so before they hand in their hard copies.

REFERENCES AND FURTHER READING

The Internet handbook for school users. (Stock No. B1084). ERIC ED375821. Arlington, VA: Educational Research Service

The Internet manual for classroom use. (Stock No. B0187). Arlington, VA: Educational Research Service.

Warschauer, M. (1995). *E-mail for English teaching: Bringing the Internet and computer learning networks into the language classroom.* Alexandria, VA: TESOL. Retrieved from http://www.lll.hawaii.edu/~ markw

A Vocabulary Quiz Given by Students to Themselves

Jeffrey A. Uhr

Levels	*High beginning +*
Aims	*Demonstrate acquisition of new vocabulary*
	Reinforce the relationship between words and various meanings
	Speak and listen in class
	Practice synonyms, circumlocution, and public speaking techniques
Class Time	*Variable*
Preparation Time	*Minimal*
Resources	*Vocabulary handout*
	Master spelling list

his quiz harnesses apprehension about quiz taking as well as allays the fear of public speaking. In this way, students are motivated to absorb a word's definition so that they can describe the word—without using it—in front of the class. In studying for the quiz and taking it, the students must access more than one possible definition for each word. In taking the quiz, students learn new angles on the meanings of words or, at least, are mildly amused when their fellow students give their uniquely worded definitions.

PROCEDURE

Preparation

1. In class, explain the concept of synonyms as a way to infuse variety into language use. Explain *circumlocution* (describing a word in other terms when you don't know what the word is) as a communication strategy.

2. Also in class, introduce public speaking techniques (e.g., volume of voice, the need to face listeners, strategies for dealing with the stress of public speaking, eye contact).

3. Outside class, prepare a vocabulary handout:

- Include two vocabulary words for each student in the class plus 3–4 more words in case a student disqualifies a word (e.g., for 20 students, 2 × 20 = 40, and 40 + 4 = 44 words).

- Include some words that are very easy to define.

Several Days Before the Quiz

1. Hand out the vocabulary list. Go over the particular definitions of the words that the students are supposed to focus on. If possible, say the definitions in a variety of ways. The more ways the words are explained, the better.

2. Encourage the students to practice saying the definitions aloud.

3. Explain the rules of the quiz:

- The definer must define the word for the rest of the class, but cannot use the word or any word containing it in their definition. If they do, that word is disqualified, and they will receive another one.

- The rest of the students must listen to the definition and write the word being defined. They receive 1 point for each correctly defined word they write.

- The definer receives 3 points for each word that three-fourths or more of the students guesses correctly.

- The definer has 2 minutes to define the word. If the definer cannot do so in that time, 2 points are deducted from the score, and the definer's turn is finished.

4. Ask class members at random to repeat the rules as a means of assessing their comprehension. Encourage clarification questions.

The Day of the Quiz

1. Have the students arrange their chairs in a circle, if possible.

2. Ask the students to clear their desks except for one sheet of paper and a writing tool.

3. Repeat the rules of the quiz.

4. Show a student a word chosen randomly from the master list. Mark that word in some way on the list. Roll or fold the master list so that the definers cannot see words defined previously.

5. Have the student define the word for the class. Keep track of the time. If the

student has not defined the word within 2 minutes, note that and move on to the next student—who must try to define the same word.

6. After a student successfully defines a word, ask if there are any questions or comments. Have the rest of the students write down the word on their quiz papers.

7. Repeat Steps 4–6 with the next student (move clockwise or to the first student's left). Continue until all the words have been defined.

8. Collect the students' papers.

FEEDBACK AND SCORING

Score the papers as follows:

1. Give 1 point for each correct word on the quiz paper.

2. Give 3 points to the definer for each word that three-fourths or more of the class guessed correctly.

3. Deduct 2 points from the definer's score for any definitions that took more than 2 minutes.

CAVEATS AND OPTIONS

1. Allow more time for the first administration of a quiz of this type than for subsequent ones because the rules will need to be explained and it is necessary to ensure that the students understand them.

2. The lessons contained within this type of quiz are most effective if the quiz is administered repeatedly throughout the semester.

3. Require the students to give their definitions in sentence form. For example, in defining the word *computer*, the student must say something like, "This is a machine that you write into and play video games on."

4. Encourage the class to ask questions of the definers while adhering to the same rules about using the word.

5. Using previously studied words, give a review quiz by following the same procedure, but require class members to call out the definitions. Award 1 point to the first correct response heard. (Note that this version of the quiz could be biased toward or against certain personality types.)

Check It Out: A Library Research Checklist

Sylvia Mulling

Levels	*Advanced*
Aims	*Understand the qualities of an acceptable library research paper in the U.S.*
	Understand how teachers evaluate research papers objectively and consistently
Class Time	*20 minutes*
Preparation Time	*30 minutes*
Resources	*Manilla envelopes*

ere's a way to facilitate the process of researching and writing a paper for students and teachers alike. Students use the checklist to guide, record, and revise their research; teachers use it to evaluate both the process and the product of the students' work, and everybody's job becomes clearer and simpler.

PROCEDURE

1. When introducing the research paper, distribute a copy of the checklist (see Appendix) to each student. Go over it carefully, explaining each of the steps and criteria. Explain how the students should use the checklist and how it will be used in evaluating their papers (see **Feedback and Scoring** below).

2. Tell the students to use the checklist as a guide and record while carrying out their research by checking off (in the spaces on the left) each step in Part A as they complete it and each requirement for the paper in Part B as they meet it.

FEEDBACK AND SCORING

1. Use the checklist (see Appendix) to evaluate the students' papers by writing (in the spaces on the right) the number of points awarded to the student for each step of the process and for each criterion.

2. The number of points assigned will vary from teacher to teacher. If desired, share the point values with the students.

3. To give feedback, pass back the completed checklists to the students, and explain the scoring system.

CAVEATS AND OPTIONS

1. The checklist reflects one such set of requirements and criteria for library research papers and may be adjusted, as needed.

2. Note that the checklist does not specify how the students are to carry out the steps and meet the criteria for the finished paper; be sure to give the students this information.

3. The checklist is not intended to substitute for other types of responses to the students' work. For example, when either the process or the product is faulty, give specific instructions for revision.

4. Use Part B of the checklist to evaluate either the first or the final draft of the research paper, or both. For example, return it with the first draft accompanied by instructions for revision, and when it is returned with the final draft, then revise the evaluation to reflect any improvement.

REFERENCES AND FURTHER READING

Moulton, M., & Holmes, V. (1994). Discovery writing: ESL student research with a purpose. *TESL Reporter, 27*, 15–20.

Reid, J. (1993). *Teaching ESL writing*. Englewood Cliffs, NJ: Prentice-Hall Regents.

APPENDIX: *Checklist for a Library Research Paper*

Name _____

Check off each requirement in the space at left when you complete it. When I evaluate your paper, I will write in the number of points you receive for each requirement. Put this paper in your manilla envelope (on top of all your other papers) and turn it in each time.

A. Steps to be turned in: You must also meet all the requirements described in Part B.	Date due		
Turn in your manilla envelope with *all* research paper materials in it each time.	Sect. 01	Sect. 04	Points
____ 1. Topic and research question	9/25	9/26	1.____
____ 2. Source cards and photocopies of sources	10/11	10/10	2.____
____ 3. Stack of note cards and copies of highlighted sources	10/23	10/24	3.____
____ 4. Title, thesis statement, and outline	11/6	11/7	4.____
____ 5. First draft, (revised) outline, and reference list	11/15	11/21	5.____
____ 6. Final draft, title page, outline, and (revised) reference list	12/6	12/5	6.____

B. Requirements for the library research paper			
_____ 1.	You have used from 5–8 sources of sufficient variety and quality.	1. _____
_____ 2.	There is a fair match between the content of your sources, note cards, outline, and paper.	2. _____
_____ 3.	You have presented at least four pages of evidence that supports your final thesis; your paper is at least six pages long.	3. _____
_____ 4.	You have written your paper according to the principles of formal academic writing; you have written in a plain style.	4. _____
_____ 5.	You have used direct quotation only for a good reason; you have used quotation marks; you have quoted exactly.	5. _____
_____ 6.	You have smoothly integrated material taken from your sources into your own writing.	6. _____
_____ 7.	You have given credit where credit is due in parenthetical textual citations and in the correct form.	7. _____
_____ 8.	You have listed *all* of your sources in the correct form in the list of references.	8. _____
_____ 9.	You have produced your paper according to the guidelines in chapter 10.	9. _____
_____ 10.	You have carefully read your paper aloud to yourself and have corrected as many language and mechanical (spelling, punctuation, capitalization, form) errors as possible.	10. _____
_____ 11.	You have carefully proofread your typed paper before turning it in.	11. _____

Tense Excitement Throwing a Die

Trevor Ballance

Levels	*Beginning*
Aims	*Demonstrate ability to distinguish spoken past tense -ed forms*
Class Time	*10–15 minutes*
Preparation Time	*5–20 minutes*
Resources	*Die*

In this activity, students try to fill in 12 spaces on their sheet with words that have the appropriate spoken past tense endings. To do the activity, the students must be familiar with the regular past tense endings of /t/, /d/, and /ɪd/. By introducing a chance element, the teacher can make the assessment competitive and exciting for the students, easily assess the students' understanding of the different pronunciations involved, and test words relevant to the needs and abilities of the class.

PROCEDURE

1. Give the students each a copy of the handout (see Appendix). Explain that they will choose words from the six columns in the chart below the squares and write one word in each of Squares A–L according to the pronunciation of its past tense ending. They can fill in the squares in any order.

2. Roll the die and call out the number. Tell the students to look in the appropriate column, choose one word, and write it in one of the squares that matches the pronunciation of *-ed* as marked in the bottom right-hand corner of each square. For example, if number 1 is rolled, the students choose among *laughed, cried, cleaned,* and *wanted.* If they choose the word *laughed,* they have the option of writing the word in Square A, D, G, or K.

3. After the students have chosen a word and written it in a square, tell them to check off (or cross out) the word from the column so that they do not use it a second time. As the options decrease, the students may find that on some occasions they are not able to fill in a square. Most students, however, should complete the sheet at about the same time.

FEEDBACK AND SCORING

1. Collect the students' sheets, and simply check that the word written in each square matches the phonetic past tense ending in the bottom righthand corner.

2. Identify any problem areas to focus on in future sessions.

CAVEATS AND OPTIONS

Play the game in groups of 3–6 students. Have the students take turns rolling the die one at a time. In each case, the number rolled applies only to their own sheet. The students attempt to be the first to complete the sheet.

APPENDIX: *Sample Handout*

Name _____

A		B		C		D	
	/t/		/ɪd/		/d/		/t/
E		F		G		H	
	/ɪd/		/d/		/t/		/ɪd/
I		J		K		L	
	/d/		/ɪd/		/t/		/d/

1	2	3	4	5	6
laughed	listened	opened	danced	robbed	played
cried	departed	walked	studied	played	carried
cleaned	brushed	shopped	closed	washed	splashed
wanted	climbed	emptied	called	mounted	shampooed

Who Is He?

Mika Kirimura

Levels	Beginning
Aims	Comprehend, practice, and demonstrate learning of the comparative form
Class Time	15 minutes
Preparation Time	5 minutes
Resources	Magnets

This assessment activity focuses on the comparative form in English. The students learn to understand as well as practice it, and the teacher monitors the students' learning of comparatives.

PROCEDURE

1. Make or find six pictures of men with different physical characteristics, each with a dog having different physical characteristics. Label each picture with the man's name; call one of them *John*. Write one of the other names on each card. With the magnets, arrange the pictures on the blackboard so that John is at the upper left (see Appendix A) to make it easier for the students to compare the other men with John.

2. Have the students each pick a card. Ask them not to show it to the other students.

3. Show the students how to describe the men by using John and Mark as examples. Make sure to use the third-person singular pronoun *he*, not the name *Mark*, so that you don't give away the answer (e.g., say *He has a smaller dog than John does*, not *Mark has a smaller dog than John does*).

4. Have one student describe the person on her card by comparing the man on the card to John. Remind the student to use the pronoun *he* in the description.

5. Have the other students raise their hands to answer when they know which person is being described.

FEEDBACK AND SCORING

Rate the students' ability to use the comparative by using the checklist (see Appendix C).

CAVEATS AND OPTIONS

1. Make sure the students know that the pictures on the blackboard are all men with dogs. To make the task easier, list the characteristics to compare (see Appendix B).

2. Make sure the students use the third-person singular pronoun *he* when making a comparison.

3. Have the students do this activity in small groups, preferably with no more than five students.

4. Give each student a sheet of paper with John's picture on the left and a blank space on the right. Describe the missing person by comparing the man on the card to John, and have the students listen to your description and draw a picture.

APPENDIX A: *Pictures*

John

Mark

Dave

Kevin

Craig

Tom

APPENDIX B: *Characteristics to Compare*

face	length of hair	height
legs	shoes	size of dog
clothes	body size	age

APPENDIX C: *Checklist for Student Performance*

Circle one score for each criterion.

	Poor					Good
Uses regular comparison -*er* correctly	0	1	2	3	4	5
Smoothly uses regular comparative with *more/less*	0	1	2	3	4	5
Uses irregular comparatives such as *better*	0	1	2	3	4	5
Uses correct nouns for comparison	0	1	2	3	4	5
Uses ... *has* ... *than* ... format	0	1	2	3	4	5
Makes comparison points clearly	0	1	2	3	4	5
Total score						____/30

Assessing Writing From Sources

Zuzana Tomaš

Levels	*Intermediate to advanced*
Aims	*Integrate academic sources into L2 writing*
Class Time	*10–15 minutes per paraphrase or quote*
Preparation Time	*5 minutes to copy rubric*
Resources	*Source-based text*

Effective writing from sources is paramount to L2 learners' academic success, especially in secondary and tertiary contexts. The assessment of this important skill usually comes at the end of the writing process, however, and frequently results in the teacher discovering major problems, including plagiarism. Teachers are often unsure how to provide effective formative, continuous feedback on source-based writing (Tomaš, 2010). When they do offer feedback, it is often too indirect for L2 writers to understand (Hyland, 2001). This task provides an assessment tool that allows L2 writing teachers to continuously assess students' integration of academic sources into their writing.

PROCEDURE

1. Introduce the exercise by reminding students that when they write from sources or peer review source-based assignments, they need to remember that the information from sources should be integrated well with the writer's own ideas.

2. Ask students to exchange drafts of their (source-based) papers.

3. Distribute a copy of the assessment rubric (see Appendix) to each student.

4. Allow students time to assess at least one paraphrase or quote by completing the rubric.

FEEDBACK AND SCORING

Ask students to return papers and rubrics to their partners and discuss their feedback.

CAVEATS AND OPTIONS

1. The teacher can distribute one rubric per quote or paraphrase or adapt the rubric by inserting additional columns that would allow students to record points for several different paraphrases and/or quotes.

2. The initial implementation of this task in the classroom may require the teacher to discuss the rubric with the students and model how to use it to assess the integration of paraphrases or quotes. This modeling can be done collaboratively with the students.

REFERENCES AND FURTHER READING

Hyland, F. (2001). Dealing with plagiarism when giving feedback. *English Language Teaching Journal, 55*(4), 375–382.

Tomaš, Z. (2010). Addressing pedagogy on textual borrowing: Focus on instructional resources. *Writing and Pedagogy, 2*(2), 223–250.

APPENDIX: *Rubric*

	2	1	0	Points
Content	The paraphrase/quote successfully builds on the content of the surrounding text and provides relevant evidence for the writer's point.	The paraphrase/quote partially relates to the content of the surrounding text and provides some evidence for the writer's point.	The paraphrase/quote does not relate to the content of the surrounding text and does not provide relevant evidence for the writer's point.	
Attribution	The paraphrase/quote is appropriately attributed to the original source.	The paraphrase/quote is attributed to the original source with a minor mistake.	The paraphrase/quote is not attributed to the original source.	
Flow/Transitions	The paraphrase/quote transitions well and does not interrupt the flow of the text. The logic of the writer's point is easy to follow.	The paraphrase/quote transitions with minor difficulty, causing a small interruption in the flow of the text. It is possible, however, to follow the writer's logic.	The paraphrase/quote does not transition well and/or the flow of the text is completely interrupted. The logic of the writer's point is difficult to follow.	
Vocabulary	For paraphrase: The level of formality in the paraphrase is the same as in the surrounding text. For quote: Vocabulary in the sentences that introduce or explain the quote is appropriate.	For paraphrase: The level of formality in the paraphrase differs somewhat from the surrounding text (e.g., there may be one non-academic synonym in the paraphrase). For quote: Vocabulary in the sentences that introduce or explain the quote is slightly problematic.	For paraphrase: The level of formality in the paraphrase differs significantly from the surrounding text. For quote: Vocabulary in the sentences that introduce or explain the quote is highly problematic (e.g., non-academic).	
Grammar	For paraphrase: The paraphrase is grammatically correct. For quote: Grammar in the sentences that introduce or explain the quote is appropriate.	For paraphrase: The paraphrase makes the surrounding text slightly ungrammatical. For quote: Grammar in the sentences that introduce or explain the quote is slightly problematic.	For paraphrase: The paraphrase makes the surrounding text grammatically incorrect. For quote: Grammar in the sentences that introduce or explain the quote is inappropriate.	
TOTAL POINTS				__/10
COMMENTS				

Using Reformulation to Assess Paragraph Rhetorical Structure

Zuzana Tomaš and Holly Andrews

Levels	*Intermediate to advanced*
Aims	*Use paragraph reformulation to make writing sound more natural*
Class Time	*30 minutes*
Preparation Time	*5 minutes*
Resources	*Nothing additional*

A frequent complaint about advanced, largely grammatically correct L2 writers' compositions is that they do not sound natural or nativelike. Although teachers can *reformulate*, meaning rewrite parts of L2 writers' texts in more natural ways (Cohen, 1983; Lapkin, Swain, & Smith, 2001; Myers, 1997), rewriting multiple compositions is not realistic for most L2 writing teachers. This reformulation-based task asks students not to write but, instead, to identify improved components within selected paragraphs. Writers become more aware of how paragraphs are structured in academic writing in English.

PROCEDURE

1. Pass out copies of the assessment task (see Appendix) to students.

2. Read the instructions with the students and answer questions.

3. Allow time for completion of the task.

FEEDBACK AND SCORING

1. Ask students to compare their responses in small groups prior to discussing the task with the whole class.

2. Concepts the teacher may want to comment on are topic sentence, coherence/ transitions, unity, support, and concluding sentence.

CAVEATS AND OPTIONS

1. An appropriate follow-up activity to this task is asking students to revise paragraphs similar to paragraph A in the Appendix.

2. Teachers can adapt this task by focusing on a specific subset of components they are teaching.

REFERENCES AND FURTHER READING

Cohen, A. (1983). Reformulating compositions. *TESOL Newsletter, 6*(12), 1, 4–5.

Lapkin, S., Swain, M., & Smith, M. (2002). Reformulating and the learning of French: Pronominal verbs in a Canadian French immersion context. *The Modern Language Journal, 86*(4), 485–507.

Myers, S. (1997). Teaching writing as a process and teaching sentence-level syntax: Reformulation as ESL composition feedback. *TESL-EJ, 2*(4), 11–16.

V

APPENDIX: *Assessment Task*

TASK: Tong, an ESL student, wrote paragraph *A*. Later he revised it and wrote paragraph *B*. Describe the differences between Tong's paragraphs *A* and *B* using the concepts identified in the box below.

A. I love dancing. It brings me relaxation. Like me, many people use dancing for relaxation. But for dancers dancing can mean stress. Often this stress comes from dancers trying to maintain or lose weight. They are doing this because they know what the expectations of ballet are! They must be athletic and strong, but also very slim, and elegant. Dancers need a lot of energy for training, but also lean body because the expectations of ballet are not to be overweight. They are also expected to devote many hours of hard training to ballet. Some of my friends train up to 5 hours a day! They hardly ever have time to go and see a movie or read a book. Also, they usually cannot travel because when they do they miss training. But one of my good friends is very good at juggling things and he always finds time for ballet as well as his friends, and traveling. The worst thing is that many of these ballet dancers starve themselves to keep their weight down.

B. Most people consider dancing as a form of relaxation, but for a professional ballerina, dancing often brings a high level of stress. A large part of this stress is related to maintaining a certain weight. This is because ballerinas are expected not only to be athletic, but also to stay lean, graceful, and elegant. In other words, dancers need bodies that are strong, energetic, and slender in order to meet the technical and aesthetic demands of ballet. Therefore, most dancers have to constantly watch what they eat since gaining extra pounds can lead to a loss of opportunities to perform, a loss of a job, or even the end of one's career. A close friend of mine is a good example of the dangerous eating habits of some ballet dancers. He typically has a cup of coffee for breakfast, a cigarette for lunch, and an apple for dinner! While ballet brings pleasure to audiences around the world, those who perform are not always as happy and healthy as they seem.

> Concepts you can comment on: topic sentence, coherence/transitions, unity, support, and concluding sentence.

Part VI

Alternative Ways of Assessing Oral Skills

- **Listening and Note-Taking**

- **Speaking**

- **Pronunciation and Connected Speech**

Part VI: Alternative Ways of Assessing Oral Skills

EDITOR'S NOTE

In the Editor's Note to Part V, I discussed how the written and oral channels of communication and the modes of producing or receiving a message are related to each of the four language skills. Naturally, those distinctions are as related to this part of the book, on oral-channel skills, as they are to Part V, on written-channel skills.

In this final section, I would like to take up an issue that is also related to both Part V and Part VI: performance assessment. As mentioned in Part V, language tests were traditionally designed to measure the four language skills separately. Language tests were also designed to be taken with paper and pencil insofar as that was possible. Given recent trends in language teaching toward notional-functional or task-based syllabuses and toward more practice with authentic communication and language use, it is no surprise that the majority of contributions in this part of the book and in Part V (as well as elsewhere in the book) propose assessment activities that require students to actually do something with the language. Such assessment activities are often called *performance assessments*.

Performance assessments should meet four conditions: The students should be asked to do something with the language; in the process they should be performing some sort of meaningful task; the tasks should be as authentic as possible; and the tasks must typically be rated and scored by qualified judges. Those four characteristics can serve as a working definition for performance assessments, and a quick look through this book will convince you that many of the contributions are performance assessments according to that definition. But why would teachers go to all the trouble of doing performance assessments?

In brief, performance assessments allow teachers to (a) assess the students in contexts that simulate authentic language use, (b) compensate for the negative effects of traditional paper-and-pencil tests, and (c) promote positive feedback by assessing the same language points and activities that students are learning in the everyday classroom.

Unfortunately, several disadvantages of performance assessments must also be overcome, including the facts that performance assessments can take considerable time to administer, can cause reliability as well as validity problems, and can increase the risk of test security breaches. By incorporating some of the suggestions here, teachers can minimize all of these problems. For instance, the *administration time problem* can be solved in part by integrating the performance assessment activities right into the class time, just as any other activities are. That

VI

is the strategy advocated by many of the contributions in this book. The *problems of reliability* that are inherent in the use of raters can be mitigated by selecting only those who are qualified, using two or more of them at a time, giving clear guidelines, training, and retraining them from time to time during the rating process, carefully monitoring the ratings as the raters produce them, and revising all of these steps before doing the ratings in other classes or during other terms. The *validity problem* can be at least partially overcome by carefully matching the assessment tasks to the sorts of teaching points and learning activities that are going on in the particular course and by assessing the students a number of times throughout the term. Finally, the *security problem* can be minimized by creating a variety of tasks, with different students performing different tasks, and by setting up conditions so that students who have already performed are unable or, at least, unlikely to communicate the nature or content of the task involved to students who have not yet performed theirs.

The majority of the assessment activities in this part of the book are performance assessments, and they are all focused on the oral channel. That is not to say that the written channel is not used at all, but the oral channel is the main one used in these activities. Naturally, many of the assessment activities elsewhere in this book also involve the oral-channel skills, but in those cases, oral skills are not the primary focus. The first section in this part of the book includes assessment activities focused on listening and note-taking; the second section contains activities focused on speaking and pronunciation; the third section focuses on pronunciation and connected speech.

The five assessment activities in the listening and note-taking section are designed for several different purposes: to help students feel more comfortable and confident when speaking with native speakers ("We Are Here to Communicate!"); to assess students' bottom-up listening skills ("Watch Your Listening"); to help students recognize key words and pertinent details, find main ideas and supporting details, and make inferences from the language contained on video recordings ("The Couch-Potato Diagnostic Listening Test"); to encourage note-taking, to assess students' abilities to quickly locate main ideas and details in a written text, as well as to assess how students follow aural directions ("LSS: Listen and Skim/Scan"); and finally, to assess students' academic listening and note-taking abilities ("Welcome to English 101").

The six assessment activities in the speaking section are designed to provide criteria for students to use in rating their class presentations and those of their peers ("Presentation Check"); to assess students' communicative speaking abilities ("Guess What My Favorite Animal Is"); to help students plan a skit project and assess their own performance ("Skit Assessment"); to motivate students and assess their linguistic and pragmatic skills ("Karaoke-Dokey"); to assess pragmatics while recording important information in messages in various contexts and registers ("Assessing Pragmatics Using Recorded Voice Messages"); and to examine improvement in students' oral reading fluency over time ("Measuring Reading Fluency").

The four assessment activities in the pronunciation and connected speech section are designed to help instructors rapidly evaluate pronunciation in class ("Assessing Production and Reception of Minimal Pairs"); to assess students' ability to identify the stressed words in a sentence ("Sentence-Stress Telegrams"); to examine students' ability to identify and reproduce appropriate word-level stress ("Repeat if Correct"); and to assess the students' comprehension of reduced forms in spoken North American English ("Reduced-Forms Dictations").

REFERENCES AND FURTHER READING

Buck, G. (2001). *Assessing listening.* Cambridge, England: Cambridge University Press.

Luoma, S. (2001). *Assessing speaking.* Cambridge, England: Cambridge University Press.

Norris, J. M., Brown, J. D., Hudson, T., & Yoshioka, J. (1998). *Designing second language performance assessments.* Honolulu, HI: National Foreign Languages Resource Center, University of Hawai'i at Mānoa. Retrieved from ERIC: ED 451 701

Shohamy, E. (1995). Performance assessment in language testing. *Annual Review of Applied Linguistics, 15,* 188–211.

We Are Here to Communicate!

Shanti L. Arnold

Levels	*Intermediate +*
Aims	*Become comfortable speaking with native speakers*
Class Time	*30 minutes–3 hours*
Preparation Time	*0–30 minutes*
Resources	*Audio recordings*

Many language students around the world study English for years in high school and college, but they feel uncomfortable speaking it when confronted with a native speaker. This discomfort is often due to a lack of confidence. The assessment activity described here enables students to practice speaking to native speakers in order to build up their confidence so they can feel proud of their language ability. Furthermore, teachers can use this assessment activity to check that the students have grasped lessons taught in the classroom—from syntax and semantic knowledge, to politeness and turn-taking skills, to the ability to maneuver the topic smoothly (Fraser, 1990; Gumperz, 1992; Janney & Arndt, 1992).

PROCEDURE

1. Decide on the topic and the main points to be assessed (e.g., grammatical structure, specific vocabulary, turn-taking skills).

2. Tell the students how the assessment activity works, including

    •   what they will need (an audio recording device)

    •   how to conduct the interview

    •   when the audio recording is due

    •   what points they will be graded on (see Appendix)

3. Have the students conduct and audio record interviews with native speakers outside class.

FEEDBACK AND SCORING

1. Collect the audio recordings from the students on the due date, or have them email a copy for the teacher to download.

2. Grade the audio recordings according to the criteria decided on, or use the chart in the Appendix.

CAVEATS AND OPTIONS

1. Summarize clear questions or discussion points to use in the interviews so that the students have an outline to follow.

2. Let the students know what they are being graded on, or some students may turn in material that cannot serve as the basis of a reliable grade.

3. For greater reliability in grading, enlist another person or several other people to listen to the audio recordings and grade them.

4. In addition to the communicative assessment discussed above, take a whole-language approach and develop other tests and activities (Rigg, 1991). For example,

   • have the students write journals or papers about their discussion with the native speaker or their feelings about doing the assessment activity

   • before the activity, have the students brainstorm questions and role-play how they think the discussion will go

   • for a bigger project, group the assessment activities and lessons around one subject, such as foreigners' ideas about a country, or a guide to a country (or, in the case of ESL students, a guide to the United States) for foreigners. Then have the students publish within their school a book on the subject based on what they find out from their interviews (Fried-Booth, 1982).

5. Adapt the activity for beginning-level students by simplifying the topic and task.

VI

REFERENCES AND FURTHER READING

Fraser, B. (1990). Perspectives on politeness. *Journal of Pragmatics, 14*, 219–236.

Fried-Booth, D. (1982). Project work with advanced classes. *ELT Journal, 36*, 98–103.

Gumperz, J. (1992). Contextualization and understanding. In A. Duranti & C. Goodwin (Eds.), *Rethinking context* (pp. 230–252). Cambridge, England: Cambridge University Press.

Janney, R. W., & Arndt, H. (1992). Intracultural tact versus intercultural tact. In R. J. Watts, S. Ide, & K. Ehrlich (Eds.), *Politeness in language* (pp. 21–41). Berlin, Germany: Mouton de Gruyter.

Rigg, P. (1991). Whole language in TESOL. *TESOL Quarterly, 25*, 521–542.

APPENDIX: *Scoring Card*

Circle the appropriate number:

(1 = no competency; 2 = some competency; 3 = competency; 4 = above-average competency)

Fluency (smoothness of speech, lack of significant pauses)	1	2	3	4
Grammar (accuracy of grammar, especially the structures taught in class)	1	2	3	4
Vocabulary (use of varying vocabulary, especially words taught in class)	1	2	3	4
Pragmatics (e.g., appropriate levels of politeness, turn-taking skills)	1	2	3	4
Comprehensibility (ability to make self understood despite other problems)	1	2	3	4

Total _____

(A = 16-20; B = 11-15; C = 6-10; Fail = 5)

Watch Your Listening

Charles Browne

Levels	*Low intermediate +*
Aims	*Demonstrate bottom-up listening skills*
Class Time	*10–15 minutes*
Preparation Time	*20 minutes*
Resources	*Video clip with 15- to 20-line two-person dialog*

One of the keys to using video successfully in the ESL classroom is to carefully add relevant previewing, viewing, and postviewing activities. Cloze-type activities such as this one can both motivate students and help develop their listening skills. Because the students know they will be receiving a grade, they are usually very motivated to work together and listen carefully. As a result, the quiz functions as both an effective learning activity and an assessment device.

PROCEDURE

1. Locate an appropriate video recorded dialog. Dialogs from movies or TV dramas are preferable to those from commercially produced ESL videos.

2. Type up the dialog, leaving 3–4 blank lines in the middle for one of the speakers. Each blank should be one sentence long. If one speaker's turn is several sentences long, leave one of the middle sentences blank to give the students more context to work with.

3. In class, instruct the students to fill in the blanks with the exact words the speaker is saying. If desired, tell the students that they will not lose points for spelling mistakes but that there will be one point taken off for each word that is missing or wrong (see Feedback and Scoring, Step 2).

4. Play the video at least four times from beginning to end without pausing.

5. Collect the papers.

VI

FEEDBACK AND SCORING

1. Develop an answer key for the words that the speaker said in each blank, and correct the students' answers.

2. Because the focus is on listening and meaning, decide whether or not to count misspellings as incorrect.

CAVEATS AND OPTIONS

1. This quiz works best as a semi-regular classroom activity. A good balance seems to be two intensive listening activities followed by a quiz. Over time, this sequence significantly improves the students' ability to follow natural-speed dialogs without the use of subtitles.

2. If the class is small, let the students replay the video as many times as they want within a given time period (typically no more than 15 minutes).

The Couch-Potato Diagnostic Listening Assessment

Steve Golden

Levels	*Intermediate*
Aims	*Demonstrate strengths and weaknesses in recognizing key words and pertinent details*
	Find main ideas and supporting details
	Make inferences
Class Time	*75 minutes*
Preparation Time	*3 hours*
Resources	*Two video clips*

tudents worldwide are watching more hours of video per week than any other group at any other time in the history of the human race. If these students truly are the video generation, then using video as a means of language instruction and assessment is clearly the way to win students' interest and increase their motivation. This diagnostic assessment capitalizes on their interest in video for the purpose of analyzing and surveying the students' mastery of several bottom-up and top-down listening microskills, including recognizing key words and pertinent details as they are linked in the speech stream (bottom-up), finding main ideas and supporting details (top-down), and making inferences from the information provided (top-down).

PROCEDURE

Preparation

1. Locate two appropriate video clips, each 30–60 seconds long, from authentic sources (i.e., materials originally made for native speakers of English). Choose video clips that are short and focused rather than feature-length films:

   - Special television news reports or programs are excellent, as the visuals set the context of the topic within seconds. Note that special reports

VI

often contain vocabulary specific to a given topic or field. Try to choose video clips on a subject the students have had exposure to in class.

- Movies or scenes from television programs can work well, especially in a functional curriculum. Choose specific scenes for the contexts the students are studying (e.g., how to greet friends, how to say goodbye).

- Commercials are short and therefore must use language and visuals to create a scene or context within seconds. Commercials can be purchased in "greatest-hits" compilations that you are legally permitted to use for educational purposes.

2. Prepare a listening assessment (see Appendix A) such that each video clip corresponds to the microskills listed in the Aims.

Part 1 (20–25 minutes)

1. Ask the students to sit where they can see the video and hear well and to clear their desks.

2. Play the first video clip. Have the students watch and listen without taking notes.

3. Hand out Part 1 of the listening assessment (see Appendix A, Part 1). Read the instructions for Part 1 to the students.

4. Play the video clip once again. Have the students take notes on their listening assessment handouts.

5. Ask the students to complete Part 1 of the handout, then collect it when they have finished. Allow 8–10 minutes to complete the exercise.

Part 2 (20 minutes)

Repeat Steps 1–5 above using Part 2 of the listening assessment (see Appendix A, Part 2) and the second video clip. Allow 10–12 minutes to complete the exercise.

Part 3 (20 minutes)

1. Play the second video clip again. Have the students watch without taking notes.

2. Hand out Part 3 of the listening assessment (see Appendix A, Part 3). Read the instructions to the students

3. Allow the students 15 minutes to complete Part 3, then collect it.

FEEDBACK AND SCORING

1. Score Parts 1–3 separately, and put all three scores and comments on a scoring sheet (see Appendix B).

2. Although the activity is designed to assess listening skills, it does not have to be scored as if it were a discrete-point test. If desired, break down the students' proficiency assessment by microskill, score each skill separately, and add up the scores to arrive at one integrated listening score.

3. Hand back the sheet to the students with the listening assessment.

CAVEATS AND OPTIONS

1. Although it is normal for the students to feel that video clips played at natural speed are far too fast, once they are taught listening skills and strategies, they will be able to listen both for the gist and for key information, thereby enabling them to communicate better with native speakers in real situations.

2. Rather than rewinding the video recording during the administration of the assessment, record each video segment for as many consecutive viewings as required. For example, record the first video clip two times in a row. Or, use a downloaded video that will play as many times as desired.

3. Be sure to check the video equipment before you use it.

4. If desired, make helpful suggestions, such as using strategies available in the students' L1, thereby encouraging autonomous language learning (Wenden, 1991). Similarly, if it will benefit the learners' understanding and if the situation permits, have the scoring sheet translated into the learners' L1.

REFERENCES AND FURTHER READING

Brown, H. D. (1994). *Teaching by principles*. Englewood Cliffs, NJ: Prentice Hall Regents.

Richards, J. (1989). *The language teaching matrix*. Cambridge, England: Cambridge University Press.

Stempleski, S., & Tomalin, B. (1990). *Video in action*. Hemel Hempstead, England: Prentice Hall International.

Wenden, A. (1991). *Learner strategies for learner autonomy*. Hemel Hempstead, England: Prentice Hall International.

VI

APPENDIX A: *Sample Listening Assessment*

Part 1

The students watch a video clip featuring a woman and a travel agent discussing the woman's itinerary.

INSTRUCTIONS: Watch the video clip. Fill in the chart.

Day	Time	Place	Action
Thursday			
			visit the Great Wall
		Hong Kong	
	7:30 a.m.		

Part 2

The students watch a video clip from a news story called "Sneaker Wars."

INSTRUCTIONS: Watch the video. Circle the main ideas in Column A. Then draw lines from those main ideas to the supporting information in Column B.

A	B
Sneakers are popular with trendy teenagers.	The colors and styles change every season.
Sneakers appeal to many different types of people for different reasons.	Nike and Reebok both have design teams.
Nike and Reebok like to compete with one another.	Women wear them to work, kids love to play in them, and athletes wear them to compete.
Nike is more serious about sports than Reebok.	Both Nike and Reebok have testing centers to keep up with the latest technology.
Fashion is a key element of sneaker sales.	The presidents of Nike and Reebok refuse to meet.

Part 3

The students watch a video clip of a man on the telephone talking to Bob (not pictured). They cannot hear Bob's end of the conversation.

INSTRUCTIONS: Watch the video. Answer the following questions in 1–2 words.

1.   What is the topic of conversation?_____

    _____

2.   Is Bob indoors or outside? _____

3.   Is Bob the boss or the caller?_____

APPENDIX B: *Scoring Sheet*

	Part	Score
1.	Recognizing key words	___ / ___
2.	Finding main ideas	___ / ___
3.	Making inferences	___ / ___
	Total	___ / ___

VI

LSS: Listen and Skim/Scan

Kim Hughes Wilhelm

Levels	**High beginning +**
Aims	**Use note-taking strategies**
	Demonstrate ability to quickly locate main ideas and details in written text
	Follow aural directions
Class Time	**10–20 minutes**
Preparation Time	**10–20 minutes**
Resources	**Two 1-page texts**
	Index cards (optional)
	Highlighting pens (optional)

This assessment activity primarily measures students' abilities to quickly and successfully locate main ideas and details in a written text, as well as to listen and follow directions in an integrated listening and reading task. The students also learn to read quickly under pressure, use reading skills and strategies, and listen and respond to the teacher's directions. Students employ note-taking strategies when they attend to the next bit of aural information before finishing with the first. With LSS (Listen and Skim/Scan), students feel that they are able to make progress in both listening and reading, and they see its application, particularly when they are studying English for academic purposes.

PROCEDURE

1. Prepare questions on the details or main ideas in one of the texts (see Appendices A and B). The first time the instructor does this activity, prepare a maximum of 10 questions. Also prepare directions that encourage the students to interact with the reading as they respond (see Appendices A and B).

2. Teach the students how to speed-read. For example, give them the following instructions:

   • Use an index card to move at a steady pace through the passage. Do not backtrack.

- Allow your eyes to hit each line only 2–3 times. Focus on the subject, the verb, the direct object of the main clause, and noun clauses.

- Use a "typewriter return" to quickly jerk your eyes to the beginning of the next line.

- Remember that the power positions of a reading are the beginning and the end (the first and last paragraphs).

3. Tell the students they are going to have 2–4 minutes to speed-read a text and that they will need to listen to directions and follow them to show that they can find main ideas and details in the text. (Decide on a length of time based on how long the reading is and how quickly the good readers in the class finish.)

4. Hand out the second text. Time the students as they speed-read it.

5. Give the students the directions. Move fairly quickly through the items (i.e., move on when the fastest 3–4 students seem to have found the answer). Encourage the students to jot down notes to help them remember the directions for answers they can't find quickly enough.

6. Collect the papers promptly so that the students don't have much time to go back over their answers. Remember that they are being assessed on listening and reading ability under timed circumstances, wherein the pressure should encourage improvement in speed, reading skills, and focused listening.

FEEDBACK AND SCORING

1. Identify the frequency of correct and incorrect answers for each question. Discuss with the students the questions they most frequently missed. Try to identify why the students missed them and which questions may have been confusing or appropriately answered with an answer different from the one you selected.

2. Help the students be aware of the following strategies and assess their own ability to use them.

- Speed-reading: Review the techniques, and ask the students to assess their abilities in each category as well as their overall reading speed. Ask if they need more guidance or practice.

- Focused listening to directions: Give the directions orally again, and ask the students to list (verbally or on paper) key words for the task as they listen. Do it a second time and, if needed, write the key words chosen by the instructor on the chalkboard. Discuss any directions that the students found confusing or difficult.

VI

- Skimming/scanning to locate answers or key words in text: Note that the order in which the questions are asked may differ from the order in which the answers appear in the text.

3. Ask the students to figure their scores. Perhaps ask for a hand count (e.g., ask *Who got more than eight correct? fewer than five?*) to note who is most and least successful with this activity. The hand count also helps less proficient students be more aware of their need to improve.

CAVEATS AND OPTIONS

1. Do LSS regularly (at least twice a week).

2. Do LSS very quickly (for 5 minutes at end of the period, or as a transition from one activity to another) after the students are familiar with the format.

3. Consider using LSS as a warm-up or extension activity for other content-based materials.

4. Progress from reading for details and literal information to reading for main ideas (see Appendices A and B).

5. Consider using 2–3 LSS activities the first and second weeks of class as diagnostic assessments to quickly identify students who need practice in listening, skimming, and scanning.

APPENDIX A: *Sample LSS (Details)*

EAP2 Core Unit 2: Laws of Ecology

Miller, G. Tyler, Jr. (1994). Nutrient Cycles. *Living in the Environment* (8th ed., pp. 78–79). Belmont, CA: Wadsworth.

DIRECTIONS: Speed-read for 45 seconds to become familiar with the main structure of the reading "Nutrient Cycles." Listen and follow directions as you then locate details. (7 points possible)

Teacher's Questions

1. What percent of organism mass is made up of macronutrients? Circle.

2. How many micronutrients are there? Circle.

3. What is another word for nutrient cycles? Circle.

4. What "drives" nutrient cycles? Circle two answers.

5. What is an example of a nutrient that cycles quickly? Circle. One that cycles slowly? Circle.

APPENDIX B: *Sample LSS (Main Ideas)*

EAP2 Core Unit 3: Biodiversity

Miller, G. Tyler, Jr. (1994). "Protecting Coastal Zones." *Living in the Environment* (8th ed., p. 139). Belmont, CA: Wadsworth.

DIRECTIONS: Speed-read for 2 minutes to become familiar with the main structure of the reading "Protecting Coastal Zones." Listen and follow directions as you then locate answers. (13 points possible)

Teacher's Questions

1. Is the purpose of this article to persuade or to inform? Circle *persuade* or *inform* on Line 1 below the reading.

2. Locate the thesis statement. Highlight it and put a star next to it.

3. What is the controlling idea of Paragraph 1? Highlight it.

4. What is Paragraph 2 about? Write it in one or two words on Line 2 below the reading.

5. What kind of structure is used in Paragraph 3 (e.g., example, compare/contrast, amplification)? Write your answer on Line 3 below the reading.

6. What is Paragraph 4 about? Write it in one or two words on Line 4 below the reading. Is this a natural process? Put an *X* next to the line that tells you.

7. How many solutions to beach erosion are offered by the writer? Circle the solution or solutions offered.

Teacher's Answers

1. Persuade

2. Last sentence

3. "...(W)e are destroying or degrading the very resources that make coastal areas so enjoyable"

4. Contamination

5. Compare/contrast

6. Beach erosion; last line of paragraph 4

7. Prevent development; allow development only behind protective dunes

VI

Welcome to English 101

Lia M. Plakans and Cynthia L. Myers

Levels	*Advanced*
Aims	*Demonstrate academic listening and note-taking abilities*
Class Time	*20 minutes*
Preparation Time	*3 hours*
Resources	*Audio recording*

This activity assesses students' academic listening with authentic materials and tasks. It can be used in a classroom as a pretest to identify students' problem areas in academic listening and note taking or as a posttest to determine students' acquisition of academic listening skills. The listening material simulates a first-day-of-class lecture in an academic course at a university. Students listen to a teacher introducing the syllabus for a new semester; as the syllabus lecture is played via audio recording, students identify what is most important and take appropriate notes, as if they were taking notes in the course.

PROCEDURE

1. Prepare a syllabus for the hypothetical class, including details on office hours, required textbooks, grading policies, and course requirements. Use a variety of items, including numbers (e.g., *office hours every Tuesday from 4:30 to 5:30*) and key terms (e.g., the name of the textbook spelled out). Write a script based on the syllabus as it would be presented on the first day of a course. Build in enough repetition to make note taking possible (e.g., *Good afternoon. I am your teacher, Sara Branch. That's Branch, B-R-A-N-C-H*).

2. Audio record the lecture. If appropriate for the level of the students, pause after each piece of information.

3. Review the audio recording. Improve unclear or ambiguous sections.

4. Pilot the activity by having a representative group of students listen to the lecture and take notes.

5. Use the activity by playing the audio recorded lecture while the students take notes.

FEEDBACK AND SCORING

1. Use the results from the piloted assessment activity to create a scoring key.

    *   Either score each piece of information, or score items representing several levels of difficulty. For example, out of a possible 40 items, choose 20 that include several pieces of information missed by few students on the pilot, several missed by many students, and several in the middle range of difficulty.

    *   Choose items to score based on whether they would be essential for the students to understand for success in the course.

    *   Use answers from the piloted activity to compile alternative responses to the exact answer (e.g., misspelled textbook name, used *papers* instead of *pages*).

2. Score the activity using the key.

CAVEATS AND OPTIONS

1. If resources are available and classroom dynamics permit, video record the lecture, which would add nonverbal cues to the listening activity and which result in an even more authentic classroom simulation.

2. Use the activity to practice certain skills. For example, focus on page numbers, and have the students practice hearing the difference in stress between, for example, the words *fifty* and *fifteen*.

3. Follow the activity with comprehension or vocabulary-in-context questions to assess other listening skills.

4. Include this style of assessment activity in a placement test for a series of academic listening classes.

VI

Presentation Check

David Progosh

Levels	Intermediate +
Aims	Assess peers and self in class presentations
Class Time	20 minutes
Preparation Time	60 minutes
Resources	Library materials, magazines, newspapers

This presentation check guides students in the process of researching, organizing, and delivering a class presentation and aids in determining a grade for their work.

PROCEDURE

1. Tell the students that they are to prepare a 3–5 minute presentation to the class. One possible topic is travel (e.g., *What country would you like to visit? Find some information about the country you want to visit and tell the class about it.*).

2. In class, discuss what makes a good presentation. Start by giving the students your criteria (see Appendix A).

3. Hand out copies of the Presentation Self-Check and Peer-Check (see Appendices B and C) so that the students have a clear set of guidelines on which they will be assessed.

4. Assign a due date, and set a schedule for the presentations.

5. In class, assist the students in preparing their presentations so that you can monitor the amount and quality of their research, organization, and preparation.

6. On presentation day, have the students fill out the presentation check forms for themselves and all other students as the presentations proceed. Take notes so that the instructor can compare grades with the ones they assign later.

FEEDBACK AND SCORING

1. Collect the self-check and peer-check forms, tally the scores, and give each student a grade.

2. Use the forms—and have the students use them—to identify areas that need improvement.

CAVEATS AND OPTIONS

1. Always keep in mind that the purpose of the presentation check is to clarify criteria and standards, thereby aiding the students in monitoring their own learning and creating a cooperative classroom environment.

2. In large classes, divide students into groups on presentation day to speed up the procedure.

3. If desired, solicit the students' ideas in developing criteria and standards for both self-check and peer-check forms.

APPENDIX A: *Sample Tips for Making a Good Presentation*

*   **RESEARCH.** Find a book, such as an encyclopedia, and take notes on your topic. Write down important dates, names, events, and vocabulary. Find out interesting or unusual facts to share with others.

*   **ORGANIZATION.** Organize your presentation. Talk about your subject in a logical progression (e.g., chronologically, thematically, by cause and effect).

*   **PREPARATION.** Before class, practice delivering your presentation aloud. Work on pronunciation, intonation, fluency, and other aspects of the presentation. Ask a friend to listen to you and make suggestions on how to make your presentation better.

*   **PRESENTATION.** During your presentation, try to be calm and relaxed. Never read notes! Use the look-up-and-say technique. Make eye contact. Get the audience involved. Invite questions.

APPENDIX B: *Presentation Self-Check*

Name _____

DIRECTIONS: Look at the following questions and rate your presentation.
Circle the number that best describes it.

1. Research: I researched my subject using books, magazines, or other sources of information.

not at all		*a little*		*a lot*
1	2	3	4	5

2. Organization: I organized my research in a logical way and included interesting facts.

not at all		*a little*		*a lot*
1	2	3	4	5

3. Preparation: I practiced my presentation to work on pronunciation, intonation, fluency, and other aspects.

not at all		*a little*		*a lot*
1	2	3	4	5

4. Presentation: I was well prepared and got others involved in a discussion on my topic.

not at all		*a little*		*a lot*
1	2	3	4	5

5. I helped others learn new information and vocabulary through my presentation.

not at all		*a little*		*a lot*
1	2	3	4	5

6. Overall, I think my presentation was

bad	*below average*	*average*	*good*	*excellent*
1	2	3	4	5

Total: _____ /30

APPENDIX C: *Presentation Peer-Check*

Name of presenter _____

Write down a question you would like to ask the presenter. _____

_____

_____

Look at the following questions and rate the presenter.

Circle the number that best describes the presentation.

1. Research: The presenter researched the subject.

not at all		*a little*		*a lot*
1	2	3	4	5

2. Organization: The presenter was well organized.

not at all		*a little*		*a lot*
1	2	3	4	5

3. Preparation: The presenter was well prepared.

not at all		*a little*		*a lot*
1	2	3	4	5

4. Presentation: The presenter got me involved in a discussion on the topic.

not at all		*a little*		*a lot*
1	2	3	4	5

5. The presenter helped me learn new information and vocabulary through the presentation.

not at all		*a little*		*a lot*
1	2	3	4	5

6. Overall, I think the presentation was.

bad	*below average*	*average*	*good*	*excellent*
1	2	3	4	5

Total: _____ /30

Guess What My Favorite Animal Is

Rieko Shimazaki

Levels	*Beginning; secondary school*
Aims	*Demonstrate ability to speak communicatively*
Class Time	*50 minutes*
Preparation Time	*20 minutes*
Resources	*Map of a zoo*

This assessment activity is designed specifically for students who have mastered 3 years of English at the high school level but are not good at speaking. The purpose of the activity is to assess their ability to use language communicatively.

PROCEDURE

1. Ask the students to name animals that they know about.

2. Hand out the map of the zoo. Ask the students which animals are found in a zoo.

3. Ask the students to choose their favorite animals and to think about the animals' features. Write difficult or unfamiliar words on the blackboard, and explain them to the students.

4. Divide students into pairs.

5. Have the students guess what their partner's favorite animals are by using *wh-* questions.

6. Have the students change partners and repeat Step 5.

FEEDBACK AND SCORING

1. Take each pair aside, and have one of the students interview the other about his favorite animal using *wh-* questions.

2. Rate one student's performance according to the scale shown in the Appendix.

3. Have the students reverse roles. Rate the other student's performance.

4. If desired, assign numbers for the purpose of grading. For instance, with a scheme like *Excellent = 5, Good = 4,* and *Poor = 3* for each of the four rating categories, a maximum score of 20 points (and a minimum of 12) would be possible.

APPENDIX: *Rating Scale*

Pronunciation	Excellent	Nativelike
	Good	Accurate enough to understand
	Poor	Hard to understand
Grammar and vocabulary	Excellent	Native-like fluency in English grammar and precise vocabulary usage
	Good	Some grammar problems and some vocabulary misuse, but they don't interfere with communication
	Poor	Severe grammar problems and inappropriate use of vocabulary
Body language	Excellent	Effective use of body language such as eye contact, hand movements, facial gestures, and loudness of voice
	Good	Inadequate use of body language
	Poor	Lack of body language
Communication	Excellent	Communicates well, understands partners' questions correctly, and answers to the point
	Good	Takes time to communicate, some misunderstanding, but manages to communicate
	Poor	Finds it hard to communicate

VI

Skit Assessment

Sayoko Okada Yamashita

Levels	*Any*
Aims	*Plan a skit project*
	Assess own performance
	Learn to participate actively
Class Time	*2–3 hours*
Preparation Time	*3 hours*
Resources	*Video recording device*

Performing a drama or skit is one of the language learning activities typically included in a communicative syllabus. Students have to take initiative in such an activity, and teachers need to monitor them carefully. One difficulty is how to assess such an activity and produce scores. The skit project suggested here will help both students and teachers logically assess the project.

PROCEDURE

Introducing the Project

1. Tell the students that they will be putting on a skit for the rest of the class and that they can include anything they like, including artwork, dancing, and music.

2. Explain that the expected time for each skit will be 2 minutes times the number of members in the group. That is, each member of the group should speak for at least 2 minutes in the group's skit. For instance, if a group has four members, the total time for the skit will be approximately 8 minutes (2 minutes × 4 people = 8 minutes).

Planning the Skit

1. Have the students form skit groups of 3–6 students (10 minutes).

2. Tell the students to discuss the theme of their skit and to give their skit

group a name (e.g., "September Wind," "Tom Sawyer's Adventure") related to that theme (15 minutes).

3. Have the students write and submit a 200- to 300-word summary of their skit (20–30 minutes, or for homework).

4. Tell the students to make a list of words in their skit (with their definitions) that might be difficult for the other students to understand (for homework).

5. Have the students write a scenario (30 minutes, or for homework).

Monitoring and Commenting on the Skit

1. Pass out the Skit Assessment Sheet (see Appendix A) to each group. Explain to the students that they will fill in each step on the sheet according to the schedule.

2. Make appointments with each group for counseling. Include at least three separate 15-minute appointments to cover (a) a summary, (b) a scenario, and (c) a rehearsal. Once the appointments are made, make a schedule of appointments and give it to each student.

3. Give the students feedback at each step. Be sure to check grammatical accuracy and word choice in the scenario step and to check appropriateness of nonverbal behavior and accuracy of pronunciation in the rehearsal step.

4. Post a checklist of the steps that all of the groups have completed.

Peer Critiquing

1. Pass out the Critical Comments Sheet (see Appendix B) at the time of the final performance.

2. Have the students write comments on the skit, language use, pronunciation, and general acting.

FEEDBACK AND SCORING

Self-Assessment

1. Have the group assess its preparation of the skit (see Planning the Skit above) using the space in the third column of the Skit Assessment Sheet (Appendix A).

2. Have the group assess its final performance (the scenario, grammatical correctness, pronunciation, language use and fluency, nonverbal expressions, and overall performance) using the Critical Comments Sheet (Appendix B).

Scoring and Grading by the Teacher

1. Give feedback to the groups for their rehearsals (in Monitoring and Commenting on the Skit above) using the Skit Assessment Sheet.

2. Grade the final performances using the Skit Assessment Sheet.

Assessment by the Other Students

1. Have the students vote on the best skit, actor, actress, music, and special talent using the Contest Voting Sheet (see Appendix C).

2. Tally the votes and announce the results in class.

3. Give prizes as appropriate.

CAVEATS AND OPTIONS

1. Be sure to give each group (not each student) a Skit Assessment Sheet so that the students know what they should do next at all times. In addition, because the activity lasts about a week and has an irregular schedule (i.e., the regular language class might continue along with the skit project), it is crucial for the students to record each step on the Skit Assessment Sheet.

2. Replace scoring or grading by the teacher(s) with a participation grade (i.e., pass or fail).

REFERENCES AND FURTHER READING

Maley, A., & Duff, A. (2005). *Drama techniques in language learning: A resource book of communication activities for language teachers* (3rd ed.). Cambridge, England: Cambridge University Press.

APPENDIX A: *Skit Assessment Sheet*

Step			Date	Sign
1	Group			
2	Members			
3	Theme (goal of the project)			
4	Title			
5	Summary			
6	Vocabulary list	Use separate sheet.		
7	Scenario	Use separate sheet.		
8	Rehearsal	LOW HIGH Language 1 2 3 4 5 Grammar 1 2 3 4 5 Pronunciation 1 2 3 4 5 Fluency 1 2 3 4 5 Nonverbal 1 2 3 4 5 Overall acting 1 2 3 4 5 Comments:		
9	Final performance	Overall grade A B C Comments:		
10	Prizes			

APPENDIX B: *Critical Comments Sheet*

Comment on the following.

1. Scenario _____

2. Pronunciation _____

3. Language use and fluency _____

4. Nonverbal expression _____

5. Overall performance _____

APPENDIX C: *Contest Voting Sheet*

Vote for the following prizes.

1. Best Skit (Write the group's name.): _____

2. Best Actor:_____

3. Best Actress: _____

4. Best Music (Write the group's name.): _____

5. Special Talent: _____

VI

Karaoke-Dokey

Judy Yoneoka

Levels	*Beginning +*
Aims	*Become interested in a task*
	Demonstrate linguistic and pragmatic skills
Class Time	*10–20 minutes*
Preparation Time	*Variable*
Resources	*Satisfactory location*
	Karaoke sound system, audio recordings, and song handouts

This assessment procedure can be used with students in a university-level oral English course. Dictations based on the songs should be assigned as homework each week, reviewed in the next class, and then used as the basis of paired conversation and journal writing. For their final assessment, students can choose either a paired conversation in front of the teacher, like the ones they practice in class, or a final party in which they will be expected to sing one of the songs in front of the other students. This activity motivates students in non-English-speaking countries who are fulfilling a course requirement in English, but see no immediate need for or applications of English in their daily lives. The activity also assesses linguistic skills, such as pronunciation, intonation, and use of reduced forms, and pragmatic skills, such as the ability to understand and effectively interpret and convey emotion in English.

PROCEDURE

1. In advance, find a suitable location (a karaoke place or a room with the appropriate equipment at school).

2. Two classes before the evaluation date, pass around a sign-up sheet (see Appendix) on which the students can mark their first, second, and third choices for songs to sing. Be sure to provide space for the students to indicate any special considerations (e.g., whether they have to arrive late or leave early on that date).

3. In the class before the evaluation date, provide the students with a list of songs they will be responsible for and the order in which they will be expected to sing.

4. Gather in the designated place at the designated time, and let the show begin!

FEEDBACK AND SCORING

1. Evaluate the students on the following factors: pronunciation (20%); liaison, reduction, intonation, and rhythm (30%); delivery, including eye contact, voice projection, stage presence (20%); and expression of content, meaning, and emotions conveyed in the song (30%). These criteria were consistent with rating sheets often used for marking students' performances in recitation and speech contests. (Adapt percentages, as desired.)

2. Incorporate peer evaluation into the assessment procedure.

CAVEATS AND OPTIONS

1. This activity is most suitable for beginners and false beginners. It could be used with intermediate- or advanced-level students, however, with any of the following modifications:

   - Require memorization.

   - Have the teacher (or other students) choose the song, using a lottery-style selection process.

   - Include a follow-up question-and-answer or short-speech period.

   - Require all participants to use English exclusively throughout the evening.

2. Use this procedure in conjunction with another assessment option, as not everyone is comfortable with karaoke!

REFERENCES AND FURTHER READING

Kanel, K. R. (1995). *Pop song listening*. Tokyo, Japan: Seibido.

VI

APPENDIX: *Sample Sign-Up Sheet*

Your name _____ Your number _____

Please circle either 1 or 2.

1. I plan to take the English song test. I will sing the following song:
    (Mark your first, second, and third choices with 1, 2, and 3)

    ____ 1. "Love Me Tender"   ____ 8. "Help"

    ____ 2. "Be My Baby"   ____ 9. "Sailing"

    ____ 3. "Imagine"   ____ 10. "Faith"

    ____ 4. "Locomotion"   ____ 11. "Let It Be"

    ____ 5. "Yesterday Once More"   ____ 12. "Woman"

    ____ 6. "Hard to Say I'm Sorry"   ____ 13. "Are You Lonesome Tonight?"

    ____ 7. "I Just Called to Say I Love You" ____ 14. "Bridge Over Troubled Water"

    You will be graded on the following:
    *   Pronunciation (20%)
    *   Liaison, reduction (20%)
    *   Delivery (30%)
    *   Expression (30%)

    Please note: Singing ability will *not* be evaluated. If you feel more comfortable chanting the words, that is fine.

    Any notes, questions, or comments? _____

    _____

    _____

    — OR —

2. I plan to take the conversation test with:

    Name of partner _____

    Student Number _____

    I (will/will not) _____ come to the karaoke party.

Assessing Pragmatics Using Recorded Voice Messages

Mira Malupa-Kim

Levels	*Adults, intermediate to advanced*
Aims	*Assess pragmatics by recording appropriate messages in various contexts/settings/registers*
	Review imperative verbs
	Practice stress and intonation
	Practice relaying important information in a concise manner
Class Time	*Variable*
Preparation Time	*60 minutes*
Resources	*Audio recording device or language lab*

Leaving voice messages is a part of U.S. daily life. In many cultures, leaving messages on answering machines is not a common practice. This activity will help students feel confident in recording messages and choosing the appropriate language for various transactions.

PROCEDURE

Preparation

1. Depending on the level and language learning goals, create a variety of situations where students need to record a voice message (e.g., responding to a friend's dinner party invitation, rescheduling a doctor's appointment, scheduling a meeting with a professor, responding to a job inquiry, making bank or credit transaction inquiries).

2. Record new messages or actual messages received from friends to create samples. Include dialog scripts to illustrate appropriate language and provide copies of these scenarios and dialogs to students.

Assessment

1. Give a short introduction on telephone culture in English—differences in receiving/making calls. Brainstorm common vocabulary/words/phrases used in leaving messages.

2. Have students listen to (or read) voice message samples. Tell students to note how phone numbers are given, area codes, transaction types, informal/formal language, and so forth.

3. First have students practice leaving messages to a friend. Then assign different types of situations.

FEEDBACK AND SCORING

1. Teachers evaluate the students' messages based on speaking, appropriateness of language, content of message, pausing, volume, and conciseness of the message (see Appendix).

2. As a follow-up activity, the teacher may select some recorded messages for listening and note-taking practice.

CAVEATS AND OPTIONS

1. This activity works best in language lab settings using a Sound Recorder in PCs/Macs or other built-in recording software (i.e., Audacity). The sample messages can be made available; handouts should be provided online or distributed in hard copies with step-by-step instructions.

2. In small classes, the teacher needs to provide digital recorders or students may use their own mobile devices to record (if using mobile devices, students should not make actual calls!).

3. For lower proficiency levels, concentrate on one function (e.g., inviting someone to a party) but assign students to invite different types of people— a friend, a classmate, or a professor—to clearly assess pragmatic aspects of the language. This is also an appropriate activity for Business English classes.

REFERENCES AND FURTHER READING

Celce-Murcia, M., & Olshtain, E. (2000). *Discourse and context in language teaching.* Cambridge, England: Cambridge University Press.

Kessler, G. (2010). Fluency and anxiety in self-access speaking tasks: The influence of environment. *Computer Assisted Language Learning, (23)*4, 361–375.

Malupa-Kim, M. F. (2009, March). *Enhancing speaking and pronunciation classes using the sound recorder.* Presented at TESOL Convention, Denver, CO.

APPENDIX: *Sample Rubric*

(adapted from rubistar.com)

Name:_____

Context/Situation: _____

CATEGORY	4	3	2	1
Speaking	Speaks clearly and distinctly all the time.	Speaks clearly and distinctly all the time, but mispronounces a few content words.	Speaks clearly and distinctly most of the time. Mispronounces some content words.	Often mumbles or cannot be understood OR mispronounces most of the content words.
Appro-priateness of the language	Language is appropriate throughout the given context/situation.	Language is appropriate for the most part for the given context/situation.	Language is somewhat appropriate for the given context/situation.	Language is not appropriate for the given context/situation.
Content	Message is complete and clearly stated.	Message is complete but a few details lacking.	Message is complete but some details lacking and/or not clear.	Message is not complete and/or not clear.
Pauses	Pauses were effectively used 3 or more times to improve meaning and/or impact.	Pauses were effectively used once to improve meaning and/or impact.	Pauses were intentionally used but were not effective in improving meaning and/or impact.	Pauses were not intentionally used and/or impact.
Volume	Volume is loud enough to be heard throughout the presentation.	Volume is loud enough to be heard at least 90% of the time.	Volume is loud enough to be heard at least 70% of the time.	Volume often too soft to be heard.
Timing	Message is delivered briefly and concisely.	Message is delivered briefly and concisely, but some pauses in between.	Message is delivered with a lot of pauses in between.	Message is delivered, but too long.

Additional Feedback: _____

_____

_____

_____

VI

Assessing Pragmatics Using Recorded Voice Messages | 367

Measuring Reading Fluency

Jeff Popko

Levels	*Intermediate to advanced*
Aims	*Measure improvement in reading fluency over time*
Class Time	*Varies*
Preparation Time	*30 minutes*
Resources	*Reading passages*
	Recording devices
	Copy of the assessment text (can be electronic)
	Projector
	Mobile computing device

PROCEDURE

At the beginning of the course, demonstrate to the students the idea of reading while listening (Popko, 2011) by projecting the text (using a laptop, or any projection system) while playing a recording. Use a reading textbook that comes with audio of the reading texts at the intermediate level, and e-books paired with their unabridged audiobook versions (e.g., Clinton, 2011; Gladwell, 2005). A portion of the class includes a group reading-while-listening session every week using the target materials.

1. Choose a passage that takes 2–4 minutes to read from the target text (either from the course textbook or from authentic texts at the target reading level).

2. Demonstrate the technology to students by reading a passage aloud while recording yourself (with any mobile computing device or phone).

3. Then, play the recording back as the students read along with the projected text.

4. Distribute the assessment text via email to the students.

5. Ask the students to read the passage silently until they feel comfortable with the text.

6. Have the students make and submit a recording.

    • If this is done as a homework assignment, students can practice as often as they wish. Ask students to submit their recording before the next class.

- If students do not have a recording device, perhaps schedule them to come during office hours or go to a media lab in the library to record.

7. Listen to the recordings, marking the reading text for targeted problems (e.g., mispronunciation, skipping words, repetitions).

FEEDBACK AND SCORING

Rate the assessment using a rubric (see Appendix). Rating can be numerical (based on the number of targeted problems recorded), or holistic (using a 5-point Likert scale), or both.

CAVEATS AND OPTIONS

1. Consider having the students record themselves again at the end of the course as a post-assessment.

2. This activity is typically used in university advanced and academic reading courses. Most of the students, therefore, have digital recording devices of some sort, and are familiar with the technology. A computer lab in which each student has a computer with headphones equipped with microphones would allow in-class assessment. At lower levels there are apps that will allow students to record picture stories (e.g., Momotaro) with tablets or smart phones.

3. Perhaps allow advanced students to participate in the creation of the scoring rubric (Popko, 2009).

REFERENCES AND FURTHER READING

Clinton, W. (2011). *Back to work: Why we need smart government for a strong economy.* New York, NY: Knopf.

Gladwell, M. (2005). *Blink: The power of thinking without thinking.* New York, NY: Little, Brown, & Co.

Popko, J. (2009). Demystifying presentation grading through student-created scoring rubrics. In T. Stewart (Ed.), *Insights on teaching speaking in TESOL.* Alexandria, VA: TESOL.

Popko, J. (2011). Reading while listening to build receptive fluency. In N. Ashcroft & A. Tran (Eds.), *Teaching listening: Voices from the field.* Alexandria, VA: TESOL.

VI

APPENDIX: *Fluency Assessment Rubric*

Student Name: _____

	Pre-assessment	Post-assessment	Change
Text			
Word count			
Numeric indicators			
Speed			
Pronunciation errors			
Long pauses			
Holistic indicators			
Stress patterns			
Intonation			
Volume			
Clarity			

Assessing Production and Reception of Minimal Pairs

Neil McPhee

Levels	*Beginning to intermediate*
Aims	*Become motivated to produce well-formed minimal pairs*
	Understand breakdowns in attempts to produce and interpret minimal pairs
	Rapidly demonstrate pronunciation
Class Time	*50 minutes*
Preparation Time	*15 minutes*
Resources	*Nothing additional*

Some classes are too large to permit one-on-one assistance with pronunciation, yet many students really need help on basic sound formation. Lost in a sea of badly produced words, students compound their misunderstanding and make few attempts at nativelike pronunciation. This assessment activity provides students with enjoyable practice in minimal pairs, as participants can give each other feedback on performance and demonstrate to the class how poor pronunciation can greatly affect communication.

PROCEDURE

1. Decide on the minimal pairs for students to contrast (e.g., *ship/sheep*; *right/light*; *heart/hat*; *rocket/racquet*). Devise a picture to represent each word in each contrast (e.g., ♥ for heart, ∏ for hat; ⇑ for rocket, ¶ for racquet; → for right, Ω for light). Think of a lexical set that needs reviewing (e.g., *shops: bank, café*).

2. Make a diagram (see Appendix) and make copies for the students.

   • On a piece of paper, make a 1-inch border on all sides. Prepare a binary tree in the center:

   • Place an arrow labeled *Start* pointing at the root node of the tree.

VI

- From this node make two branches that each lead to an alternative in the first minimal-pair contrast (e.g., *heart/hat*; see Appendix, Diagram 1).

- Give these two nodes (*heart* and *hat*) two branches that lead to the alternatives in the second minimal-pair contrast (e.g., *right/light*; see Appendix, Diagram 2).

- Give each of the lowest nodes two branches that lead to the alternatives for the next minimal-pair contrast (e.g., *rocket/racket*). Include one alternative only at the end of each branch (see Appendix, Diagram 3).

- Repeat until all the minimal pair contrasts have been diagramed.

- In the margin around the tree, write down members of the lexical set that the students need practice with. Connect every lexical item in the set (e.g., *shop*) to a different one of the lowest nodes.

3. Present the minimal pairs in class as usual, remembering to practice perception before production. When necessary, illustrate good and bad habits.

4. Give the students the handouts. Give the L1 equivalent or a definition for one of the words in the margin, and ask the students to find the word (e.g., for *bank*, *a place to keep money* or for Japanese students, *ginko*). Tell the students to write the name in their L1 above the English version.

5. Repeat this process for all the other lexical items. Provide remedial help on vocabulary as required.

6. Direct the students' attention to the *Start* arrow in the center. Explain that the students must listen carefully, follow the lines with their finger, and find out where you are going. For example, if you call out one alternative from each of the minimal pairs in turn (e.g., *heart, right, rocket),* the students must follow the line from the last node to the shop and then call out the shop's name when asked where you are now.

FEEDBACK AND SCORING

1. Some students will take the wrong path through the tree. By tracing the path they have taken and seeing where it diverges from the instructor's, note where the student's perception was faulty.

2. Give feedback as necessary, showing where the instructor's path and theirs diverged, and offer helpful suggestions (e.g., lip-read). Repeat Steps 5 and 6 until the students are familiar with the procedure.

3. Divide the group into pairs. Have the students take the role of listener or speaker, freeing the instructor to circulate and give personal assistance as required.

CAVEATS AND OPTIONS

1. Review any number of phonemes in this manner.

2. At the beginning of a course, use this assessment activity diagnostically to swiftly assess which problem areas need the most attention.

REFERENCES AND FURTHER READING

Avery, P., & Ehrlich, S. (1992). *Teaching American English pronunciation*. Oxford, England: Oxford University Press.

APPENDIX: *Sample Diagrams*

Diagram 1

Diagram 2

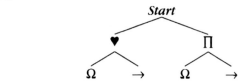

Diagram 3

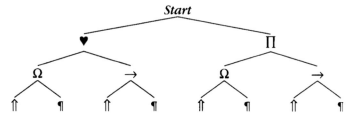

Sentence-Stress Telegrams

Larry Davis

Levels	***High beginner to intermediate***
Aims	***Become comfortable in identifying which words receive stress within sentences***
Class Time	***10–15 minutes***
Preparation Time	***10–15 minutes***
Resources	***Nothing additional***

This assessment activity examines the ability of students to identify the stressed words in a sentence. Such stressed words are important for establishing the rhythm of English sentences, where words receiving emphasis are separated by roughly equal intervals of time. (For stressed words with more than one syllable, the syllable receiving primary stress receives emphasis.) Besides assessing awareness of sentence-level stress, this activity can also be used to raise awareness of the fact that stress usually falls on the content words within a sentence.

PROCEDURE

1. Prepare a list of sentences that are appropriate for the students' level. For each sentence, underline or circle the words that are stressed.

2. Read each sentence; students should write down only the words that are stressed (telegrams). So, a sentence like *The cat chased the dog* becomes *cat chased dog*.

3. Ask students to give their telegrams for the sentence; write these on the board. Then, write the full sentence and correct telegram on the board. Continue until all of the sentences have been covered.

FEEDBACK AND SCORING

1. For informal assessment, see **Procedure** Step 3.

2. This exercise can be done as a more formal quiz, with students handing in their telegrams of the sentences for scoring. Telegrams can be scored as correct/incorrect, or partial credit given by awarding a point for each correct word.

CAVEATS AND OPTIONS

1. To make the assessment easier, rhymes or other materials with a strong beat may be used and the beat emphasized when reading each sentence. Students can also be encouraged to repeat the sentence and clap out the beats in order to identify the stressed words.

2. The assessment can be done in pairs in which one student reads a sentence and the other writes down a telegram.

3. Depending on the speaker's intent, one or more of the stressed words in an utterance may be given additional prominence. For example, the sentence *The boy ate the apple* would be the answer to the question *What did the boy eat?*, whereas *The boy ate the apple* would be a reply to the question *What did the boy do with the apple?*

4. For lower-level learners, it is probably best to use simple declarative statements, avoiding strong emphasis on any particular word.

REFERENCES AND FURTHER READING

Brown, J. D. (2012). *New ways in teaching connected speech.* Alexandria, VA: TESOL International Association.

Celce-Murcia, M., Brinton, D. M., & Goodwin, J. M. (2010). *Teaching pronunciation: A course book and reference guide* (2nd ed.). Cambridge, England: Cambridge University Press.

Repeat if Correct

Larry Davis

Levels	**Beginning to intermediate**
Aims	**Become comfortable in identifying and producing word-level stress**
Class Time	**20 minutes**
Preparation Time	**15–20 minutes**
Resources	**Nothing additional**

In English, the stress placed on the different syllables has an important effect on the intelligibility of multisyllabic words. This assessment examines students' ability to both identify and reproduce correct word-level stress. It can be used with whole classes to provide a quick assessment and feedback, or used with individuals for more formal assessment.

PROCEDURE

1. Prepare a list of sentences with each containing a word that will be the target of the assessment. Decide whether the word will be pronounced with correct stress or incorrect stress, and underline the syllable to be emphasized. For example, in the sentence "The teacher will *collect* the assignment tomorrow" the target word is *collect* and the stress is incorrect (the second syllable should be stressed, not the first). For longer multisyllabic words, the primary and secondary stress can be adjusted to create incorrect pronunciation; double and single underline can be used to represent primary and secondary stress, respectively. (Or, any other consistent marking system can be used.) See the Appendix for examples of incorrect sentences.

2. Practice reading the sentences out loud a few times to ensure the intended pronunciation will be reliably produced.

3. Write the target word for the first sentence on the board. Tell the students that a sentence containing this word will be read out loud. If the word is pronounced with stress on the correct syllable, then they should repeat the sentence out loud. If the word stress is incorrect, they should remain silent.

4. Read the first sentence out loud. Note the approximate number of students who repeat the sentence and the approximate number who pronounce the target word correctly. Feedback can be given immediately after each item by telling students whether the sentence is correct or not, and by having the class as a whole say the sentence out loud, correctly pronouncing the target word. Continue until all of the sentences have been read.

5. The number of students who repeat the sentence provides an estimate of students' ability to recognize correct word stress, while the repetition gives an indication of their ability to produce correct stress.

FEEDBACK AND SCORING

1. See **Procedure**, Steps 4 and 5.

2. Students may also be assessed individually. In this case, the student can be asked to simply indicate whether the pronunciation is correct or not, and then asked to repeat the sentence using correct pronunciation, with a point awarded for each task.

3. Finally, the assessment can be done as a more formal listening quiz, where students are given a quiz sheet and must mark the correct sentences.

CAVEATS AND OPTIONS

Word stress may vary within different sentence contexts. Word-level stress may be minimized in words that are unstressed within the sentence, or may vary with sentence-level intonation. Care should be taken so that the target word is stressed in the sentence, and that the sentence intonation pattern (e.g., statement or yes/no question) does not alter or obscure the word stress.

REFERENCES AND FURTHER READING

Brown, J. D. (2012). *New ways in teaching connected speech.* Alexandria, VA: TESOL International Association.

Celce-Murcia, M., Brinton, D. M., & Goodwin, J. M. (2010). *Teaching pronunciation: A course book and reference guide* (2nd ed.). Cambridge, England: Cambridge University Press.

APPENDIX: *Sample Incorrect Sentences*

(target word in *italics*)

Oil is a major *export* of that county. (correct form: *export*)

She *introduced* her friend. (correct form: *introduced*)

My friend is the *president* of our club. (correct form: *president*)

If you have a question, ask the *professor* (correct form: *professor*)

I don't like *romantic* movies. (correct form: *romantic*)

Reduced-Forms Dictations

James Dean Brown and Ann Hilferty

Levels	***Any***
Aims	***Demonstrate comprehension of reduced forms in spoken North American English***
Class Time	***10–15 minutes***
Preparation Time	***2 hours***
Resources	***Digital recorder/player***

Years ago, one of the authors was asked by a student, "Please to speak more slowly." The author had heard that request so many times that it irritated him, and without thinking, he fired back, "No! You listen more quickly!" That was the beginning of the development of a series of lessons which culminated in the reduced-forms dictation described here and used in speaking classes as weekly quizzes and as part of the final exam. (See Brown & Hilferty, 1995, for more information on what reduced forms to teach and how to teach them; see Brown & Hilferty, 1986, for an evaluation of this project.)

PROCEDURE

Create the Dictation

1. Write a dialog between two people that includes all of the reduced forms to be assessed. Make it as natural sounding as possible. For instance,

    DAVID: Whenerya goin' ta Tokyo, Janice?

    JANICE: I'm gonna go on Saturday, David.

    DAVID: Boy! I wish I were gettin' ouda here fer awhile. Ya gotcher plane ticket?

    JANICE: Na. I gotta gedit tamara.

    DAVID: Whaddaya hafta do in Tokyo?

    JANICE: I gotta giv'em some drawings, but I also wanna do some sightseeing.

    DAVID: Where'll ya go?

VI

JANICE: I wanna gedouda Tokyo 'n see Nikko.

DAVID: 'kay, ava good time.

JANICE: 'kay, g'bye.

2. Locate two native speakers who have very different voices (perhaps a male and a female) and who can read such a dialog naturally.

3. Have the native speakers record the dialog three times, each time at a fast but natural rate of speech. The first time, have them read fast and straight through the dialog. The second time, have them read fast but stop after each turn and give the students ample time to write out the full forms. The last time, have them read fast and straight through to give the students a chance to review their work.

4. Prepare a reduced-forms dictation sheet with the speakers' names on it and include directions (see Appendix A).

5. Also prepare a scoring sheet with directions (see Appendix B).

Administer the Dictation

1. Hand out the Reduced-Forms Dictation (Appendix A) .

2. Read the directions to the students. Ask the students if there are any questions. If so, answer them.

3. Play the recording. Walk around the classroom to double-check that the students are writing the full forms of the words they are hearing.

FEEDBACK AND SCORING

1. Have the students exchange papers.

2. Pass out the Reduced-Forms Scoring Handout (see Appendix B). Read the scoring directions to the students.

3. Have the students correct each other's dictations.

4. Collect all the dictations. Check the corrections, compile and record the scores, and give the students feedback in the next class on how they did as a group and individually.

CAVEATS AND OPTIONS

1. The students may find this novel form of assessment difficult at first, but typically they quickly come to understand the value of such assessment activities.

2. Administer reduced-forms dictations periodically so that both the instructor and the students can monitor their progress. With low-level students, start with dialogs that are read more slowly but with all the appropriate reduced forms, and gradually administer faster and faster dictations.

REFERENCES AND FURTHER READING

Brown, J. D. (2012). *New ways in teaching connected speech.* Alexandria, VA: TESOL International Association.

Brown, J. D., & Hilferty, A. (1986). Listening for reduced forms. *TESOL Quarterly, 20,* 759–763.

Brown, J. D., & Hilferty, A. G. (1995). Understanding reduced forms. In D. Nunan & L. Miller (Eds.), *New ways in teaching listening* (pp. 124–127). Alexandria, VA: TESOL.

Brown, J. D., & Kondo-Brown, K. (Eds.). (2006). *Perspectives on teaching connected speech to second language speakers.* Honolulu, HI: National Foreign Languages Resource Center, University of Hawai'i at Mānoa.

Celce-Murcia, M., Brinton, D. M., & Goodwin, J. M. (2010). *Teaching pronunciation: A course book and reference guide* (2nd ed.). Cambridge, England: Cambridge University Press.

VI

APPENDIX A: *Reduced-Forms Dictation Handout*

DICTATION DIRECTIONS: This is a reduced-forms dictation. That means you will hear natural English with all its reductions. Your job is to write down the full forms of all of the words to show that you understand what the speakers are saying. Do *not* write contractions like *can't* or *don't*. You will hear the dictation three times: once read straight through, then again with pauses to give you time to write, then one last time straight through so that you can check your work. Do your best.

DAVID: _____

JANICE: _____

DAVID: _____

JANICE: _____

DAVID: _____

JANICE: _____

DAVID: _____

JANICE: _____

DAVID: _____

JANICE: _____

APPENDIX B: *Reduced-Forms Scoring Handout*

SCORING DIRECTIONS: Score only the full forms of words that are underlined in the dialog below. It is not necessary for the words to be spelled 100% correctly, but they must be readable and have the correct grammatical endings. Circle each word that is correct on your colleague's dictation. Then count up the total number of circled words. The maximum score possible is 50.

DAVID: When are you going to Tokyo, Janice?

JANICE: I am going to go on Saturday, David.

DAVID: Boy! I wish I were getting out of here for a while. You got your plane ticket?

JANICE: No. I have got to get it tomorrow.

DAVID: What do you have to do in Tokyo?

JANICE: I have got to give them some drawings, but I also want to do some sight-seeing.

DAVID: Where will you go?

JANICE: I want to get out of Tokyo and see Nikko.

DAVID: Okay, have a good time.

JANICE: Okay, goodbye.